HATE
SPEECH

Rita Kirk Whillock
David Slayden
EDITORS

SAGE Publications
International Educational and Professional Publisher
Thousand Oaks London New Delhi

For information address:

SAGE Publications, Inc.
2455 Teller Road
Thousand Oaks, California 91320
E-mail: order@sagepub.com

SAGE Publications, Ltd.
6 Bonhill Street
London EC2A 4PU
United Kingdom

SAGE Publications India Pvt. Ltd.
M-32 Market
Greater Kailash I
New Delhi 110 048 India

Printed in the United States of America

Library of Congress Cataloging-in-Publication Data

Main entry under title:

Hate Speech / edited by Rita Kirk Whillock, David Slayden.
    p. cm.
    Includes bibliographical references and index.
    ISBN 0-8039-7208-3 (c: alk. paper). ISBN 0-8039-7209-1
(p: alk. paper)
    1. Hate speech—United States. 2. Oral communication—Social aspects—United States. 3. Freedom of speech—United States.
4. United States—Social conditions—1980-   I. Whillock, Rita Kirk.
II. Slayden, David.
P95.54.H38 1995
302.2'242—dc20   95-9038

95 96 97 98 99 10 9 8 7 6 5 4 3 2 1

Sage Production Editor: Astrid Virding
Sage Typesetter: Janelle LeMaster

HATE
SPEECH

Contents

Acknowledgments   vii

Introduction   ix

1. Elite Discourse and the Reproduction of Racism   1
   Teun A. van Dijk

2. The Use of Hate as a Stratagem for Achieving
   Political and Social Goals   28
   Rita Kirk Whillock

3. The Gay Agenda: Marketing
   Hate Speech to Mainstream Media   55
   Marguerite J. Moritz

4. Work-Hate: Narratives About Mismanaged Transitions
   in Times of Organizational Transformation and Change   80
   H. L. Goodall, Jr.

5. Symbolism and the Representation of Hate in
   Visual Discourse   122
   David E. Whillock

6. Acts of Power, Control, and Resistance:
   Narrative Accounts of Convicted Rapists   142
   Peter M. Kellett

7. Hating for Life: Rhetorical Extremism and
   Abortion Clinic Violence   163
   Janette Kenner Muir

8. Holy Wars and Vile Bodies:
   The Politics of an American Iconography   196
   David Slayden

9. There's Such a Thing as Free Speech:
   And It's a Good Thing, Too   226
   Stephen A. Smith

   Afterword: Hate, or Power?   267
   David Theo Goldberg

   Author Index   277

   Subject Index   282

   About the Contributors   291

Acknowledgments

This book originated with an awareness, however uncomfortable and uninvited, that hate crimes and incidences of hate speech were either on the rise, or being increasingly covered in the media, or both. Hate is, to say the least, an unpleasant topic. Its existence and perpetuation raises questions and often forces conclusions we would otherwise prefer to ignore. That we were able to bring this questioning into the open has been the result of an uncommon generosity—both financial and intellectual—of several people and organizations. Here, we pay them our thanks, if not exactly their due.

The Sam Taylor Foundation

The Southern Poverty Law Center

John Gartley

Phil Seib

Patrick Brantlinger

Christa Mallick, editorial assistant

Shannon Lindsey, our research assistant

Sophy Craze, our editor at Sage

Introduction

Hate is recently much among us and while the increase in expressions of hate—whether hate speech or acts of violence—has been typically accounted for as the result of cultures clashing and merging, such a narrative's use of simple cause-effect reasoning fails to address numerous questions raised by hateful acts and expressions, including how hate is perceived, rationalized, acted upon, invoked, and institutionalized. The implications of this "crisis" model of hate are that hateful expressions are extra-societal phenomena: isolated instances of extreme, disruptive, illegitimate, irrational, antisocial behavior. Once hate is conceived of as abnormal, the response that follows is often clinical: Incidences of hate are described and then arguments made for its repression or eradication (the admission of hate crimes into criminal codes, for example). But seeing hate as an extreme expression that arises only in moments of cultural tension encourages us to ignore its role in the subtle negotiations that take place daily in complex, modern society, indulging the comfortable notion that hate is a pathological practice of "others."

Although the crisis model is no doubt one notable way of understanding hate, it is not the only one. This text proceeds from a basic and perhaps controversial assumption: that hate is an integral part of society, that it has numerous functions within the public and private discourses by which a society discovers and comments on itself. In short, this text is organized around the idea that hate has specific uses within and throughout societies and that it is indeed used.

As we began to explore hate as a dialectical phenomenon, we discovered that current information about the rhetorical functions and dimensions of hate is limited. The narrow focus on hate as a topic is due, at least in part, to characterizing it as an extreme emotional response that many would prefer to subdue rather than explore. In contrast to studies on love—hate's positive antithesis—hate has not received much scholarly attention, except for theological discussions. But each culture has approved objects of hatred. We may hate liars and thieves. We hate those who murder. We may even hate those who hate others. In other instances, whole cultures may be induced, invited, or permitted to hate people or ideas they fear, or who are perceived as threats to dearly held values (as was demonstrated in the McCarthy hearings of the 1950s).

Rather than approach the subject holistically, much of the previous work has focused on specific acts of hatred (such as the Holocaust or the racial intolerance of the 1960s), the legal protection for expressions of hate, and the various "-isms" associated with hate (such as racism or sexism). To date, no effort in the communication field has been made to bring together the various approaches to study the rhetorical expression and strategies of hate. Nor has anyone examined the implications for this kind of discourse on the dialectic process. From the beginning of this project, our intention was to address these deficits. We drew upon the unique insights of leading scholars from a variety of disciplines, asking them to join in a collaboration directed by the goal of understanding hate as a communication phenomenon. As a result, this book cuts across traditional academic boundaries in the social sciences and humanities. This exploration of the multiple facets of hatred in society considers—in addition to the more spectacular incidents that usually command media attention—the subtle means by which hate is conveyed and examines how it is naturalized, credentialed, and hidden in everyday discourse. Whether we apply the lessons learned from such exploration to Ice-T's *Cop Killer,* the rhetoric of David Duke, or the various topics covered here, the common purpose is to expose something about the subject-object relationship of hate and, once exposed, to consider the questions that arise. What are the differences, if any, between being angry and hating? Does hate exist only in expression? What distinguishes exchanges of anger from hateful discourse? How is hate used by those in power as well as by the disenfranchised?

What we discovered through this study is compelling. As routine expressions of hate are pushed out of public discourse they reemerge in more subtle and less newsworthy ways. Yet their impact remains significant and common attitudes toward hate are complicit in a marginalization of hate—in the United States and elsewhere. Public use of blatantly derogatory language against minority groups in our newscasts, classrooms, or places of worship is tolerated rarely. When such expression is permitted, its use is to provide context to society's lesson that hate is outside bounds of routine expression and is predicated on a common recognition of the destructive force of hate speech and hateful acts. This common recognition is due at least in part to awareness of atrocities, an awareness kept alive in public memory by the periodic reintroduction of dark segments of history through specialized museums—the National Holocaust Museum in Washington, D.C., for example, or the Museum of Racism in Birmingham, Alabama—or productions, such as the documentary *Night and Fog,* or the popular film *Schindler's List,* whose commercial success supports the conclusion that societal reinforcement of anti-hate messages has experienced considerable success. Laws have been passed that add penalties for transgressions designated as "hate crimes," establishing a protected class for women, minorities, and persons with disabilities; and such laws have been made possible by growing public rejection of intolerance. That a hate crime is now newsworthy further supports the contention that intolerance is publicly rejected, and the increase of public protesting against the protestors indicates a decline of fear in confronting hateful opponents. At a Klan march outside of Atlanta only a few years ago, the Klan was outnumbered 4 to 1. Indeed, Klan marchers had to be protected by the National Guard. Public disdain can even be noted by collective actions to deny fringe groups an arena for agitative rhetoric. At a Skinhead rally in one Texas town, for example, people were asked by local officials to stay at home so that speakers could not provoke a public incident and, thus, receive news coverage. The media showed up, but few others did; consequently, the rally was subjugated to back-page coverage and failed to spark the kind of recruitment excitement organizers sought.

In the past few decades, numerous efforts have been made to deride acts of hate, vilify the leaders of hate groups, and isolate hate mongers from power, so much so that society might be considered successful in its attempts to teach lessons against hate. And credit for the success of these initiatives must be given to civil rights pioneers like Morris Dees who, along with other members of the legal team at the Southern Poverty Law Center, not only took up the cause of those denied voice but established a national program for teaching tolerance to school-age children. There are numerous organizations that support efforts for better relations among members of society, such as B'nai B'rith, The Anti-Defamation League, and private research resources including the Sam Taylor Foundation, which provided research funding for this project.

On the face of it, then, marginalizing hate speech or acts is the trait of a just and honorable society, and progress has generally been made toward that distinction. Yet no one could reasonably argue that hate has been eradicated; indeed, hate still exerts its influence in a wide range of power relations. This study acknowledges the continued prevalence and force of hate as an operational tactic; it explores how a culture's values are established and reinforced by examining the positioning of a culture's objects of hate. In the struggle to define a culture's core values (and the consequent objects of its disdain), controversy inevitably arises. Current debates over a variety of social issues—abortion, gay rights, community standards, family values, affirmative action—may provide insight into what happens when members of a culture divide bitterly over substantive issues. How are the opponents positioned? And what appeals are made to the masses—however *mass* might be conceived—who provide consensus and determine the outcome?

Among the hate-related issues for students of persuasion are how argumentative standards of judgment for opposing arguments are placed, how a different standard is indicated as being more valid, and what impact this polar rhetoric has on the dialectical process. Perhaps one of the more significant facets of hate is its expansiveness: It is more encompassing, as Aristotle noted, than lesser emotions such as anger, which is directed against individuals. Hatred may also take aim at whole classes of persons or a people. The fact that we may (and do) hate whole classes of persons or objects denies their individuality. In fact, to arouse feelings of hatred successfully, objectification based on generic description and definition are necessary.

In understanding the operation of hate speech, one initial premise must be made clear: The deliberate use of hate by rhetors is an overt attempt to win, to dominate the opposition by rhetorical—if not physical—force. In this book we argue that strong negative emotions such as hate are used to polarize particular groups in order to organize opposition, solidify support, and marshall resources toward forcing a "final solution" to a thorny problem. This polarization predisposes audiences to negate likely opposing claims, typically utilizing a literal and often highly symbolic object of hatred at which anger is focused. Far from the notion that it is used only as a propaganda technique in state-controlled cultures, any culture (and any group, dominant or subordinate) can and does use hate speech to establish in-groups and out-groups. Because the practice of assigning blame is not exclusive to a particular culture or single group within a culture, a primary emphasis in this study is the naturalization of hate, how acts and utterances that at first seem not to be hateful are, in effect, stratagems employing hate tactics in their execution. Acknowledging that hate is naturalized, that it finds subtle as well as extreme expression, that it is not simply an irrational, unseemly outburst, enables us to explore more thoroughly its uses within society and to recognize that it is culturally bound and viable and, perhaps, even necessary.

Admitting hate as a part of culture rather than extraneous to it brings us more clearly in touch with its uses. And in practice hate becomes an essential tool for the construction of identity and the acquisition of power. The various chapters of this book recognize and discuss hate as a tool used to assert—either actively or symbolically— one identity and annihilate another. Some times this act becomes tangible (abortion clinic bombings, the harassment and murdering of doctors); other times it is a narrative that remains entirely in the symbolic realm in that it is a cathartic expression but not an action—work-hate narratives, for example. An underlying question about this operation—hate as a symbolic expression of identity—is the acceptance of an aggressive confrontational imperative: Why must one identity be achieved at the expense of another? And if expressions of hate are in fact destructive, annihilistic in their very shape and intent, why do we argue that they must be admitted as part of public discourse?

It seems simplistic that with the many problems caused by or associated with hate speech—some of which this book examines—and the acknowledged power of language—hateful or otherwise—to stir the emotions, that a solution or response to the fact of hate speech would simply be to allow it, to hear it out rather than silence it. But this allowance is based on a simple recognition: That even though the language and logic that forms the speakers' arguments may be vile, reprehensible, and obscene, what they have to say is useful and valuable. As signposts, such rhetorical actions can tell us a great deal, as Steve Smith points out in Chapter 9,

> hate speech can serve an important social and political function. Irrational expressions of hate based on the status of the targets can alert us to the fact that something is wrong—in the body politic, in ourselves, or in the speakers. It might suggest that some change is necessary, or it might only warn us against the potential for demagogues. Speech codes, ordinances, and statutes would (if they could be enforced) blind us to the problems and deny us the opportunity to solve them before they broke out into actions.

Solutions that advocate eradication have heard hate speech but not listened to it.

The distinction between speech acts and actions here is significant. For while a speech act can instigate an action it is not an action; and it may be wrongly construed as the cause of an action. What gives words their power other than a relation to truth held by the listener? When one segment of society, the economically deprived, say, competing with other unskilled laborers, hears and believes that Asians are to blame for their precarious economic condition, what is the truth that is heard? It is simply that someone acknowledges the reality of their condition (this is true), says that they are not to blame (this may or may not be true), and assigns blame to another. This operation proceeds from a truth, but the causality, though faulty, removes blame from the listener to some other. It denies the need for self-transformation; it affirms the legitimacy of the feelings of injustice; and it offers a simple solution. Put simply, those who believe hate speech hear the affirmation that something is wrong and that the something that is wrong is not their fault. But legislation prohibiting hate speech is no less simplistic in its approach. Attempting to silence hate speech proceeds also from a denial. If we don't talk about it or, rather, if we don't hear it, then it doesn't exist or it might go away. Of course, this is not the case and hate speech is not the problem. The conditions that create a receptive audience for hate speech—ignorance, inequity, and fear—comprise the problem. To address these is much more difficult than attempting to silence the voices that remind us, by example, that problems exist. Suppressing hate speech is suppressing or masking the symptoms rather than treating the cause. Hate speech exists because people find it to be relevant; such speech is relevant: It articulates and typifies the felt condition of people's lives. If its logic is faulty (and it is), its visceral appeal is credible. For this reason it must be allowed and listened to and admitted as a form of public discourse. We should not try to expunge it but should instead ask why it exists and examine critically what is really being said and why. This is difficult and problematic and valuable. This is what we have attempted to do in this book.

In discussions of hate speech, disease metaphors are abundant. Extending an already overworked metaphor, we suggest that to deny hate is unhealthy, like ignoring the symptoms of an illness. And it is a commonplace that to treat only the symptoms ignores the cause. Hate speech must be recognized as a legitimate and valuable form of symbolic expression in society—not because it is true or sound, but because it identifies discontent, injustice, inequities. To deny voice, even those voices that are vile, disgusting, and hateful, is itself an act of contempt. This book is informed by the view that by talking about hate speech and by admitting it into public discourse, we can come to terms with it. Dialogue will occur, rather than isolation, exclusion, quarantine. Hate, admitted into the open and circulated beyond the confines of its narrow constituency, loses its power, faces scrutiny, is heard out.

Our own language throughout this book, wherein we examine the hate speech of others, often tends toward the evangelical. This tone is no doubt evoked by a common recognition among the authors of a need to come to terms with the practices of hate speech as well as its prevalence. Certainly hate speech is abundant. Incidents of it are increasing. If in our examination the metaphors we employ are of the spirit as well as the diseased body, perhaps there is good reason. If hate speech is the failure of an overarching vision, perhaps this narrowed perspective can be expanded; perhaps discussion is the means. If hate speech is symptomatic of the ills of society, then we should use the metaphors and step past them, as Goodall says later in this book, to engage in dialogue about the issues behind the metaphors. Hate speech is monological. Once we engage in dialogue, then we have taken a step toward addressing the problems that stimulate hate speech. And, in doing so, we have compromised its power or, to continue the disease metaphor, applied an antidote and begun the healing process.

—RITA KIRK WHILLOCK
—DAVID SLAYDEN

Elite Discourse and the Reproduction of Racism

Teun A. van Dijk
University of Amsterdam

Editor's Introduction

Polite society publicly eschews hate mongers and their evil acts. Consequently, when hate becomes a topic of conversation, the social status of the perpetrators is clearly implied. In this chapter, van Dijk contends that elites routinely attribute racism to lower-class whites or

AUTHOR'S NOTE: An earlier version of this chapter was presented at the International Conference on European Racism, September 25-30, 1990, Hamburg, Germany.

1

to the extreme Right factions in society. He then takes exception to that conclusion.

Van Dijk argues that because elites attribute the problem of racism to other social groups, they fail to recognize and deal with the racism that the dominant class imposes. He examines elite discourse in the mass media, education, politics, and business to expose inherent, institutional racism. This research is compelling and supports the argument that, although elites cloak their language in tolerance, they linguistically institutionalize the dominance of white groups over multiethnic components of society.

Van Dijk's findings are based on a program of research conducted in the Program of Discourse Studies of the University of Amsterdam, some of which he reviews here. In this analysis, he reminds us that hate can be cloaked in civility, and that language does not have to be visceral to inflict harm.

Introduction and Backgrounds

This chapter discusses some of the implications of a decade of research, carried out at the University of Amsterdam since the early 1980s, about the reproduction of racism through various types of discourse and communication. The fundamental thesis of this research program is that discourse—institutional as well as interpersonal text and talk—plays a crucial role in the enactment, expression, legitimation, and acquisition of racism in society (van Dijk, 1984, 1987a, 1987b, 1991, 1993).

White group members and white institutions are daily involved in a multitude of different discourses that express and confirm their dominance: from socializing talk and children's books during childhood, through textbooks at schools, and in the various discourses of the mass media, politics, business, and the professions. Their participation in this case may be active, as when they subtly or blatantly engage in racist talk addressed to minority group members, or in prejudiced stories among themselves about "those blacks" or "those foreigners." Or they may more passively be confronted with the portrayal of ethnic events and minorities in news reports, advertising, movies, or other media messages.

Such discourses are not simply innocent forms of language use or marginal types of verbal social interaction. Rather, they have a fundamental impact on the social cognitions of dominant group members, on the acquisition, confirmation, and uses of opinions, attitudes, and ideologies underlying social perceptions, actions, and structures. In other words, racism is socially learned, and discourse is essential in the process of its ideological production and reproduction.

The first major aim of this research framework, then, is to analyze systematically the details of some important discourse types about ethnic affairs and minorities. This discourse analytical approach goes beyond the traditional methods of content analysis and pays attention to such diverse discursive structures and strategies as topical or thematic structure (global contents), schematic organization (e.g., storytelling and argumentation), local semantic moves, style, rhetoric, and other properties of text and talk. So far, this program of research has analyzed everyday conversations, textbooks, and news reports in the press. At present we continue to extend this research toward an analysis of political (parliamentary) debates, academic discourse, and corporate text and talk.

The second aim of this research program is to examine the detailed structures, strategies, and contents of ethnically oriented social cognitions, such as prejudices and related ethnic attitudes. This cognitive "interface" allows us to link overt actions, including discourse, with social beliefs of white groups on the one hand, and with (representations of) societal structures on the other hand. It is at this point where the interaction between the micro and macro levels of racism needs to be theorized. It should, therefore, be emphasized that this approach to social cognition analysis is not some kind of individual psychology or traditional prejudice research. On the contrary, it is first of all *social* analysis, that is, analysis of the cognitions shared by members of groups or cultures.

Finally, both discourse and socio-cognitive analyses are embedded in a broader study of the societal, political, and cultural framework of racism in which structural and ideological roles and functions of racist discourse and cognitions play a role. At this level we study, for instance, the role of racist textbooks or news reports in the institutional framework of education or the mass media. Besides the study of power relations between groups, such an analysis also contributes to a more adequate insight into the cultural mechanisms involved in the reproduction of racism, ethnocentrism, and related forms of dominance.

This three-pronged approach (discourse, social cognition, and sociocultural contexts) is complex and necessarily multidisciplinary. The binding element is discourse, seen as a form of language use and communication, as social meaning and action and as a sociocultural, political, and ideological practice defining societal systems and structures. Interdisciplinary discourse analysis precisely studies the interrelations among these forms of discourse and, as a result, may provide some more detailed insights in the different modes and dimensions of the reproduction of racism in society.

Elite Racism

One important thesis of our theoretical framework has emerged from this large research program. It is the special role of the "elites." Although this notion is notoriously vague (Bottomore, 1964; Domhoff & Ballard, 1968; Mills, 1956), it will here serve to denote those groups in the sociopolitical power structure that develop fundamental policies, make the most influential decisions, and control the overall modes of their execution: government, parliament, directors or boards of state agencies, leading politicians, corporate owners, directors and managers, and leading academics (for details, see van Dijk, 1993).

Ignoring further complexities of their political analysis, we identify elites for our analysis primarily by their role in the order of discourse. That is, elites are the ones who initiate, monitor, and control the majority and most influential forms of institutional and public text and talk. They have preferential access to the mass media, may set or change the agenda of public discourse and opinion making, prepare and issue reports, carry out and publish research—thereby controlling academic discourse—and so on. In other words, the power of specific elite groups may be a direct function of the measure of access to, and control over, the means of symbolic reproduction in society, that is, over public discourse. This also means that the power of the elites is especially persuasive: Through public discourse they indirectly also control access to the minds of the public at large. This does not mean that elite opinions and ideologies are simply imposed, inculcated, or otherwise passively adopted by the public, but only that their discursive resources are such that they are better able than other social groups to influence interpretations and social beliefs and to marginalize or suppress alternatives that are against their interests (see also the discussion in Abercrombie, Hill, & Turner, 1990).

The same is true in ethnic affairs and in the reproduction of racism. Because racism is essentially defined in terms of white group dominance over variously defined minority or immigrant groups, or more generally as the dominance of European(ized) groups over non-European ones, this dominance needs to be daily reproduced in the many contexts of a multiethnic society. Indeed, despite the undeniable existence of "popular racism" (Miles, 1982; Phizacklea & Miles, 1979), we have reasons to believe that such "grassroots" racism is not always spontaneous, and less influential than usually assumed (by elites!). Rather, we shall assume that many of its elements are *preformulated*, sometimes in seemingly indirect, subtle, or even "tolerant" terms, by various elite groups. In other words, elite discourse plays a fundamental role in the ethnic consensus (the consent to participate in domination) of the white group as a whole. This thesis does not imply that there is no interaction between popular and elite forms of racism. Elite racism today is seldom overt and blatant. Rather it often takes the "modern" form of "new" or "symbolic" racism and is typically enacted in the many forms of subtle and indirect discrimination (in action and discourse) in everyday situations controlled by these elites. It is also enacted whenever elite interests are threatened, for instance in hiring and affirmative action, cultural beliefs, political power, and so on (Barker, 1981; Dovidio & Gaertner, 1986; Essed, 1990, 1991; Wellman, 1977). Because of their positive self-image as tolerant citizens, elites' racism is typically denied and therefore hard to oppose (van Dijk, 1992). One of the strategies of denial is precisely to attribute racism to the white lower class or the "poor inner cities," or to identify racism exclusively with the ideologies of the extreme Right. The fact that there are also (usually marginalized) elite groups engaged in active antiracism also shows that elites and elite racism are not homogeneous.

In the rest of this chapter I will focus on several types of elite racism, such as that of the media, politics, corporate business, and academia (for details see van Dijk, 1993). Obviously, these forms of text and talk are mutually related in many ways: The media largely focus on political discourse on ethnic affairs, while conversely both politicians and the media also use scholarly reports on immigration or minorities to support their views. Corporate discourse in turn influences political concerns (such as those about affirmative action). The discourse of the public at large, if heard at all, is often restricted to indirect representation by politicians and journalists. For example, when immigration restrictions may be legitimated because of an assumed "popular resentment," social cognitions are partly instigated by the elites in the first place. In all these relationships, the media play the central role of the information and opinion interface among the elites themselves and (largely top down) between the elites and the public at large.

Media Discourse

Despite conflicting evidence in mass communication research about the effects of the mass media, we have theoretical reasons and empirical support for the claim that mass media discourse plays a central role in the discursive, symbolic reproduction of racism by elites (Hartmann & Husband, 1974; van Dijk, 1991). Newspapers and television, as well as individual journalists and program makers, may themselves be partially dependent on other power elite groups in the definition of the ethnic situation. They may try to report "objectively" on government policies, police actions, court cases, immigration, social affairs, or crime. Yet for each of these domains they draw upon sources and source texts that are seemingly beyond their control. Journalists may have the illusion, therefore, of providing a "balanced" view of ethnic affairs. Here are a few examples to illustrate that point.

Hiring. Theory predicts. Research results show differently, however. First, as corporate or semi-state organizations, the mass media also participate in the labor market. Simple statistics show that, especially in Europe, virtually none of the media employ a substantial number of minority journalists, especially not at higher editorial or managerial levels (Wilson & Gutiérrez, 1985). Besides this form of discrimination, sometimes legitimated by alleged language or other "deficiencies" of immigrant journalists, the exclusion of minority journalists implies also that news stories or television programs are predominantly white in overall perspective, if not in content and style. Several factors similarly influence white reporters to attribute more importance and credibility to white (official) sources, such as government agencies, the police, or "minority experts."

Control and Access. One way to control minority points of view in the press is through hiring. In Europe, there are few minority journalists and, if they are hired, their position in the news room is marginal (Wilson & Gutiérrez, 1985). Minority organizations have less access to the media, less control over the definition of the ethnic situation, and less influence on their own portrayal. Analysis of quotation patterns confirms these hypotheses. Minorities are systematically less quoted in and about news that directly concerns them; or their opinions are "balanced" by those of white speakers. Indeed, minority speakers are seldom quoted alone. Also, if quoted, they are quoted in less credible modes of quotation. Accusations of discrimination and racism are typically and consistently accompanied by quotation marks or doubt words like *alleged* or *claimed.*

Research into news structures and news production has often shown that elite news actors have special access to the media because they are found to be important, newsworthy, and credible by journalists (Galtung & Ruge, 1965; Gans, 1979; Tuchman, 1978). Elite sources and news actors have organized their access by institutional discursive practices such as press releases, press conferences, and the activities of their own public relations offices. Because most elites in North America and Europe happen to be white, a dominant white view and perspective pervades in the news, with the white group systematically presented in a more favorable light.

Topics. The lack of minority journalists, the overall white interests and perspective of most reporters and editors, as well as the role of white elite groups in the shaping of news also have consequences for the selection and treatment of news topics. If covered at all, minorities are portrayed in the news primarily in terms of topics that are "interesting" for white readers.

Earlier research and our own analyses of the British and Dutch press show that this is indeed the case: Minorities are represented in terms of a very limited and stereotypical set of topics. Among the top five topics—both as to frequency and size—we usually find topics (or rather topic clusters or "subjects") such as (a) immigration; (b) violence, crime, riots, and other forms of deviance; (c) ethnic relations; (d) cultural differences; and, especially in the United States, (e) music and sports (Hartmann & Husband, 1974; Johnson, 1987; Martindale, 1986; Merten, Ruhrmann et al., 1986; van Dijk, 1983, 1991). Moreover, these topics are dealt with in such a way as to emphasize negative properties or actions of immigrants, refugees, or minorities. Immigration is seldom portrayed as a contribution to the economy or the culture. It is instead posed as a problem, a threat, or an invasion. Similarly, cultural differences such as those attributed to Muslims also tend to be characterized as problematic or threatening to "us." On the contrary, problems for "them," such as discrimination and racism, are typically mitigated or dealt with as regrettable incidents attributed to individuals or extremist groups outside of the consensus. Other topics relevant to the everyday lives of minorities (housing, education, health care) have low priority.

Local Semantic Moves. Whereas topics are defined as global semantic macrostructures of discourse, the local level of meaning in news discourse is also relevant for insight into media representation of minorities and ethnic affairs. At this level the actual description of ethnic persons and events are seldom innocent. To understand these local forms of discourse bias, we need to know the overall goals and agendas of discourse about ethnic affairs. As is also the case in everyday conversation (van Dijk, 1987a), we here find two complementary strategies: positive self-presentation and negative other-presentation.

Importantly, however, negative presentation of "them" is constrained by laws, norms, and values; as a result, explicitly and blatantly racist accounts are rare, especially in the quality press. The official norm that prohibits overt discrimination is rather well known and, up to a point, supported. To represent minorities in a negative way, therefore, the press also needs discursive forms that counterbalance such negativity, for instance, by affirming that "we are not racist, but . . ." Such disclaimers, in their various forms, are routine and involve apparent denials as well as apparent concessions ("there are also intelligent, hard-working blacks, but . . ."). In the latter case, for instance, we may expect positive success stories about individual minority group members. Functionally, this "solo" role of the individual exception reassuringly confirms for the white public that (a) some minority group members can make it, so we can't be blamed, but (b) the minority group as a whole still occupies "its place," so they are not becoming dominant.

The local semantics of racist discourse must be necessarily veiled. "Real" opinions and attitudes, especially in the public discourse of the mass media, need to be toned down or otherwise made less direct. This means that implications, presuppositions, and suggestions play an important role. Indeed, the discourse of ethnic affairs has become heavily coded in such a way that apparently neutral words are being used to avoid the racist implications of true intentions and meanings. Large sections of the Western press, in collusion with the authorities (government, ministries), now use the term *economic* refugee. This more or less neutral description, however, implies that they are not "real" refugees and also that they "only come to live here off our money," two more direct forms of prejudice expression in everyday talk. The same is true, especially in the United States, for the coded uses of words such as *broken families, teenage mothers, welfare mothers, inner-city crime, crack,* and other social problems stereotypically attributed to African Americans or other minorities. Blaming the victim is one major implication of veiled and coded elite discourse.

The Denial and Reversal of Racism. The overall contrast, also found at the level of local meanings between positive "us" and negative "them," implies that the media generally present whites not only as nonracist, but also as tolerant and helpful and the immigrants, at the least, as ungrateful and unadapted. This contrast requires a complex strategy of denial. Moves in such a strategy of denial are some of the moves mentioned above ("we are not racist, but . . ."); the systematic use of doubt signals, also mentioned above, when minorities or white antiracists accuse whites of discrimination or prejudice; the management of quotations (where minorities that could give evidence about racist practices are not quoted); and finally by reversal ("they are the real racists"). This is particularly the case in the right-wing British press, where emphatic denials of racism are routinely associated with violent attacks against the "Loony Left" as well as antiracist "busybodies" (van Dijk, 1991). Even in the liberal press, explicitly antiracist positions are seldom covered neutrally and virtually never positively. The racism of the media, more than any other form, is ignored and denied completely in those same media. The racism of other elite groups such as those in politics, corporate business, scholarship, or education, is similarly ignored or mitigated. Excesses are reported merely as painful incidents, never as structural properties of racial inequality in society at large. This is typically the case in the (few) media reports about discrimination in hiring and the workplace. Accusations of racism are often seen as more problematic than racism itself, while disturbing the fabric of in-group consensus and solidarity.

Our analysis suggests that the news media in general and the press in particular are crucially involved in the reproduction of elite racism. They do so, first of all, because of their close involvement with the power structure (Lichter, Rothman, & Lichter, 1990) and, hence, because they share in the ethnic consensus of the dominant political elites. Second, the media have their specific ways in producing, reproducing, and emphasizing an ethnic consensus. The white group is generally presented in neutral or favorable terms, especially in the domain of ethnic affairs, whereas immigrants, foreigners, refugees, or resident minorities are portrayed as the source of the problems, conflicts, and threats. Obviously, there are variations of mode and style among the different mass media. The liberal press may emphasize the positive role of white liberals as "helpers" of minority groups, whereas the conservative or right-wing press will tend to focus on the negative properties of the "aliens." Through the discriminatory patterns of hiring and access, topic selection and emphasis, quotation, local semantic strategies, and the style and rhetoric of people description, the media play their own crucial role in the legitimation and reproduction of elite racism.

Educational Discourse: Textbooks

Another major conduit for the reproduction of racism is educational discourse. After informal socialization and learning through parental talk, children's books, and television programs, lessons and textbooks provide the first encounter with the institutionalized educational communication of knowledge, beliefs, norms, and values. It is here that white children in Western countries may, sometimes for the first time, be hearing or reading about groups and peoples of color and about other cultures, continents, and nations.

Both formal and hidden curricula and their implementation in classroom interaction, formal lessons, and learning materials are similarly part of that dominant culture. Whether or not an increasing number of minority children enter the classrooms of European or North American schools, dominant educational discourse remains essentially white (Brandt, 1986). Third World peoples, cultures, and nations are viewed from a Western perspective; the same is true for minority groups and cultures within Western societies. Despite an increase of formal acknowledgments made (in several countries) to the need for "multicultural education," everyday teaching practices, the education of teachers, and the contents of textbooks are only slowly and minimally beginning to reflect such policies (Banks & Lynch, 1986; Troyna & Williams, 1986).

Textbook research in several countries has repeatedly supported this conclusion, at least for the more formal discourses of learning (Klein, 1986; Milner, 1983; Preiswerk, 1980). These studies are unambiguous in their concurrent findings that, whether more blatantly in the past or more subtly today, textbooks ignore, marginalize, inferiorize, or problematize non-Western peoples, societies, and cultures.

Our own study of social studies textbooks in the Netherlands also supports such a conclusion (van Dijk, 1987b, 1993). Despite the obvious presence of minorities in the country, half of all books in use in 1985 did not even deal with the topic of ethnic affairs. According to most textbooks in a variety of subjects, schools and society at large are still wholly "white." In that respect, textbooks in the United States have changed, so much so that a conservative backlash against multiculturalism in curricula and textbooks has become one of the potent new forms of cultural racism, for example, under the label of malicious accusations of political correctness (Aufderheide, 1992; Glazer & Ueda, 1983).

Second, in Dutch textbooks, if minority groups are portrayed at all, the focus is on a few major topics remarkably similar to those also dominant in the mass media: (a) immigration, (b) cultural difference, (c) race relations, and (d) crime and deviance. As is the case in the press, each of these topics tends to be framed in a negative perspective: that of problems, conflicts or threats to "us" (Western culture, "our" country, etc.). Immigration topics do not merely spell out the facts, such as which groups immigrated when and why, but also focus on overpopulation. Contributions to the economy due to migrant labor or the exploitation of low-wage workers are seldom acknowledged.

Cultural differences, the main topic of social studies textbooks in the Netherlands, are similarly associated with problems such as alleged lack of adaptation, strange habits, problems of language learning, or assumed deviance attributed to different religion, especially Islam, such as pathological family structure, the subordinate position of women, or irritating dietary restrictions. Whether or not the portrayal is mildly stereotypical or more blatantly prejudiced, one implication of the details of this topic is clear: "we" are obviously superior because we are more modern, more advanced, more rational, and even more tolerant. On the other hand, as with the press, discrimination and racism are hardly topicalized and safely attributed to others abroad, as when dealing with earlier segregation in the United States or apartheid in South Africa. Sometimes discrimination and racism are even blamed on minorities themselves. This is consistent with the mitigation of accounts of colonialism and slavery in history textbooks and with the way "Third World" peoples are presented with in geography textbooks; stereotyping, victim-blaming, and problemati-zation are the dominant message of such books. Racism and Eurocen-trism in textbooks are intimately related.

When minority groups are dealt with in Dutch social studies text-books, even the few lines about the major groups involved neverthe-less feature some information about crime and deviance, such as drug dealing or drug use by Surinamese or Chinese, terrorist violence by Moluccan youths, or culturally based crimes of Turks and Moroccans.

Sometimes such "information" will be followed by the disclaimer that "of course, they are not all like that."

These topics account for the vast majority of the (few and short) passages about "foreigners" in our present-day textbooks. Virtually absent is information about relevant other topics, such as social affairs, education, history, culture, and the problems experienced by immigrant minorities. If addressed at all in textbooks, minority students have virtually no possibilities of identification, particularly with the heroes of their histories.

Although the contents of Dutch textbooks in the early 1990s have been improving, the conclusions found in our research of the mid-1980s still largely hold true. The social science topic for the 1996 exam will be ethnic affairs, but the plans for that exam are virtually a reproduction of the dominant consensus on ethnic affairs. That is, it will focus on problems caused by "them," whereas the word *racism* is carefully avoided. White and black children in the Netherlands are therefore inadequately prepared for the multicultural society in which they are growing up.

The vastly influential discourses of textbooks (textbooks are the only "obligatory" types of discourse in society!) are shaped by outside ideological forces, such as those of academic disciplines, teacher training, and the mass media. Far from being independent, there are multiple relations between elite discourse in education and that in other societal domains. For textbooks, there is the additional constraint of direct or indirect influence and decisions of parents, school boards, civic organizations, publishers, business corporations, political parties, governments, the churches, and many other societal formations and institutions with an interest in their contents. Again, most of these groups or organizations are white and reluctant to accept an educational account of the ethnic or international situation that involves or implicates them in the reproduction of white or Western power directed against minorities or Third World peoples.

Finally, it should be realized that these forms of ethnocentric educational discourse not only play a role in the inclusion and reproduction of dominant culture and its associated social cognitions, they are also part of the societal functions of the school and education themselves—that is, in the preparation of children for society and the labor market. By portraying and implementing the marginalization and subordination of ethnic minority groups and their children, textbooks prepare minority children for a society in which a specific position is reserved for them: lower status and menial work. The educational statistics for most minority groups clearly reflect the school experiences and premonitions children have of this position and show how performance, achievements, drop-out (or rather "force out") rates, and diplomas attained are not only a function of socioeconomic class or the alleged educational "culture" of the group, but also dependent on the educational system and the schools themselves.

Academic Discourse

Whereas the history of the humanities and the social sciences amply shows the emphasis placed on the supremacy of white Europeans (Barker, 1981; Haghighat, 1988; Miles, 1989; Todorov, 1988; UNESCO, 1975), contemporary racism in scholarly discourse has become much more subtle and indirect and tends to focus on "cultural differences."

Apart from the rather small right-wing fringe of racist sociobiologists (for critical analysis, see, e.g., Barker, 1981; Chase, 1975), more "modern" forms of racist academic discourse often tend to focus on the "incompatibility of cultures," the "pathology" or the "culture of poverty" of the African-American family, the "underachievement" of minority children, the "fanaticism" of Moslem fundamentalism, or the "criminal" tendencies of African Americans or Afro-Caribbeans, among the many other "problems" or "disadvantages" attributed to minority groups in North America and Western Europe. In this respect, the major topics of "ethnic" research are not very different from the major topics of media coverage.

Ethnic relations, especially in Europe, are primarily studied by white academics. Obviously this has an impact on their perspective and interpretation. In the Netherlands this means, among other things, that most of these white scholars have minor interest in the issues of racism or may even deny its existence (for critical analysis, see Essed, 1987). Also, they may derogate or otherwise marginalize ethnic research by minority scholars, for example, with the argument that it is naturally "biased." At the same time, it is often not realized, or may even be denied, that ethnic relations in general and racism in particular should be theorized in terms of dominance relations and power. In this way, even if benevolently or "objectively" studying minority language, culture, social structures, or "behavior," they may unwittingly contribute to the reproduction of such ethnic power relations. Indeed, as is the case for elite racism generally, the major problem of the white elites is that their cognitions, discourse, and actions are indifferent to, if not conducive to, the change of such power relations in society.

In other words, the role of academic elites in the reproduction of racism is far from innocent. Unless they participate directly in public debate in the media, which they often do, their work may seem to be relegated to the margins of public opinion. Nothing is less wrong, however. Although sometimes delayed by years or decades, many of the beliefs and ideologies underlying or emerging from scholarly work are also communicated and represented by other elites (especially those of politics, education, and the media) and whence by the public at large, where "lay theories" of ethnic or racial differences, if not white Western superiority, have a very long life. It may well be that of all the elite preformulations of racism, those of academic discourse are ultimately, though often indirectly (through textbooks, media, or politics), most influential.

Political Discourse

In the complex structure of most Western countries, political power may officially be dominating that of other elites or organizations, whatever the power of the media or business corporations. "Ethnic affairs," however, are largely managed by local or national governments, elected bodies (parliament or city councils), and the bureaucracies that prepare, make, and implement the fundamental decisions about immigration, settlement, special employment schemes, housing programs, health care, education of minority groups or immigrants, and the regulation of ethnic relations through laws against discrimination.

Such political decision making is largely discursive. Policies, rules, regulations, laws, and general principles are informally discussed at all levels of the national or local political hierarchy and formally discussed in meetings of committees or sessions of elected bodies, and then decided upon by such institutions. Finally, they are communicated to various organizations and agencies, such as the police, the immigration service, or the schools, or to the public at large through the mass media.

In other words, political communication and discourse are crucially involved in many of the early stages of decision making about relevant aspects of ethnic affairs. Such decision making and its characterizing discourse are neither autonomous nor free from influences from other sectors in society. Input and feedback for these decision processes—and therefore for political discourse—is provided by public opinion, largely expressed or orchestrated by the mass media, hearings, advice from a large number of experts, committees, organizations or institutions, decisions of political parties, the bureaucracies or the ministries or other state institutions, opinions and actions from minority groups, as well as the various "facts" of the socioeconomic situation (like unemployment statistics), and the international situation (arrival of refugees, immigration and refugee treaties).

This complex network of relations of power, influence, and information processes also means that we cannot simply identify "political discourse" with the autonomous expressions in text and talk of politicians or political organizations. The political voice is not only, by rule, a representative voice, but also a composite voice, incorporating opinions and even the style of other powerful organizations and their elites. Despite this heterogeneity of sources and influences, which of course also exists in other domains (typically so in the mass media), we take political discourse and communication here in its narrow and restricted sense as the body of text and talk of politicians: that is, of members of the national and local executive and legislature, as well as of political parties and political organizations.

Scholarly evidence about the nature of political discourse on ethnic affairs is either regrettably scarce or does not explicitly analyze such discourses in their own right (Reeves, 1984). Many studies exist on the politics of ethnic affairs, but they tend to be formulated in the usual terminology of political opinion and decision making, not in that of discourse and communication structures and strategies. Examples of political discourse on "race" abound in the literature but only in a haphazard way—that is, by illustration. Few studies focus specifically on the political discourse on ethnic affairs and even fewer do so in terms of a discourse analytical approach or in view of an understanding of the role of discourse in the reproduction of racism in society (see, however, among other studies: Hall, Critcher, Jefferson, Clarke, & Roberts, 1978; Seidel, 1985, 1987, 1988; Wodak et al., 1990).

Political discourse about ethnic affairs is very similar, at least in certain respects, to other types of elite discourse, such as that of the media, education, or academic scholarship. One reason for this similarity is simple: Most politicians, especially in Europe, are white and have similar class and educational backgrounds as the other elites. Second, most voters are white, and most politicians will therefore (in principle) primarily think of the interests of their voters. Or conversely, it is unlikely that they make decisions that are in favor of minorities if they are not also in favor of whites. Third, most of the organizations that have organized access to and influence on political decision making are also white. Only in some specific cases, such as the case of antidiscrimination laws and affirmative action, are there decisions that seem to favor minority group members more than majority group members.

This complex set of interests and influences sets the stage for the overall white perspective of political discourse. There are many political and ideological variations—for example, between Left and Right—although in ethnic affairs such distinctions may not always be reliable indicators of ethnic attitudes. Although communist politicians, thinking of their (white) voters in poor inner-city areas, may sometimes espouse anti-immigrant views, as has been the case in France, we on the whole accept there is a correlation between the political Right and the "ethnicist Right." The "ethnicist Right" is constituted of those politicians or organizations generally in favor of further restrictions on immigration if not of repatriation, against ethnic pluralism, against special measures in favor of minority groups, and in favor of maintaining white dominant culture (Gordon & Klug, 1986).

To get a picture of the backgrounds of the dominant political discourses on ethnic affairs, let us first summarize a few findings of the Report of the European Parliament Committee of Inquiry into Racism and Xenophobia (Ford, 1990). Apart from giving a survey of extreme, right-wing racist groups and movements in Europe, it also quotes positions and statements of prominent politicians. It should be emphasized again, however, that although the focus is on politicians of the Right, racist discourse is not restricted to the Right. Also, more "moderate" conservatives and socialists may occasionally make derogatory remarks about immigrants or minorities when they see electoral advantages. Enoch Powell's comments on immigrants in the United Kingdom are well known and so is the statement of former Prime Minister Margaret Thatcher about the country being "swamped" by people of a different culture. President Mitterand, hardly known as a radical racist, also spoke of a "threshold of tolerance," while Chirac in the spring of 1991 declared that he could well understand the resentment of ordinary white people being confronted with large and ill-smelling immigrant families from North Africa. France's new prime minister, Edith Cresson, thought of solving the problem of illegal immigration by putting such immigrants en masse in a jumbo jet and transporting them back to their own countries. The list of such "bold ideas" and "slips of the tongue," reminiscent of the statements of the National Front in the United Kingdom or France or of similar parties in other countries, can be extended without any difficulty.

Thus, the Report of the EC Parliament Committee tells us that the interior minister of the Belgian government in 1987 thought of immigrants as "barbarians," a name gladly adopted by the racist Parti des Forces Nouvelles. Mr. Nolis, mayor of the Brussels borough of Schaerbeek, is the author of a racist pamphlet depicting North Africans as "terrorists," "religious fundamentalists," "drug addicts," and "barbarians." He had 150,000 copies distributed with this kind of "information" to local schools. The general resentment against immigrants in Belgium even allowed the government to ban immigrants from registering in six Brussels boroughs. In Denmark, often thought to be more tolerant, a leader of the right-wing Fremskridt Parti referred to immigrants as "the vast hoards of terrorists pouring in over us from the Middle East and Sri Lanka" and as people who "breed like rats." The public prosecutor did not find these statements serious enough for an indictment. Similar political discourse and practices are reported from other European countries where immigrant groups are harassed, attacked, and derogated, often with the tacit, or not so tacit, approval of the political or justicial elites. Most countries do not have effective antidiscrimination laws, often with the pretext that current laws are adequate to handle cases of discrimination.

Right-wing racist parties, sometimes getting more than 10% of the vote, and although systematically violating the law, are not prohibited in any European country, often with arguments that refer to their democratic rights. The democratic rights of minority groups or (other) immigrants are apparently less relevant. Right-wing racist parties play a very useful role, namely, in order to be able to take more "moderate" stands about the other parties, or to threaten immigrants to stay in line or the "forces of the Right" would take over—as was the case in the tabloid press in the United Kingdom after the "riots" in some inner cities.

Parliamentary discourse is generally of a more moderate type. In our comparative analysis of a decade of parliamentary debates about immigration, refugees, and ethnic affairs in the Netherlands, Germany, France, the United Kingdom, and the United States, we reconstructed the dominant modes of talk and opinion regarding these issues. All representatives, including those of overtly racist parties, emphatically deny that they are racist and emphasize that they are in favor of human rights, *but* that apart from being fair, they should also be strict, that is, curb immigration and be tough on "illegal aliens," otherwise the present minorities would suffer. Here are a few examples of these "mixed" arguments and messages of our democratically elected representatives (with a few exceptions, we do not identify the speakers in this case. We are interested only in general properties of political discourse on ethnic affairs.):

1. In practice we should also come to a less soft approach. (Prime Minister Lubbers of the Netherlands, in a radio interview)

This statement was one among several announcing the new minority policy of the Dutch government. Here are a few statements that could recently be heard in the British House of Commons:

2. I believe that we are a wonderfully fair country (. . .) [but] British citizenship should be a most valuable prize for anyone, and it should not be granted lightly to all and sundry. (May 15, 1990)

3. If we are to work seriously for harmony, nondiscrimination and equality of opportunity in our cities, that has to be accompanied by firm and fair immigration control. (June 20, 1990)

4. My hon. Friend and I will continue to apply a strict but fair system of control, not because we are prejudiced or inhumane, but because we believe that control is needed if all the people who live in our cities are to live together in tolerance and decent harmony. (June 20, 1990)

Similar forms of positive self-presentation, nationalist self-glorification, denials of racism, mixed with *buts* and followed by restrictive measures, especially on the Right, may be heard in the French Assemblée Nationale:

5. Our country has [for a] long time been open to foreigners, a tradition of hospitality going back, beyond the Revolution, to the *Ancien Régime*. (July 7, 1990)

6. The French are not racist. But, facing this continuous increase of the foreign population in France, one has witnessed the development, in certain cities and neighborhoods, of reactions that come close to xenophobia. In the eyes of the French unemployed man, for instance, the foreigner may easily become a rival, towards whom a sentiment of animosity may threaten to appear. (July 7, 1990)

Of course, such more veiled and indirect forms of derogation, warnings, and "firm" policies are still "moderate" compared to what the leader of the Front National, Jean-Marie Le Pen has to say:

7. We are neither racist nor xenophobic. Our aim is only that, quite naturally, there be a hierarchy, because we are dealing with France, and France is the country of the French. (July 7, 1990)

In Germany, parliamentary talk about immigrants is usually less blatant than this, but we find the same kind of "fair but firm" discourse as elsewhere, often having the same upshot:

8. (. . .) An uncontrolled increase of foreigners from non-European cultural backgrounds would further exacerbate the integration of non-European citizens, which is already difficult enough.

When one of the Green Party speakers in the German Bundestag dared to characterize the new immigration law as "racist," the Speaker of the House rather unusually intervenes as follows:

9. A chill ran down my back when our colleague Mrs. Trenz said that this bill was a form of institutionalized racism. Whereas the older ones among us had to live twelve years under institutionalized racism, Ladies and Gentlemen, I beg you, and in particular our younger colleagues, to show respect for these terrible experiences, and not to introduce such concepts to our everyday political business.

Even the concept of racism is banned from discussions in Parliament—being too reminiscent of old practices of the Nazi regime. Indeed, this denial of racism is, as we have suggested above, one of the hallmarks of elite racism. When discussing the 1990 Civil Rights Bill, one representative in the U.S. House expresses a similar idea:

10. Well, now can we also agree this afternoon that you can have different philosophies about how to achieve through law civil rights and equal opportunities for everybody without somehow being anti-civil rights or being a racist or something like that.

Just as in Western Europe, the U.S. representatives, both Republicans and Democrats, joined in calling the United States the most tolerant country in the world. Yet (especially the Republicans), at the same time did everything they could to block the new Civil Rights Bill, eventually vetoed by President Bush, because it would allow "quotas" in hiring minorities. Says another representative,

11. This nonsense about quotas has to stop because when we begin to hire and promote people on the bases of their race, we are going to bring to our society feelings of distress, feelings of unhappiness, and these emotions will accumulate and ultimately explode and destroy us.

Presented again in 1991, this Civil Rights Bill led to similar arguments and allegations about quota as it did in 1990. In other words, even when irrelevant, specific buzz words, such as *busing* and *quota* are used to prevent the civil rights of minorities from "going too far." We are all against discrimination, but minorities should not push their luck and expect to get free handouts, get hired without qualifications, or get away with easy litigation against employers—some of the tenets of the "symbolic" racism of the elites (see also the contributions to Dovidio & Gaertner, 1986).

These and similar examples from parliamentary discourse may be multiplied at random. They show, among other things, the same pattern of positive self-presentation ("we are fair," "we are not racist") and negative other-presentation of immigrants ("illegals") or other minorities ("associated with drugs," "not motivated to work") as we have found in many other forms of elite discourse. Overtly racist statements are rare, but often the consequent policies do not diverge very much from the "stop immigration" policies and discourse of the Right. Only the rhetorical packaging is sometimes more subtle.

The major problem of such political discourse is that it is often reproduced (and sometimes enhanced) by the media, and thus reaches the public at large, which has no difficulty comprehending the gist of such messages: "These immigrants don't belong here," "We should be tough in immigration," and "They should adapt to their new country," among other ideological implications. In other words, in the complex process of the reproduction of racism, the preformulation of subtle racism by the political elites plays a primary role.

Corporate Discourse

Although discrimination in business has been widely documented (Fernandez, 1981; Jaynes & Williams, 1989; Jenkins, 1986; Jenkins & Solomos, 1987), data and research results about corporate discourse of ethnic affairs are scarce. Less than political, social, educational, or academic discourse, such forms of text and talk are rarely reported in the media, if only because they are usually inaccessible to journalists. Corporations and their public relations (PR) departments have a powerful control over what is communicated to the press and are not likely to give insight into the decision making and daily practices of hiring, promoting, interaction, and business transactions involving minority groups.

Evidence from research on the experiences of minority group members, however, unambiguously shows that at the level of everyday racism, discriminatory practices in business are widespread (Essed, 1990, 1991). These practices may themselves be discursive or can be legitimated in text and talk. The dominant properties of such discourse are in line with the overall goals of capitalist business corporations: competition and profit. Thus, when minorities will be less hired or promoted, such discriminatory action will be legitimated in terms of assumed cultural, educational, or professional "deficiencies," alleged "problems" created by minority group workers, or in terms of reduced competition due to the presence of minority employees. Especially in Europe, any form of affirmative action or ethnic monitoring, proposed to counter the staggering unemployment among minority groups, is resolutely rejected as a form of intolerable infringement on the "freedom of enterprise." Claiming reduced competitiveness, corporations usually can get away with such rejections.

In order to examine the properties of corporate discourse on race, we interviewed the personnel managers of several major, sometimes multinational companies in the Netherlands. Again, at this high level, blatant racist talk to interviewers is rare. On the contrary, positive self-presentation here (better known in business as PR-talk) is rife, especially in the larger companies. They know their social responsibility, are in favor of equal opportunities, will hire minorities, but only, of course, when they can get them, when these applicants are qualified, and so on. Here are a few fragments of such talk:

12. (Does business have the responsibility to help solve the problem of minority unemployment?) Yes, oh yes. I think I see this as a task of the whole society, and X is part of that, so we should contribute our bit. But the buck should not be passed to business alone.

13. (Opinion about a target of a minimum of 60,000 minorities to be hired by Dutch employers, in an agreement with the unions, but:) I don't think that we would immediately give preference to hiring a lot of aliens. Because we do not operate, uhh, after all we are a business company. We are there to function economically.

14. Positive action, yes, that, uhhh . . . positive discrimination. Yes, as I already said before, I don't believe in that. I only believe in economic stimuli. Uhhh . . . I don't think you should formulate a policy if there is no rationale behind it. If you do that, that is irrational behavior. We should combat that with the intuition of business interest.

In the same vein, any discrimination in the company is denied or reduced to regrettable small incidents, affirmative action resolutely rejected as against principles of the free market and the laws of making profits, and government intervention and legislation forcefully resisted. At the same time, minority unemployment, especially in the Netherlands, is more than 3 times as high as majority unemployment, and may reach more than 50% for certain minority youths.

Conclusions

We started from the assumption, detailed in our earlier work, that discourse plays a prominent role in the reproduction of racism. More specifically, this chapter further elaborates the thesis that it is not primarily "popular" racism, but elite racism that is particularly influential in this reproduction process. The media, educational, academic, social, corporate, and political elites, among others, control or have access to widely published types of text and talk and may thus preformulate, though often in more "moderate" terms, the kind of modern racism that will then be taken up and be legitimated by large segments of the general population.

The media play a central role in this process, because they both relay political or corporate discourse to the public, while at the same time contributing their own slanted perspective of ethnic affairs. Minority journalists, especially in Europe, are scarce: Minority groups are much less quoted, or quoted more negatively; topics focus on stereotypes about minorities, such as crime, drugs, cultural differences, and generally the problems that immigrants and minorities cause.

The same is true in textbooks, which similarly stereotype people from non-European countries as being poor, dependent, without initiative, and as having bizarre habits, but above all as being responsible for their own misery. More sophisticated but hardly different is the message that comes across in many white academic studies of minorities, which also tend to focus on "deviance" or "deficits" and are typically interested in the kind of topics that confirm widespread stereotypes.

Political discourse is focused on control, that is, on the restriction of immigration and on the limitation of the civil rights (and welfare) of minorities, although often with the mixed message of positive self-presentation ("we are fair") that characterizes virtually all elite discourse on minorities or race relations. Corporate discourse, finally, similarly engages in PR-talk about minorities but at the same time argues against any form of compulsory affirmative action that may restrict the freedom of the labor market.

All of this elite text and talk is obsessed by the possible accusation of discrimination, bias, or racism and emphatically denies it. The elites have the unshakable self-image of being specifically tolerant, unlike ordinary people. At the same time, they need arguments, reasons, and legitimation to keep (too many) non-Europeans from entering the country, the city, the school, the university, the scholarly journal, the company, or politics. To do that they have recourse to a number of standard arguments about equality and equal rights (primarily of their own white group), about quality (never mentioned when the minority of white men were favored by positive discrimination), social order, and so on. In sum, given that it is articulate, seemingly well-argued, apparently moderate and humane, and given its power of control and access to the means of ideological production, elite discourse about ethnic affairs effectively establishes, maintains, and legitimates the ethnic consensus, and consequently the dominance of the white group in the increasingly multiethnic societies of Western Europe and Northern America.

References

Abercrombie, N., Hill, S., & Turner, B. S. (Eds.). (1990). *Dominant ideologies*. London: Unwin Hyman.

Aufderheide, P. (Ed.). (1992). *Beyond PC towards a politics of understanding*. Saint Paul, MN: Graywolf Press.

Banks, J. A., & Lynch, J. (Eds.). (1986). *Multicultural education in Western societies*. London: Holt, Rinehart & Winston.

Barker, M. (1981). *The new racism*. London: Junction Books.

Bottomore, T. B. (1964). *Elites and society*. London: C. A. Watts.

Brandt, G. L. (1986). *The realization of anti-racist teaching*. London: Falmer.

Chase, A. (1975). *The legacy of Malthus: The social costs of the new scientific racism*. Urbana: University of Illinois Press.

Domhoff, G. W., & Ballard, H. B. (Eds.). (1968). *C. Wright Mills and the power elite*. Boston: Beacon.

Dovidio, J. F., & Gaertner, S. L. (Eds.). (1986). *Prejudice, discrimination, and racism*. New York: Academic Press.

Essed, P. J. M. (1987). *Academic racism: Common sense in the social sciences* [CRES Publications, No. 5]. University of Amsterdam: Centre for Race and Ethnic Studies.

Essed, P. J. M. (1990). *Everyday racism*. Claremont, CA: Hunter House.

Essed, P. J. M. (1991). *Understanding everyday racism: An interdisciplinary theory*. Newbury Park, CA: Sage.

Fernandez, J. P. (1981). *Racism and sexism in corporate life*. Lexington, MA: Lexington Books.

Ford, G. (1990). *Report of the Committee of Inquiry in Racism and Xenophobia*. Brussels: European Parliament.

Galtung, J., & Ruge, M. H. (1965). The structure of foreign news. *Journal of Peace Research, 2*, 64-91.

Gans, H. (1979). *Deciding what's news*. New York: Pantheon.

Glazer, N., & Ueda, R. (1983). *Ethnic groups in history textbooks*. Washington, DC: Ethics and Public Policy Center.

Gordon, P., & Klug, F. (1986). *New right, new racism*. London: Searchlight Publications.

Haghighat, C. (1988). *Racisme "scientifique": Offensive contre légalité sociale*. Paris: L'Harmattan.

Hall, S., Critcher, C., Jefferson, T., Clarke, J., & Roberts, B. (1978). *Policing the crisis: Mugging, the state and law and order*. London: Methuen.

Hartmann, P., & Husband, C. (1974). *Racism and the mass media*. London: Davis-Poynter.

Jaynes, G. D., & Williams, R. M. (Eds.). (1989). *A common destiny: Blacks and American society*. Washington, DC: National Academy Press.

Jenkins, R. (1986). *Racism and recruitment: Managers, organisations and equal opportunity in the labour market*. Cambridge, UK: Cambridge University Press.

Jenkins, R., & Solomos, J. (Eds.). (1987). *Racism and equal opportunity in the 1980s*. Cambridge, UK: Cambridge University Press.

Johnson, K. A. (1987). *Media images of Boston's black community* [Research report]. Boston: University of Massachusetts, William Monroe Trotter Institute.

Klein, G. (1986). *Reading into racism*. London: Routledge & Kegan Paul.

Lichter, S. R., Rothman, S., & Lichter, L. (1990). *The media elite: America's new power brokers*. New York: Hastings House.

Martindale, C. (1986). *The white press and black America*. Westport, CT: Greenwood.

Merten, K., Ruhrmann, G., et al. (1986). *Das Bild der Ausländer in der deutschen Presse [The image of foreigners in the German press]*. Frankfurt, Germany: Dagyeli Verlag.

Miles, R. (1982). *Racism and migrant labour*. London: Routledge & Kegan Paul.

Miles, R. (1989). *Racism*. London: Routledge & Kegan Paul.

Mills, C. W. (1956). *The power elite*. London: Oxford University Press.

Milner, D. (1983). *Children and race: Ten years on*. London: Ward Lock Educational.

Phizacklea, A., & Miles, R. (1979). Working class racist beliefs in the inner city. In R. Miles & A. Phizacklea (Eds.), *Racism and political action in Britain* (pp. 93-123). London: Routledge & Kegan Paul.

Preiswerk, R. (Ed.). (1980). *The slant of the pen: Racism in children's books*. Genève: World Council of Churches.

Reeves, F. (1984). *British racial discourse: A study of British political discourse about race and race-related matters*. Cambridge, UK: Cambridge University Press.

Seidel, G. (1985). The concept of culture in the British and French New Right. In R. Levitas (Ed.), *The ideology of the New Right* (pp. 43-60). Oxford, UK: Basil Blackwell.

Seidel, G. (1987). The white discursive order: The British New Right's discourse on cultural racism, with particular reference to the *Salisbury Review*. In I. Zavala, T. A. van Dijk, & M. Diaz-Diocaretz (Eds.), *Approaches to discourse* (pp. 39-66). Amsterdam: John Benjamins.

Seidel, G. (1988). The British New Right's enemy within: The anti-racists. In G. Smitherman-Donaldson & T. A. van Dijk (Eds.), *Discourse and discrimination* (pp. 131-143). Detroit: Wayne State University Press.

Todorov, T. (1988). *Nous et les autres: La réflexion française sur la diversité humaine*. Paris: Seuil.

Troyna, B., & Williams, J. (1986). *Racism, education and the state*. London: Croom Helm.

Tuchman, G. (1978). *Making news: A study in the construction of reality*. New York: Free Press.

UNESCO. (1975). *Race, science and society*. Paris: UNESCO.

van Dijk, T. A. (1983). *Minderheden in de media* (Minorities in the media). Amsterdam: SUA [Socialistische Uitgeverij Amsterdam].

van Dijk, T. A. (1984). *Prejudice in discourse*. Amsterdam: John Benjamins.

van Dijk, T. A. (1987a). *Communicating racism*. Newbury Park, CA: Sage.

van Dijk, T. A. (1987b). *Schoolvoorbeelden van racisme: De reproduktie van racisme in maatschappijleerboeken* [Textbook examples of racism: The reproduction of racism in social science textbooks]. Amsterdam: Socialistische Uitgeverij Amsterdam.

van Dijk, T. A. (1991). *Racism and the press*. London: Routledge & Kegan Paul.

van Dijk, T. A. (1992). Discourse and the denial of racism. *Discourse & Society, 3,* 87-118.

van Dijk, T. A. (1993). *Elite discourse and racism*. Newbury Park: Sage.

Wellman, D. T. (1977). *Portraits of white racism*. Cambridge, UK: Cambridge University Press.

Wilson, C. C., & Gutiérrez, F. (1985). *Minorities and the media*. Beverly Hills, CA: Sage.

Wodak, R., Nowak, P., Pelikan, J., Gruber, H., De Cillia, R., & Mitten, R. (1990). "Wir sind unschuldige Täter." *Studien zum antisemitischen Diskurs im Nachkriegsösterreich*. Frankfurt, Germany: Suhrkamp.

The Use of Hate as a Stratagem for Achieving Political and Social Goals

Rita Kirk Whillock
Southern Methodist University

Editor's Introduction

In the previous chapter, van Dijk helps us understand how elites impose racism on societal structures, even if they unwittingly do so to protect their own vested interests. In this chapter, Rita Kirk Whillock explores the use of hate appeals as intentional persuasion. She makes the case for the existence of what she defines as a "hate stratagem."

Whillock argues that hate appeals are used consciously to inflame the emotions of followers, denigrate the out-class, inflict permanent and irreparable harm on the opposition, and, ultimately, to conquer. Using political campaigns as context, she references examples like the Willie Horton advertisement in the 1988 presidential election and the antigay advertisement used by Patrick Buchanan in the 1994 race. The bulk of the analysis, however, centers on the use of a hate letter widely circulated in a statewide election in an Alabama governor's race.

Through this analysis, Whillock explores how people can use public prejudices and stereotypes as motives to action. In this case, action is taken at the ballot box but it could just as easily be used to create civil unrest or perpetuate violent acts in other contexts. Whillock argues that by understanding hate as a stratagem for victory, we are capable of exposing and defusing its power.

Dirty politics reached an all-time low in 1988 when racial fears became the substance of national debate during a presidential election. The Bush campaign, seeking to define issues that would demonstrate philosophical differences between Republicans and Democrats, zeroed in on an issue that indicated a Dukakis weakness in both polls and focus group analysis. That issue was the Massachusetts furlough policy.

Though the policy was not substantially different from that of programs in 26 other states, the conflict centered on the fact that Governor Dukakis opposed the death penalty. Some reasoned that because many felons released through the furlough program were already serving the maximum sentence allowed by law, other crimes they might commit while on furlough would result in no greater punishment. In essence, felons were given no incentive to stay straight and no stiffer punishment if they committed crimes again.

Both Democrats and Republicans saw the furlough program as a campaign issue. What the Democrats did not expect was the divisive advertisement aired by an independent committee called "Americans for Bush."

The advertisement featured Willie Horton, a convicted murderer, who raped and brutalized a woman while on furlough. Significantly, Willie Horton was black and the woman he raped was white. Why did race matter? The more brutal crime was the one for which Horton was serving a prison term. Horton stabbed a 17-year old student more than 24 times, "cut off his sexual organ, stuck it in his mouth, cut his arms and legs off, and stuck the guy in a trash can" (Atwater, quoted in Runkle, 1989, p. 115). The real issue should have been why such a person would be released from jail for any reason.

The advertisement pointed out a different set of issues, one that struck at the heart of the American psyche. According to Susan Estrich, campaign manager for Dukakis,

> Whether it was intended or not, the symbolism was very powerful . . . you can't find a stronger metaphor, intended or not, for racial hatred in this country than a black man raping a white woman. And that's what the Willie Horton story was. (Estrich, quoted in Runkle, 1989, pp. 115-116)

That perception is culturally and historically rooted. Almost a hundred years ago, one author argued,

> Rape is the most frightful crime which the negroes commit against white people, and their disposition to perpetrate it has increased in spite of the quick and summary punishment that always follows. . . . This proneness of the negro is so well understood that the white women of every class, from the highest to the lowest, are afraid to venture any distance alone . . . for rape, indescribably beastly and loathsome always, is marked, in the instance of its perpetration by a negro, by a diabolical persistence and a malignant atrocity of detail. (Bruce, 1889, p. 83)

This historical image was invoked by the story of Willie Horton. It is an image grounded in fear, history, and the nightly news. For many, the face of crime in America is black and Willie Horton with his Manson eyes personified that fear.

Significantly, the timing of the Horton spot coincided with a Bush furlough advertisement that claimed Massachusetts prisons were revolving doors for convicted felons. The timing is relevant because voters frequently interspersed the two and thought they remembered Horton's face in the revolving door advertisement. They had help.

Several factors combined to produce an indelible impression on the American voter. First, the Horton advertisement made sensational headlines. The advertisement received national news coverage not only at the time it was first aired, but almost every time it was mentioned by party officials or in a political speech. Second, the spot aired for 10 weeks. Few political advertisements are run for this length of time, particularly not ones produced and financed by independent committees. Third, though channeled through an independent committee, the advertisement was the subject of state Republican party fliers and Bush references throughout the campaign.

The Bush campaign tacitly distanced itself from the race issue until they saw the effect the advertisement was having upon voters. At one point Lee Atwater, Bush's campaign strategist, claimed that "by the time we're finished they're going to wonder whether Willie Horton is Dukakis' running mate" (Runkle, 1989, p. 117).

The ethics controversy over the Horton spot dominated much of the political talk during the 1988 general election. Should the Bush campaign have asked that the advertisement be withdrawn? Should the campaign have exercised more control over state party organizations who were giving it even more play? Perhaps we will never know for sure if the Horton spot was instigated at the urging of the Bush campaign or not. What we do know is that it was a deliberate racist appeal and once the race card was played, it was exaggerated for maximum effect by Bush supporters.

The Willie Horton advertisement was not the first time that racial hatred has been introduced in a political campaign, nor will it be the last. Its significance is that it has caused many scholars to reconsider how such feelings can be manipulated for specific effects. Is there a strategy for using hate? Throughout this chapter, I use examples of hate issues in political campaigns as evidence that there is.

One thing should be clear, however: We cannot detect the intent of a rhetor unless he or she provides that information to us. Most often, we are only able to analyze the effects. Yet by studying those effects, we can begin to discover how hate can be used for specific rhetorical ends.

The Strategic Uses of Hate

In normal discursive environments, a communication strategy may be employed that aims to accomplish some specific goal. Given the military implications of the term *strategy,* it is usually perceived as having characteristics of both aggressive positioning and thoughtful defense. In a communication context, the term may be viewed as symbolic warfare (King, 1987, p. 27). Using this rhetorical paradigm, an argumentative strategy might be viewed as discourse involved with the clash of reasoning, supported by emotional appeals and designed to induce compliance.

A rhetorical strategy is different, however, from a stratagem. A *stratagem* is "an artifice or trick in war for deceiving and outwitting the enemy, a cleverly contrived trick or scheme for gaining an end" (Gove, 1986, pp. 225-226). Hate speech is an example of such a stratagem. Rather than seeking to win adherence through superior reasoning, hate speech seeks to move an audience by creating a symbolic code for violence. Its goals are to inflame the emotions of followers, denigrate the designated out-class, inflict permanent and irreparable harm to the opposition, and ultimately conquer.

Why would an unscrupulous rhetor invoke hate appeals into the political process? The answer is simple: to win. Campaigns frequently find themselves frustrated by the fact that they cannot get people to concentrate long enough to talk with them about a subject rationally. Jokes permeate political campaigns about the anti-intellectual nature of the American voting public. Consequently, campaigns spend a great deal of money trying to figure out what people are willing to listen to and responding to the "issue of the day" in order to get media coverage.

The tension is not just between campaigns and the voting public, but also between campaigns and the press. For example, a viable issue in an election might be the way the infrastructure of a community needs to be rebuilt to sustain community growth. Yet candidates complain that when they talk about drainage projects and sewage repairs, the story is buried in the paper and rarely covered on the nightly news. Thus, the criteria of newsworthiness creates tension between the campaign and the press.

Many veteran campaigners believe that the press is more interested in sensationalism than educating the public or supporting democratic values. Roger Ailes, one-time strategist for both Reagan and Bush, has dubbed this phenomenon the "orchestra pit theory of politics": "If you have two guys on stage and one guy says, 'I have a solution to the

Middle East problem,' and the other guy falls into the orchestra pit, who do you think is going to be on the evening news?" (Ailes, as quoted in Runkle, 1989, p. 136).

Politics is loaded with sensational pratfalls. When candidates are not successful in generating media coverage and they cannot find a way to make the public take notice, the climate is ripe for drastic methods.

Hate appeals, unlike pratfalls into an orchestra pit, have a shelf life that exceeds the introduction of the appeal itself. A hate appeal works initially because it is flashy and attracts media attention because of its "explosive and revolutionary character" (Ellul, 1965, p. 73). Importantly, hate stratagems work quickly to produce results. The groundwork for the invocation of hate appeals is often already established through cultural and historical stereotypes. These lessons of childhood, regionalism, race or religion are deep-seated and often invisible from an individual's thought-stream. Once tapped, however, they serve to produce familiar choice patterns.

To explain how hate stratagems can be used in political campaigns, we must first take note of the creation and use of stereotypes and then examine how hate appeals use negative stereotypes to achieve specific rhetorical goals.

The Creation and Use of Stereotypes

People use stereotyping—or classification schemes—almost every day (see, e.g., Bodenhausen & Lichtenstein, 1987). Identifying distinguishing characteristics of people by broad classifications is an attempt to describe some essential property of groups. Although such classification schemes can provide a certain degree of understanding about others, they also deny individuality and heighten differences in ways that can produce fear and alienation (see Staub, 1989, pp. 59-60).

By choice, people will often isolate themselves from designated groups ascribed negative traits or whose values oppose their own. People have a natural tendency to congregate with others with whom they share common attitudes and values (see Asch, 1951). Together, these factors result in polarization between groups. Such polarization occurs whenever people become accustomed to the comfort of similar others, isolate themselves from those who are different, and begin constructing barriers to maintain a "proper" social distance from the designated out-group.

The significance of this self-polarizing behavior is that it creates conditions ripe for hate appeals. By defining out-groups and finding comfort in the conformity of others "like us," out-groups can be just as isolated as they might have been in the controlled setting of the propagandist. This situation may be even more devastating in terms of results because followers are not forced to be isolated. The isolation is self-imposed. To maintain the social order, isolated groups begin to construct self-justifying reasons for their behavior.

None of this becomes threatening or alarming until the groups are forced to compete for some limited rewards, or circumstances develop where one group may gain power (and perhaps domination) over the other (Brehm, 1966; Brehm & Brehm, 1981). For example, Lawrence Bobo explains how blacks and whites in this country have become combatants. He contends that the "American social organization allows and fosters in whites the belief that blacks, in so far as they demand changes in the racial status quo, are a threat to their lifestyles as well as to other valued resources and practices" (Bobo, as quoted in Roth, 1990, p. 32). Once perceptions like this take root, struggles for dominance occur. Such struggles rarely result in a negotiated settlement. Instead, each group begins to develop more reasons to justify and sustain its distrust of the other group (see Rothbart, 1981; Russell & Russell, 1968). Unless the process is halted, feelings of enmity among groups may develop. Concurrently, actions of a single individual become symbolic of the behavior of an entire class of people. In this way, hate is self-perpetuating: "Hate once provoked continues to reproduce itself" (Ellul, 1965, p. 73).

In the initial stages, then, isolation of the designated out-group is useful in order successfully to instill negative stereotypes (see Duster, 1971, p. 27). Perhaps this accounts for why many studies of hate have been associated with propaganda. In that particular setting of controlled communication, rhetors often have the power physically to isolate people from the objects of their hatred. For example, during the Holocaust, Hitler's army isolated Jews in places like the Warsaw ghetto and eventually to concentration camps. In this way, he physically isolated them. Yet Hitler also played upon self-imposed isolation.

Of the six million Jews sent to concentration camps only a half million were "German Jews." The rest were from countries in German-occupied "foreign" lands (Porpora, 1990, p. 43). The differences Hitler depicted were the result not only of religion but also of nationality. By using physical and perceptual separation, Hitler was able to reduce the opportunities for followers to disconfirm the stereotypes he offered. "The Jews" became an isolated, faceless, amorphous crowd.

Isolation, no matter how it is imposed, allows stereotypes to be created that magnify the differences of the out-class, often grotesquely. Moreover, the descriptions do not need to be truthful: "Any statement whatever, no matter how stupid, any 'tall tale' will be believed once it enters into the passionate current of hatred" (Ellul, 1965, p. 74).

One significant facet of stereotyping is that it permits description—and perhaps action against—whole classes of people (see Brewer & Kramer, 1985). This helps to explain why hate is more encompassing than lesser emotions such as anger. Aristotle (1984) notes that whereas anger is directed against individuals, hatred is broader. It may also take aim at whole classes of people (p. 1382a). Individuals, then, become symbols of the group they represent. So important is the symbolic value of these classifications that one way a "hate crime" is identified in American courts of law is by the "symbolic status" of the victim (see Grimshaw, 1969; Nieburg, 1972; Sterba, 1969).

The power of stereotypes is also shown by the fact that they override specific, disproving examples. Individuals whom we may know who do not fit those stereotypes are viewed as exceptions to the rule, or are different because they have risen above their natural instincts to become more "like us." Indeed, Allport (1958) notes that "people who hate groups in the abstract will, in actual conduct, often act fairly and even kindly toward individual members of the group" (p. 32).

Once these stereotypes become grounded and the differences established, stereotypes can be used to accomplish particular rhetorical objectives.

Using Stereotypes to Invoke Hate Appeals

The use of hate as a rhetorical stratagem allows the rhetor to accomplish four specific goals: to inflame the emotions, denigrate the designated out-class, inflict permanent and irreparable harm to the opposition, and ultimately, to conquer. To demonstrate these appeals, the text of a letter circulated in the 1990 Alabama Democratic gubernatorial primary is included at the end of this chapter.

Rarely do we find such a blatant example of the use of hate appeals. In this instance, there can be no doubt that the author's purpose was to use hate to tip the balance of the election. Not known is that author's identity nor the specific intent of the letter.

During the Democratic primary, official campaign stationary for the Flippo campaign was ordered under false pretenses, stolen, and then used for this letter. It was sent to Flippo supporters across the state. The Flippo campaign denied involvement—as the letter claimed it would—and offered a reward for the arrest and conviction of the perpetrator. Because the letter was sent through the mail and the intent was clearly to influence the outcome of the election, a federal mail fraud and election tampering investigation was conducted. To date, no one has been arrested for this crime.

Conspiracy theories abound regarding the author's intent. There are those who believe what the letter said: that someone within the Flippo campaign sent the letter. Others believe that it was written by someone within the Bishop campaign, since the letter harms him the least. Some argue that it was instigated by the Republican party to throw the Democrats into disarray. Importantly, no one knows for sure what the motive was. We only know that it cast suspicions on everyone; caused much pain to candidates, their families, and their supporters; and encouraged untold numbers of people to turn away from the political system.

The only way the letter can serve a greater moral purpose is to expose the hate stratagem used so that such appeals will lose their impact and voters can understand the way even an unknown rhetor has attempted to manipulate their passions.

Inflaming the Emotions

In order to engage the emotions of an audience, a rhetor must first help the audience coalesce into a group. The objective for the communicator is to help individual audience members understand what links them together. Typically, the use of the hate stratagem invites audiences to be linked through the bonds of common experience.

Individuals may feel threatened by any number of issues, from the rising power of an ethnic group to the loss of political structures that have favored their particular values or religious heritage. Individuals may be drawn together by the simple act of acknowledging each other's pain. In a Jesse Helm's advertisement the story is told of a white man rejected for a job reserved for someone else (we assume a black man) because of an Affirmative Action hiring quota. Perhaps, as in a Patrick Buchanan attack against the National Endowment for the Arts, the audience is told about public money supporting arts projects by gays, a lifestyle that stands in opposition to many people's religious beliefs. The stratagem takes root each time the story depicts an injustice to "others like us" and depicts the perpetrator as a member of some out-class.

The rhetor may invoke cultural truisms that link people to a common heritage, draw upon the bonds of common experience, or unite the audience against a common enemy. Whatever the means, the rhetor's task is to acknowledge the audience's feelings and validate them by linking audience members to others who have similar experiences.

Drawing these linkages may be overt or subtle but the effect is clear. By acknowledging individuals' pain and anger, the rhetor provides them with "the sense that they are being recognized and respected" (Lerner, 1992, p. 37). Individuals no longer feel alone or isolated. Most important, once people become united they have no need to feel shame about expressing their feelings. Like a river breaking through a dam, the freeing of emotions long bottled up produces an exhilarating effect.

Once drawn together, the audience becomes empowered in ways individuals were not (King, 1987, pp. 39-44). One of the manifestations of that power is the ability to assign blame for their pain (see Burke, 1966, p. 39). People seem to have a need to defer responsibility for their misfortunes, to blame someone or something beyond their personal control. This action permits the audience to explain their misfortunes while also allowing them to maintain positive images of themselves. Even if the charges are not wholly accurate, the audience becomes engaged in a fantasized community that extols their own virtues while exonerating themselves from any blame for their own misfortunes. As King (1987) notes, "The kind of participation that ensures loyalty is group action in which one does not indulge in the luxury of critical reflection. It is experiential, but not analytic" (p. 24).

The other, and more devastating, effect for those blamed for the audience's misfortunes—the designated out-class—is that these emotional expressions are not diffused but targeted toward the object of their hatred. The rhetor can stoke the fires of that hate by leading the audience to believe that the out-class is a threat to their lifestyles, values, or beliefs (see, e.g., Averill, 1982).

Once the audience accepts that a particular group is responsible for their misfortunes, the threat of future harms against them become more real. The cycle of "they harmed us, we blame them, they continue to threaten us, we must respond" produces a schism between the groups that eventually leads to a breakdown of the dialectic process.

As adherents of a hateful message begin to coalesce into a unified group, they become more certain of the rhetor's claims. From peer reinforcement to testimonials that provide additional anecdotal evidence, the designated out-group becomes further distanced and the claims against them become more vitriolic.

In the hate letter reprinted here, note this cycle of harm-blame-threat intended to provoke an audience response. The author blames Hubbert (a Democrat) for the election of Guy Hunt (the first Republican governor since reconstruction). The harm, we are told, is that the democratic process was subverted when Hubbert "anointed" a nominee instead of letting people elect one. The threat is that he will exercise this kind of power again. Similarly, the author blames liberal teachers and blacks for subverting the political process. The harm is that these groups have ignored the audience's values in previous policy decisions. For example, they have already overlooked instances of corruption such as vote fraud and kept "perverts and incompetents in the classroom." The threat is that the audience can expect more abuses as this group assumes even more power.

Importantly, the use of *synecdoche*—linking smaller events to larger ones and then arguing that the part stands for a larger whole—invites the audience to believe that the examples the rhetor offers are not atypical. Isolated events, then, take on greater significance because they are understood in light of a larger scheme or plan. King (1987) argues that the use of synecdoche is powerful because it makes "a small event appear far more critical than it ordinarily appears" (p. 29).

Typically, the use of synecdoche by hatemongers implies that there is some great conspiracy at work. In the hate letter the rhetor argues that, "It is no secret that behind the scenes gubernatorial politics in Alabama can get mean and nasty." We learn that *they* "have been working for months trying to soil" *our candidate's* "character and reputation." Once that stage has been set, specific examples are provided as "evidence" of a conspiracy. For example, the letter claims that Hubbert was "responsible for the appointment of the 'gang of five' who took the nomination away from Graddick"; that the teachers and blacks "on the State Democratic Executive Committee conducted a purge of conservative and moderate legislators in 1983"; that if their candidate is elected, the liberal teachers and blacks will "control not only the Democratic party, but also the legislature"; and that the opposition and his cronies will "control the state education budget and use their power to force institutions to give kickbacks in return for their appropriation." The author describes a powerful conspiracy working against the people of the state that is depriving them of their legal voice.

The author leads the reader to believe that the only way such abuses can be stopped is if they unite and correctly assess blame so that action can be taken against these perpetrators of evil.

Denigrating the Out-Class

Political wisdom states that it is more effective to give voters one good reason to vote against an opponent than a host of reasons to vote for the candidate you want them to support. One way that can be accomplished is to designate the opponent and his or her supporters as the cause of the voter's misfortunes. Jacque Ellul (1965) notes,

> Whether the object of hatred is the bourgeois, the Communist, the Jew, the colonialist, or the saboteur makes no difference. Propaganda of agitation succeeds each time it designates someone as the source of all misery, provided that he is not too powerful. (p. 73)

The confirmation of these out-groups as the source of misery works to produce significant effects. The depth of feeling against members of the out-group is extreme. Aristotle notes that whereas anger can be cured with time, hatred cannot. Hate moves people beyond feeling. Those who hate have no feeling toward the objects of their attack. They do not care if these persons suffer, for "they would have them cease to exist" if that were possible (Aristotle, 1984, p. 1382a). Indeed, once the source of misery is identified, "it must be rooted out if the people of the nation are to achieve the human satisfactions and community that they seek" (Lerner, 1992, p. 39).

Once the out-group has been designated, the rhetor can begin inoculating the audience against rebuttal (for an explanation of the inoculation techniques see McGuire & Papageorgis, 1961; Petty & Cacioppo, 1977). Hate appeals cannot succeed if the audience believes that the instances cited are atypical or are of little material consequence to their daily lives. The rhetor needs to predispose an audience to construct arguments against opposing claims. One way to achieve this is to set up a situation where each response offered by the out-class is predictable.

In the hate letter, note the number of instances where the author in essence tells the reader how a candidate is likely to respond to these charges. James, we are told, will claim to be a conservative, not a liberal. Yet the author implies that we can determine his liberal leaning by his activities: "Although he presents himself as a conservative businessman's candidate, there were at least seven tax increases during the James administration." The author warns that James will tell you that he is honest, but then the author claims James shredded public records. The author predicts James will tell you he is religious, then argues that "his real life is anything but Christian" and points to alleged extramarital affairs. In this way, the audience is given arguments to use when a supporter of an opposition candidate makes a claim or the candidate tries to defend himself. Essentially, the rhetor narrows the ground on which a member of the out-class can persuasively argue.

Another strategy the rhetor may use is to vilify the out-class in ways that make it difficult to elicit the support of others in mounting a response. The villains in a hate story must, therefore, be made to appear as evil, opposing the values of the audience. In this letter, for example, gays are not only different because of their sexual habits. The letter leads the reader to believe gays are sinister, seeking to impose themselves on society's truly innocent: the children. In the letter, we learn that "Hubbert hired a Montgomery lawyer to fight the dismissal of a junior high school teacher in Huntsville who had been convicted of sodomy with three young boys."

Similarly, we are told that liberals are more than people with differing views of government. The letter leads the audience to believe they are spineless ("In the face of black voter fraud Siegelman as attorney general looked the other way and left it to federal officials to prosecute"), extremist ("he supported McGovern in 1972 and Dukakis in 1988, worked for liberal Congressman Al Lowenstein, and took a campaign contribution from Jane Fonda"), and drug-users ("Siegelman claims to be a leader in the war on drugs even though he has admitted that he used marijuana"). Black leaders are depicted as carpetbaggers who helped in the "purge" of conservatives and moderates from the legislature. Blacks are typified by the actions of one leader who routinely abuses power to get "lucrative land deals and other perks and rip-offs."

By portraying the out-class in extreme ways, few people from the same out-class will find the strength to support those under attack. Hate works in part by displacing responsibility for a person's problems and selecting a suitable scapegoat; generally one who is weaker, and often found alone without "group support" so that he or she is more easily preyed upon. In the hate letter, note that to defend the actions of the out-class, a person would also have to account for the actions of those extremists whose actions have produced the enmity. Blacks would have to support a carpetbagger while gays would have to defend child molesters. Too often, out-groups are not willing to bear that responsibility nor effective enough to change the rhetorical situation. The result is that whole groups are convicted based on the actions (or supposed actions) of the few. Members of the out-class become more isolated and less likely to congregate for fear of being labeled in such negative ways.

Significantly, as stereotypes take hold, these acts of self-isolation make members of the out-class more vulnerable to attack. Studies of hate crime in the United States, for example, find that in general, there are a number of perpetrators, usually outnumbering victims two-to-one (see Berk, Boyd, & Hammer, 1992, pp. 131-132). Victims found in a weakened state are more vulnerable to attack.

Ultimately, the audience is asked to target its hatred and to retaliate against members of those groups who are responsible for the breakdown of societal values.

Inflicting Permanent and Irreparable Harm

One characteristic of hate crimes in the United States is that the perpetrators rarely *take* something of value from those they seek to harm. Instead, something of value is defaced or destroyed. This characteristic is also applicable when hate appeals enter public discourse.

The most notable application of this principle is how the hate appeals attempt to destroy the validity of characteristics the victim uses to create his or her identity. The criticism it offers, then, is not designed to improve the opponent, but to deface or destroy him. In the hate letter, note how the author chooses to attack the candidates. Siegelman claims to be a Christian, we are told. The implication is that this is a positive identity. But we learn that his wife is a Jew, an obviously negative attribute to the author because the question is asked: "Do you think the people of Alabama want a Jew family living in the Governor's mansion?" The criticism—that his wife is Jewish—is a defining characteristic and one that will not go away as if it were some bad habit that needed to be broken. To attack his wife on these grounds is to defame her very worth as a person. Yet the damage is not limited to his wife. The author of the letter also implies that Siegelman is an unworthy Christian since he has married a Jew. Being closely associated with a member of a designated out-class implies that Siegelman may be "one of them" and not "one of us." A power relationship is also implied. Using this warped logic, marrying a Jew makes Siegelman a weaker Christian but his wife is depicted as no less a Jew. The Siegelmans are thereby labeled a "Jewish family" that will change the social order of the state house.

James and Bishop are similarly attacked for personal characteristics. Again, the author of the hate letter identifies traits for which there is no reasonable defense. We are told that James is inept, ignorant, stupid, dishonest, and immoral while Bishop is a hot-tempered, ignorant red-neck. The question that analysts must ask is "How do you mount a defense against those charges?" There are many anecdotal pieces of evidence to support the presence of these characteristics in many people. On balance, how would a person prove that these were *not* defining characteristics? The answer is that there is no ready defense strategy. As with the Siegelman example, the charges levied against the candidates are designed to inflict permanent and irreparable harm. That goal is achieved whatever response is mounted.

In each of these charges, the problems cited do not reside with systems or processes that can be corrected, but in the inherent negative characteristics of particular groups of people: the "liberal establishment," the blacks, the Jews, the gays. We are led to believe that these groups have harmed our society and—barring some conversion experience—that these perpetrators of evil will continue to wreak havoc until they are replaced with more suitable representatives.

More importantly, there is no effective response. When the hate stratagem is applied, members of the targeted group are routinely placed into a defensive-avoidance position. Strategies may include a denial of the charges ("that is untrue"), a defense ("the teacher's union routinely provides legal counsel for any member charged with an offense that may threaten his or her job"), a counterattack ("we don't have to resort to smear campaigns to win"), or atonement ("we're sorry that you feel that way, give us a chance to show that we are not like the stereotype you've described").

Both defensive and avoidance strategies are ineffectual in responding to the out-group treatment of the hater. The use of response strategies implies that the opposition will respond to a reasoned defense, or at least find an unreceptive climate for future attacks. By contrast, the stratagem of hate is designed to conquer, not to negotiate. The result is that rather than defusing a crisis, victim responses often escalate the problem. They fuel the fires of hate by proving that the message had the harmful effects intended.

Too often, no response is offered by groups whose combined voice might convey strength. Out-groups may be distinguished by some class or category, but they may not comprise a unified group that interacts with one another. Indeed, members of the designated out-group may even refrain from associating with one another in an attempt to avoid being stigmatized by negative labels. The real value of an out-group to the hate monger is symbolic. Yet, the hate stratagem cannot be fully understood until we also recognize the desire of the rhetor to conquer the opponent.

The Quest to Conquer

Each of us probably has the desire to remove from our lives those things that create unwanted pain. Similarly, as a society we might prefer to banish murderers, robbers, and rapists. We take this action not only because these perpetrators commit evil acts but because they have brought pain to those we love. So strong is the relationship between love and hate that Allport (1958) argues that hatred cannot exist "unless something one values has been violated. Love is a precondition of hate" (p. 32).

In the hate letter, note how the author identifies the objects of love that have been harmed by these villains. The most obvious is the candidate for whom the letter is supposedly written. Others include a democratically elected government, a government that represents conservative and moderate interests, the state's children and their education, Christian values and heritage, competent management of government funds, and honest leaders. Hate appeals offer a kind of retribution for the pain inflicted upon us or threatening those institutions we cherish.

Sometimes it is possible literally to exterminate those we hate. Yet groups can also be similarly banished if stripped of their power, possessions, and influence. Such actions quite literally negate the group's social existence.

The quest to define and distance ourselves from things, people, or actions we find abhorrent is a natural phenomenon. Burke's claim that we define ourselves by what we are *not* supports this assumption. These negations are evident in all societies and may extend to whole classes of people when objects are designated for disdain and societal taboos established. The stratagem of hate attempts to mirror this negating process. The true goal of the stratagem is to remove the offending agent entirely, or to negate its very existence. Yet a fine distinction must be drawn. The issue is not that groups are different. It is that hate appeals make use of the difference to destroy the lines of communication that might help foster a climate for peaceful coexistence (Memmi, 1971, p. 187).

Once suitable issues are detected for hate appeals, rhetors can make use of the deeply embedded cultural truisms that influence our actions, including the way we vote. In American politics, for example, race, religion, and ethnicity are issues that serve hate stratagems well. These are issues that voters care about (see Dennis, 1981). First Amendment protections of religion, the abolition of slavery, and the immigration of millions from nations around the world all serve as examples of the clashes and challenges that have defined our national character. These clashes have resulted in strong views and cultural stereotypes that are easily invoked. Rhetors can prey upon these tendencies to influence election outcomes with incentives provided by hate appeals. We know, for example, that American voters have strong preexisting views on race that predisposes them to accepting certain tales as true. Evidence suggests that whites avoid contact with blacks, making most of their assumptions from stereotypic ideas about them (see Carter & Helms, 1990; Dennis, 1981). These views are reflected in voting decisions. Numerous studies show that in this country, voters typically vote for members of their own racial group (see Chubbick, Renwick, & Walker, 1970; Gaertner & McLaughlin, 1983; Hahn & Almay, 1971; Lieske & Hilliard, 1984; Pettigrew, 1972; Vanderleeuw & Engstrom, 1987). American voters, then, already hold biased views toward members of other ethnic groups. Hate appeals merely raise the consciousness level so that voters do not forget to act on their prejudice.

Hate appeals invite people to participate, to act out their hate. By withholding a vote from particular candidates or casting it in favor of another, the vote becomes both a voice and an instrument of negation. Those who accept the validity of the hate letter message, for example, would clearly understand whom they should vote against. On another level, we could also speculate that people who found the entire episode morally repugnant might vote against the whole group of Democrats, including the one the letter is supposed to help. Although we do not know the motive of the author, we can easily surmise the intent was to harm the out-classes and defeat those who would represent their interests.

The danger imposed by rhetors of hate messages is that they argue with the intent of annihilation. Stratagems do not work incrementally to produce measured results over time. They are revolutionary in spirit and effect. In extreme situations, riots, strikes, and demonstrations are to be expected as the end result once the out-group discovers it has no legitimate way to respond. Yet these acts of desperation do not resolve problems or lead to recognition for the out-class. They only provide evidence for the rhetor's claims and more justification for the rhetor's quest to eliminate the out-class entirely.

Hate appeals are often used when more rational approaches have failed to produce the desired effects. They are a winner-take-all device. Once carried out, the feelings aroused cannot be satiated and the object of the hatred can no longer be condoned. By utilizing hate speech, the rhetor attempts to subvert opposing arguments and to narrow the valid argumentative ground on which opponents might construct a claim. Critical to an understanding of this communication is that once hate is unleashed, and the dialectical process breaks down, recovery is virtually unattainable. Ellul (1965) notes,

> What has been unleashed cannot be brought under control so easily, particularly habits of violence or taking the law into one's own hands—these disappear very slowly. This is even more true because results achieved by revolution are usually deceptive; just to seize power is not enough. The people want to give full vent to the hatred developed. (p. 76)

The fact that hatred is so deep-seated means that it is not responsive to restorative persuasion. It only fuels the desire to annihilate the enemy.

Against Trivializing Hate

In American society, the routine expression of a powerful negative emotion such as hate is treated as a societal taboo. Parents teach children to avoid saying they hate someone and social stigmas are cast on those haters whose message is viewed as deviant from social norms. Rather than acknowledging the magnitude of the feeling, the term is frequently trivialized by equating it with dislike—as when we "hate" a sweater or the rain. We might assume that the act of hating, except in rare circumstances, is considered outside the bounds of our culture's mores. Perhaps this is because the culture recognizes the severity and power of this emotion.

I argue that hate is not viewed as outside the bounds of societal interest. From societal sanctioning of the Salem witch-hunts or the McCarthy hearings, to outrage over Wounded Knee and Mi Lai, American history is replete with examples of how society has attempted to come to terms with acts of hatred. Such struggles will continue to exist as long as we keep trying to define (or redefine) our culture's core values and the consequent objects for its disdain.

Whether casting a ballot in favor of or against a candidate or proposition or taking some specific action like laying in front of an abortion clinic, rhetors use hate appeals to provide the audience with a sense of purpose, to reinforce the notion that their actions make a difference. Rhetors create an increased urgency to talk, fight, stand up for beliefs, or support (or reject) a particular candidate. The result is that an individual's life becomes filled with a greater sense of purpose and urgency. The audience becomes empowered through the consensus of people with whom a person identifies. The use of hate can be powerful and has the potential, when used appropriately, to achieve positive outcomes.

More notable, however, is the use of hate stratagems to divide and conquer. Rhetors may use hate appeals to accomplish selfish goals, blame others, and legitimize power dominance: "and the hatred it offers him is not shameful, evil hatred that he must hide, but a legitimate hatred, which he can justly feel" (Ellul, 1965, p. 152).

Far from the notion that it is only used as a propaganda technique in state-controlled cultures, hate speech can be used to establish in-groups and out-groups in any culture. Strong negative emotions such as hate can be used to polarize particular groups to solidify support and marshal resources toward forcing a "final solution" to a thorny problem.

Political campaigns provide fertile ground for using hate appeals to win value clashes. The very nature of the political process is to establish majority domination and control. As discussed in other chapters of this book, current debates over social issues such as abortion, gay rights, or affirmative action provide insight into what happens when members of a culture are bitterly divided over substantive issues.

This chapter uses illustrations from both the 1988 presidential election and the 1990 Alabama Democratic gubernatorial primary to demonstrate how hate appeals created a divisive climate. Because of the invocation of hate appeals, good people were harmed and whole groups of people became less trustful of others' motives and less respectful of other's differences. The authors of these hate messages were successful: They subverted rational argument, denigrated whole groups of people, irrevocably harmed the opponent, and ultimately, succeeded in breaking down the tentative bonds of trust between differing groups.

In order to stop ourselves from responding to hate appeals, we must first understand how we are manipulated by them. Perhaps then we will better understand the need to expose these appeals, for only members of the dominant class have the power to expose hate as a stratagem for victory; only members of the in-class have the power and the voice to defend the out-class against stereotypic depictions and false injury claims.

(References begin on page 53)

▨FLIPPO
FOR GOVERNOR

TO: Flippo Contributors and Supporters

SUBJECT: Flippo Auxiliary Communication Team (FACT)

DATE: May 14, 1990   CONFIDENTIAL

    Although you may not have been able to give Ronnie significant financial support, you now have an opportunity to make a valuable contribution that will cost only a few minutes of your time each day.

    The Democratic primary for Governor is just three weeks away. Now that voters are beginning to pay more attention to the candidates, the campaign is entering a new and critical stage. The Flippo campaign and all of the other candidates will be on television with extensive advertising during these final days. Television commercials, however, are only one source of information for voters. Word of mouth communications from friends and acquaintances can be just as important. That is why we have formed FACT, the Flippo Auxiliary Communication Team.

    FACT is extremely important, but also extremely sensitive and confidential. Because fundraising has been so successful, we can buy access to voters' living rooms to deliver Ronnie's positive message through paid television advertising. Voters also need to know why they should <u>not</u> vote for our opponents, but obviously Ronnie does not want to be associated with negative campaigning. For that reason, <u>it is essential that you keep the existence of FACT and any communication relative to FACT confidential.</u> Understandably Ronnie, campaign manager Joe McLean and press secretary Steve Cohen must treat FACT as unofficial and unauthorized. Nevertheless we want <u>you</u> to know that what you are doing is very important and deeply appreciated.

    It is no secret that behind the scenes gubernatorial politics in Alabama can get mean and nasty. James, Siegelman and especially Hubbert staffers have been working for months trying to soil Ronnie's character and reputation. Since this is likely to be a very close election, it is time we fight fire with fire. Attached are a few "talking points" for you to use in your private conversations. Voters need to know this information so they are not tricked by our opponent's slick advertising campaigns. Remember, your job is not to spread lies or rumors, just FACT.

Mailing Address:
Post Office Box 245 / Florence, Alabama / 35631-0245
(205) 760-1990 / FAX (205) 760-8877
Office Location: 120 West Mobile Street

Paid for by Flippo For Governor. Mims Rogers, Treasurer 8

FLIPPO AUXILIARY COMMUNICATION TEAM

Gubernatorial Campaign FACT Sheet

Paul Hubbert

1.   More than any other person, Paul Hubbert was responsible for
      the election of Guy Hunt in 1986. It was Hubbert who talked
      Baxley into contesting the election and who was responsible
      for the appointment of the "gang of five" who took the
      nomination away from Graddick. It was Hubbert who insisted
      a new primary not be held but that Baxley be anointed as the
      nominee of the party.

2.   Hubbert's teachers and Joe Reed's blacks on the State
      Democratic Executive Committee conducted a purge of
      conservative and moderate legislators in 1983. Instead of
      allowing the people to vote, Hubbert and Reed hand-picked
      their friends and punished their enemies.

3.   If Paul Hubbert becomes Governor, Joe Reed will become the
      second most powerful man in Alabama. As the new head of AEA
      as well as ADC, Reed's blacks and teachers will control not
      only the Democratic party, but also the legislature. What
      Joe Reed wants, Joe Reed will get...no contest.

4.   Hubbert and Reed have enriched themselves not only at the
      expense of the teachers and black voters they supposedly
      represent, but the taxpayers as well. Hubbert has pocketed
      enormous sums of money as a middle man for teacher's health
      insurance, while Reed uses his political clout to intimidate
      officials at Alabama State University into giving him
      lucrative land deals and other perks and ripoffs. Reed and
      Hubbert already control the state education budget and use
      their power to force institutions to give kickbacks in
      return for their appropriation.

5.   In 1985, Hubbert hired a Montgomery lawyer to fight the
      dismissal of a junior high school teacher in Huntsville who
      had been convicted of sodomy with three young boys.
      Hubbert's lawyer argued strongly that the teacher should be
      allowed to keep his job and stay in the classroom. There
      are numerous examples where Hubbert and Reed have fought to
      keep perverts and incompetents in the classroom teaching our
      children.

Don Siegelman

1.   Siegelman's left wing leanings are no secret to those who
      keep up with politics, but many of your friends and

acquaintances may not know about him or may need reminding. Make sure they know he supported McGovern in 1972 and Dukakis in 1988, worked for liberal Congressman Al Lowenstein, and took a campaign contribution from Jane Fonda.

2. Siegelman tries to present himself as a champion of election reform when in fact all he has done throughout his political career has been to cater to labor and black voter groups. As secretary of state he forced through changes in the law that liberalized voter registration and absentee voting In the face of black voter fraud Siegelman as attorney general looked the other way and left it to federal officials to prosecute.

3. Siegelman claims to be a leader in the war on drugs even though he has admitted that he used marijuana. Is this the kind of example you want to set for your children?

4. Siegelman claims to be a Christian but his wife, Lorie, is a Jew. Do you think the people of Alabama want a Jew family living in the Governor's Mansion? Be certain that you inform the members of your church.

Fob James

1. Although he presents himself as a conservative businessman's candidate, there were at least seven tax increases during the James administration. In 1980 he increased property taxes by 10 mills and added four cents per gallon to the tax on gas and oil. As Governor, James also increased the coal severance tax, motor vehicle tax, cigarette tax, alcoholic beverage tax, transient occupancy tax, and in 1982 approved a bill calling for a property reappraisal (resulting in tax increases) across the state.

2. As Governor, James was politically inept. Virtually every major proposal he presented was shot down because he was incapable of making the political process work. In an appalling display of ignorance, James accidently pocket vetoed the work of an entire special session of the legislature. By failing to deliver the bills to the secretary of state before the deadline, he accidently vetoed 22 crime bills and wasted $300,000 of taxpayers' money for the special session.

3. Although James has the image of being honest (even if he was stupid), Fob had his share of cronies who got rich at public expense. In fact, he was so concerned about being discovered that just before he left office Fob ordered at least 60 boxes of incriminating records shredded and disposed of—in violation of state public records laws.

James uses school prayer and his wife's involvement with
national religious organizations to appeal to Christian
voters, but his real life is anything but Christian. It is
no secret that while he was Governor, James was a heavy
drinker and maybe even a borderline alcoholic. What is not
so well known is that he is a compulsive womanizer. While
Bobbie was off at religious meetings or while Fob was
supposed to be hiding behind a duck blind in Canada, Mr.
James was pursuing another type of wildlife. Although most
of Fob's companions were recruited from the private sector,
apparently at least one female member of the Governor's
staff was called upon to "entertain" Fob several times.
Among her close friends the phrase "Fobbed again" took on
new meaning.

Charles Bishop

1.   While Bishop is hopelessly behind and not a serious
     contender, he does cut into Ronnie's north Alabama base
     slightly so its important that we offer a little ammunition
     to cut him down. Bishop portrays himself as a successful
     businessman but in reality he's nothing more than an
     ignorant redneck who got lucky and made some money. Bishop
     almost makes Guy Hunt look sophisticated.

2.   During his first term in the state senate, Bishop's payoff
     for helping Baxley get elected lieutenant governor was an
     appointment as chairman of the rules committee. His style
     was arrogant and dictatorial. He never held public
     committee meetings, and in fact the only time the committee
     met at all was when they happened to get together at one of
     the Montgomery bars.

3.   Even Paul Hubbert, who is courting Bishop for his support in
     the runoff, says privately that Bishop was so ineffective in
     the senate that it was better to have him against you than
     for you. Bishop frequently lost his temper on the senate
     floor and invited opponents to step outside so he could
     "whip their ass."

Figure 2.1.   An Example of a Hate Letter

References

Allport, G. W. (1958). The nature of prejudice. In R. M. Baird & S. E. Rosenbaum (Eds.), *Bigotry, prejudice, and hatred: Definitions, causes, and solutions.* Buffalo, NY: Prometheus.

Aristotle. (1984). *The rhetoric and the poetics of Aristotle* (W. R. Roberts, Trans.). New York: Modern Library.

Asch, S. E. (1951). Effects of group pressure upon the modification and distortion of judgments. In H. Guetzkow (Ed.), *Group, leadership, and men* (pp. 177-190). Pittsburgh, PA: Carnegie Press.

Averill, J. R. (1982). *Anger and aggression: An essay on emotion.* New York: Springer.

Berk, R. A., Boyd, E. A., & Hammer, K. M. (1992). Thinking more clearly about hate motivated crimes. In G. M. Herek & K. T. Berrill (Eds.), *Hate crimes: Confronting violence against lesbians and gay men* (pp. 123-132). Newbury Park, CA: Sage.

Bodenhausen, G. V., & Lichtenstein, M. (1987). Social stereotypes and information processing strategies. *Journal of Personality and Social Psychology, 52,* 871-880.

Brehm, J. W. (1966). *A theory of psychological reactance.* New York: Academic Press.

Brehm, S. S., & Brehm, J. W. (1981). *Psychological reactance.* New York: Academic Press.

Brewer, M. B., & Kramer, R. M. (1985). The psychology of intergroup attitudes and behavior. *Annual Review of Psychology, 36,* 219-243.

Bruce, P. A. (1889). *The plantation negro as a freeman.* New York: G. P. Putnam.

Burke, K. (1966). *Language as symbolic action.* Berkeley: University of California Press.

Carter, R. T., & Helms, J. E. (1990). White racial identity, attitudes, and cultural values. In J. E. Helms (Ed.), *Racial identity attitudes: Theory, research, and practice* (pp. 145-164). Westport, CT: Greenwood.

Chubbick, J., Renwick, E., & Walker, J. (1970). An analysis of the 1970 New Orleans mayoral election. *Louisiana Business Survey, 12,* 8-12.

Dennis, R. M. (1981). Socialization and racism: The white experience. In B. P. Bowser & R. G. Hunt (Eds.), *Impact of racism on white Americans* (pp. 71-86). Beverly Hills, CA: Sage.

Duster, T. (1971). Conditions for a guilt-free massacre. In S. Sanford & C. Comstock (Eds.), *Sanctions of evil* (pp. 24-36). San Francisco: Jossey-Bass.

Ellul, J. (1965). *Propaganda: The formation of men's attitudes.* New York: Vintage.

Gaertner, S. L., & McLaughlin, J. (1983). Racial stereotypes: Associations and ascriptions of positive and negative characteristics. *Social Psychology Quarterly, 46,* 23-30.

Gove, P. B. (Ed.). (1986). *Webster's third new international dictionary of the English language unabridged.* Springfield, MA: Merriam-Webster.

Grimshaw, A. D. (1969). Three views of urban violence: Civil disturbance, racial revolt, class assault. In A. D. Grimshaw (Ed.), *Racial violence in the United States* (pp. 385-396). Chicago: Aldine.

Hahn, H., & Almay, T. (1971). Ethnic politics and racial issues: Voting in Los Angeles. *Western Political Quarterly, 24,* 719-730.

King, A. (1987). *Power & communication.* Prospect Heights, IL: Waveland.

Lerner, M. (1992). Stopping David Duke and Patrick Buchanan. *Tikkun, 7,* 37-42.

Lieske, J., & Hilliard, J. W. (1984). The racial factor in urban elections. *Western Political Quarterly, 37,* 545-563.

McGuire, W. J., & Papageorgis, D. (1961). The relative efficacy of various types of prior belief-defense in producing immunity against persuasion. *Journal of Abnormal and Social Psychology, 62*, 327-337.

Memmi, A. (1971). *Dominated man.* Boston: Beacon.

Nieburg, H. L. (1972). Agonistics—Rituals of conflict. In J. F. Short, Jr., & M. E. Wolfgang (Eds.), *Collective violence* (pp. 82-99). Chicago: Aldine.

Pettigrew, T. (1972). When a black candidate runs for mayor: Race and voting behavior. In H. Hahn (Ed.), *People and politics in urban society* (pp. 95-118). Beverly Hills, CA: Sage.

Petty, R. E., & Cacioppo, J. T. (1977). Forewarning, cognitive responding, and resistance to persuasion. *Journal of Personality and Social Psychology, 35*, 645-655.

Porpora, D. V. (1990). *How holocausts happen.* Philadelphia: Temple University Press.

Roth, B. M. (1990). Social psychology's "racism." *The Public Interest, 98*, 26-36.

Rothbart, M. (1981). Memory processing and social beliefs. In D. L. Hamilton (Ed.), *Cognitive processes in stereotyping and intergroup behavior* (pp. 145-182). Hillsdale, NJ: Lawrence Erlbaum.

Runkle, D. R. (Ed.). (1989). *Campaign for president: The campaign managers look at '88.* Westport, CT: Auburn House.

Russell, C., & Russell, W. M. S. (1968). *Violence, monkeys and man.* London: Macmillan.

Staub, E. (1989). *The roots of evil: The origins of genocide and other group violence.* Cambridge, UK: Cambridge University Press.

Sterba, R. (1969). Some psychological factors in Negro face hatred in anti-Negro riots. In A. D. Grimshaw (Ed.), *Racial violence in the United States* (pp. 385-396). Chicago: Aldine.

Vanderleeuw, J., & Engstrom, R. L. (1987). Race, referendum, and roll-off. *Journal of Politics, 49*, 1081-1092.

The Gay Agenda

Marketing Hate Speech to Mainstream Media

Marguerite J. Moritz
University of Colorado

Editor's Introduction

The mass media is often—and erroneously—considered a neutral source of public information. Journalistic pleas for fairness and the principles of equal time for disparate voices may be lofty goals but they are rarely executed in a climate devoid of value judgments. Meg Moritz helps us understand the media's approach to controversial issues and makes us aware of how the media can be influenced by organizations perpetuating negative stereotypes.

Moritz develops her case through an analysis of the Far Right's strategies in attacking the gay and lesbian community in the United States. She helps us understand the use of implied authority pro- vided by elites such as doctors, educators, or authors. She examines the use of visceral visual images as the wallpapering that leads seemingly rational critics to (mis)interpret otherwise neutral verbal descriptions. And she explores the responsibility of the media to become more active adjudicators of images they project.

No doubt competing groups will continue to try to privilege their messages by establishing the framework in which future societal debates will be judged. Moritz challenges the reader to consider how this practice leads to mainstream endorsement of hate as targeted groups are stereotyped and marginalized.

When, in a matter of months, lesbians appear on the cover of *Newsweek, New York Magazine,* and *Vanity Fair,* when the topic of gay men in the military is taken up by *60 Minutes, Nightline,* and network news shows, when *U.S. News & World Report* offers a piece on same-sex romantic friendships of the 19th century and when gay life on college campuses is discussed in *Redbook,* one might wonder whether a revolution has taken place in the nation's most influential editorial offices (see, e.g., Bennetts, 1993; Kasindorf, 1993; Mansfield, 1993; Salholz, 1993; "Straight Talk," 1993). Indeed, the attention gays and lesbians are receiving today in the mass media is long overdue and in some senses gratifying, but there are also signs that changes won't come easily nor will they go unchallenged.

Despite "Lesbian Chic," "The Power and the Pride," "My Brother's Gay . . . Big Whoop!" and other such encouraging headlines, news media practices continue to be deeply implicated in the perpetuation of a heterosexist, homophobic culture and in the privileging of elite white, conservative male voices. One of the most obvious manifestations of this is the space and time devoted to the antigay agenda of the Radical Right.[1] When reporters present news stories on issues pertaining to African Americans or to Jews and other ethnic and religious minorities, they do not seek out the Ku Klux Klan or the neo-Nazis to represent the so-called other side. Yet when gay and lesbian issues are raised, inevitably journalists include a spokesperson who espouses an antigay agenda and invoke the rationale of objectivity to justify the practice. And, just at the time that newsroom personnel are beginning to identify their own antigay biases, the Radical Right leadership itself has become more media savvy in pushing its message. Their tactics in the 1992 elections provide perhaps the most vivid and useful examples of how a hate campaign can be manipulated, marketed, and made palatable to mass media practitioners and their audiences alike.

A Critical Test

The 1992 elections were a critical test for the antigay agenda of the Radical Right. Anticommunism had lost its compelling power and antiabortion efforts were losing ground. Perhaps sensing that the antigay message would be easier to sell to a wider constituency, fundamentalist Christian leaders around the country often launched their frontal assaults with a condemnation of homosexuality and a declaration against the growing gay rights movement.

The gay rights controversy has become the wedge issue of the right wing. Using this wedge as a point of entry, right-wingers are infiltrating mainstream institutions, raising money, and building a base of power that will ultimately serve a much broader political agenda that only begins with dismantling many of the gains of the gay rights movement (S. Nakagawa, Internet communication, 1994).[2]

Oregon and Colorado were singled out as the prime battlefields where the ideological warfare would take place. In Oregon, the ballot initiative had a take-no-prisoners tone: The *New York Times* called it the "strongest anti-homosexual measure ever considered by a state" (Egan, 1992, p. 1).[3] In essence the Oregon measure would have required state institutions, including schools, to actively work against any acceptance of homosexual lifestyles. It defined homosexuality as "abnormal, wrong, unnatural and perverse" and equated it with pedophilia (Egan, 1992, p. 1). The Colorado proposal was seemingly more limited, aiming at revoking antidiscrimination protections in Denver, Boulder, and Aspen and also at denying any court relief to gays, lesbians, or bisexuals wanting to make claims of discrimination.

In the period before the election, a wide range of campaign literature was created by various political and religious groups. One of the
more virulent efforts at persuasion in Colorado was an 18-page
booklet entitled *Death Penalty for Homosexuals Is Prescribed in the
Bible,* put out by Pastor Peter J. Peters of the Eastern Plains town of
LaPorte (Peters, 1992). Quoting extensively from the Bible, the pamphlet not only condemns gays and lesbians, saying that "intolerance
of, discrimination against and the death penalty for" (p. 3) homosexuals is directly commanded in the Scriptures, but it also criticizes the
conservative Colorado for Family Values (CFV) because their ballot
proposal did not go far enough. It was CFV that launched the antigay
initiative known as Amendment Two. Peters (1992) criticized their
efforts because, among other shortcomings, the amendment did not
deny homosexuals freedom of speech and free assembly:

> The historical record shows that forty years ago, family values in America
> would never allow homosexuals to have free speech, free assembly, safety,
> etc., and thus, the homosexual was afraid to come out of the closet. Now
> lukewarm Judeo-Christians consider it family values to allow them to do
> so. (p. 3)

This kind of hate speech, clearly identifiable and undeniably extreme, was common during and after the political campaign. As offensive as these efforts were, however, they were—precisely because of
their extremism—politically less threatening and less effective than
some of the more moderate approaches with the same objective. When
Pete Peters advocated legislation to make homosexuality a crime
punishable by death, when he called on the state to eliminate or exterminate an entire group of people, he based his claim upon a literal
interpretation of the Bible and his strongest appeal was to religious
fundamentalists. Mainstream audiences, even very conservative ones,
may not have been persuaded.

By contrast, the Radical Right has been more effective with its
antigay efforts when it has reframed the argument as a "special rights"
issue, obscured its religious motivations and connections, toned down
its language, and focused its attack on individuals and groups that most
critically challenge conventional standards for public behavior and
cultural expression:

the Religious Right has learned to adopt new tactics, concentrating on local and state politics and coalition building. It has learned to moderate its rhetoric, self-consciously appealing to "common sense" values instead of quoting scripture. In November of 1990, in fact, a symposium of Christian Right leaders was held under the auspices of the Heritage Foundation in Washington, D.C. to develop this new strategy. (J. Mozzochi, G. Leichtling, & S. Gardiner, Internet communication, 1994)[4]

Nowhere are these tactics more clearly shown than in a videotape titled *The Gay Agenda,* one of the most widely circulated and frequently discussed pieces of propaganda to emerge from the 1992 campaign. In both form and content its message pushes the hate speech debate into areas that are at once more problematic and more compelling.

Dueling Videos

The Gay Agenda is a 19-minute videotape constructed in traditional, formal news documentary style. It relies heavily on interviews with persons presented as experts and combines their comments with news footage of gay rights demonstrations and gay pride parades. In addition, the video uses footage of ads from gay magazines and still photos of a drag queen who went straight, got married, and now talks about living a happy, heterosexual life. Its audio track includes the diagetic sound of interviewees as well as the extra-diagetic sound added for a music track and for a "Voice-of-God" narrator.

The video was produced prior to the 1992 November elections and was made available in both Oregon and Colorado. Its creators have claimed that they distributed 10,000 copies in those two states alone, many of them handed out free of charge. After the election the distribution effort continued, and by early 1993 *The Gay Agenda* had started circulating in Washington, D.C. When the Commandant of the United States Marine Corps got a copy he told Congresswoman Pat Schroeder in a letter that he had it sent out to the rest of the Joint Chiefs of Staff (Flanders, 1993a, 1993b).

As the tape made the rounds in Washington, reportedly going to every member of Congress, a group called the Gay and Lesbian Emergency Media Coalition prepared a video response entitled *Hate,*

Lies and Videotape. Initially, *The Gay Agenda* video had been ignored by the mainstream news media—perhaps seen as yet another piece of predictable antigay propaganda. But the release of the response video created a legitimate space for the news media to enter. *Hate, Lies and Videotape* suddenly turned a piece of propaganda into a point-counterpoint story with both sides represented (Flanders, 1993a). The creators of the response tape were, in effect, asking the news media to take up the story, examine the evidence, and bring their conclusions to their audiences. Thus, they themselves created the license for news organizations to circulate the antigay material.

In the case of television news in particular this was an ideal story: low in cost, high in controversy, heavy on both visual interest and audience appeal, and neatly fitting into the news frame that reduces complex issues to simple cases of pro and con. Because television reporters could logically tell the story through and with material from the already available videotapes, most of the expense of production work was eliminated. Television news for years has operated under an imperative that demands not just pictures, but "good" pictures, that is, images that are highly compelling, and certainly this story provided that. After the release of the response video, stories on the so-called dueling videotapes were featured on CNN, ABC, and in the *Washington Post* and *USA Today* (Flanders, 1993a, 1993b).

Who Won?

If this indeed was a video duel, is it possible to determine how points were scored and whether either side actually won? On the level of public relations, the answer is somewhat obvious. *The Gay Agenda* won a decisive PR victory simply by being circulated in major news media outlets, particularly television. Instead of being seen by several thousand people, it was now seen by several million. Some of its more memorable visual images were excerpted on *Larry King Live,* for example, but the response video was not shown at all.

In addition, *The Gay Agenda* won a political victory because it was a more credible and convincing videotape, even though much of the factual content of that video has been either refuted or, at the very least, seriously challenged. Indeed, the video succeeds by employing the very codes, techniques, and stereotypes used in television news and documentary forms. In a sense, *The Gay Agenda* beats the news media at its own game.

Precisely because this is a videotape, its message is carried not just by the printed word or even by the spoken word. Instead, it employs production techniques of both Hollywood cinema and documentary film to create more complex visual and aural messages. The particular ways in which these are constructed and connected—complete with casting, framing, shooting, editing, and mixing devices—constitute a cinematic language with its own set of meanings and messages. Thus, an analysis of the video requires not only an examination of its language but also of its filmic codes. Such a critique necessarily raises questions about the meaning and the accuracy of mass mediated images that have been selected or constructed to represent gay and lesbian people. A review of how those images have been both created and debated by gay rights advocates and their opponents, therefore, may be useful before turning to an analysis of the video itself.

From Invisible to Outrageous

From its inception in the late 1960s and early 1970s, the organized gay rights movement in the United States has criticized mass media for ignoring gays, lesbians, and bisexuals. With its Production Code of 1934, Hollywood voluntarily accepted a virtual ban on such portrayals in narrative film (see, e.g., Russo, 1981). Although network television had no explicit prohibition, its unwritten conventions resulted in the same outcome not only in entertainment programming but also in television news. For the most part, print accounts were similarly unavailable (Moritz, 1992b). In virtually every area of mass mediated popular culture from the postwar period through the 1960s, homosexuality was placed in the absent portion of what Hartley has called the absent-present paradigm, where certain subgroups and topics are either marginalized or erased altogether (Hartley, 1982).

Those accounts that did exist were negative in the extreme. For example, the *New York Daily News* report of the Stonewall Riots in 1969—often considered a crystallizing moment for the gay rights movement—showed a blatant contempt for gays and lesbians that was characteristic of the press. Its headline, "Homo Nest Raided, Queen Bees Are Stinging Mad," captures the story in more ways than one. That same year, the detective show *N.Y.P.D.* presented television's first fictional gay character and described homosexuality as "an area of human activity feared and detested everywhere" (Russo, 1981, p. 110).

This record, of course, needs to be placed within a larger historical and cultural context. In the 1950s, Hollywood cinema was still tame and television was contentedly conservative. Married couples were shown in bed, but never in the same bed, only in twins. The word *pregnant* was off-limits for producers of *I Love Lucy* when their star's real-life pregnancy had to be included in the storyline. Small wonder gay leather men were not showing up on *Father Knows Best*.

Media practitioners are, after all, products of the culture just as much as they are producers of it:

> they no doubt have taken their cues from the larger context in which homosexuality typically has been vilified. Religion has called it immoral. Medicine considered it pathological. Government made it illegal. In that setting, the marginalization of and bias against homosexuality in all mass media are hardly surprising. (Moritz, 1992a, p. 157)[5]

Media Advocacy

With the growth of the gay rights movement in the 1970s, media advocacy became a critical issue. It first focused on inclusion and then on the elimination of socially damning stereotypes. Progress was slow in coming. Mainstream Hollywood cinema, no longer strictly adhering to its earlier self-imposed code, remained largely unwilling to take up the topic. When it did, the result was predictable. "Typically, homosexuality was portrayed at best as unhappiness, sickness or marginality and at worst [as] perversion and evil that had to be destroyed" (Fejes & Petrich, 1993, pp. 396-422).[6]

Prime-time television was similarly reticent to create gay or lesbian characters and equally likely to make them figures of contempt when it did. Fictionalized depictions of gays and lesbians were particularly problematic because they necessarily involved the creation of images when there was very little agreement among media producers, executives, or pressure group members as to what would constitute an acceptable gay or lesbian representation—acceptable to both gay and mainstream audiences.

Nonetheless, the 1970s proved to be a decade of daring on entertainment television, thanks in general to network interest in increasingly urban audiences and in particular to the pioneering works of Norman Lear. His hit series *All in the Family* took up gay themes on more than one occasion and also offered television's first lesbian storyline.

With the advent of the Reagan years, the rise of the Moral Majority —complete with Anita Bryant's much publicized antigay crusade, and with the discovery of AIDS, network television came under increasing pressure from the Christian Right. Any program themes that featured material that could be construed as anti-Christian or antifamily— including discussions of abortion, homosexuality, and sex—were legitimate targets. When the conservative Coalition for Better Television in 1981 organized a nationwide consumer boycott of programs with objectionable themes, ABC responded by scrapping a take-off on *La Cage Aux Folles,* CBS abandoned three TV movies with gay themes, and NBC turned the Tony Randall character in *Love, Sydney* into a gay man with a discreet homosexual past but an asexual present and future (Levine, 1984, pp. 225-226).

Even the growing AIDS epidemic could not provide a sufficiently compelling programming rationale at the networks in the early 1980s:

> Despite their own insistence that the networks strive to be socially relevant, topical and responsible, no network took up the subject of AIDS in a prime-time drama until NBC offered the made-for-TV movie *An Early Frost* in late 1985. . . . Because [Rock] Hudson's death thrust the AIDS story onto the front pages of magazines and newspapers around the world, network television showed heightened interest in treating the topic. (Moritz, 1992b, p. 264)[7]

As the 1980s wore on, the three networks were faced with sweeping industry changes. Cable television, VCRs, and the enormously popular Fox programming schedule all offered opportunities for entertainment that pushed the boundaries of acceptable television fare. Faced with that kind of competition, the networks themselves were increasingly willing to explore a number of formerly taboo topics, including gay and lesbian themes. *Golden Girls, Kate and Allie, Hill Street Blues, St. Elsewhere, Moonlighting, Hunter, Hotel* and *L.A. Law*—some of the biggest hit shows of the 1980s—all had episodes with homosexual characters. ABC offered one of the first recurring gay characters in prime-time history on its police comedy *Hooperman*, and *HeartBeat*, another ABC show, introduced the first lesbian character to be part of an ensemble cast (Moritz, 1992b).

But these prime-time network programs were also most vulnerable to criticism precisely because they appear during what is considered family viewing time. Prime-time network television still has the largest audience share and to a great extent still sets the parameters of acceptable entertainment. When gays and lesbians show up there, it is an entry into the most significant of public spaces.

As the decade drew to a close, the Radical Right response to these more liberal media policies was yet another national advertiser boycott—this one launched in the late 1980s by the Reverend Donald Wildman's Americans for Family Values. And the networks once again faced the dilemma of pleasing constituencies that had opposing agendas. In a 1989 article, *Advertising Age* predicted the conservative voices would win that battle and that the 1990s would be a time of "New Puritanism" on prime-time TV. Brandon Tartikoff, then head of programming at NBC, was publicly agreeing that the networks had gone too far and declaring that they were "not in the business of pushing boundaries" (Moritz, 1992b, p. 266).

While network television may not have been willing to take the lead in pushing boundaries, it could not afford to ignore the cultural shifts that inevitably take place in society and the way those shifts are represented by other mass media outlets.

> Non-network popular talk shows such as *Donahue* and the *Oprah Winfrey Show* have presented programs on gay and lesbian topics that have allowed gays and lesbians to speak out on their own behalf. In addition, the Public Broadcasting System (PBS), National Public Radio (NPR), cable networks such as HBO and public access cable have provided more exposure to gay and lesbian issues and concerns. (Fejes & Petrich, 1993, p. 401)

Newspapers and news magazines began to increase their coverage significantly as well. Thus, when gay rights became an important news and talk show topic, as it did during the 1992 campaigns in Oregon and Colorado, and as it has during the on-going debates over gays in the military, entertainment television could not help but sit up and take notice.

In this sense, there is a continual interaction between fictionalized gays and lesbians and what might be called real ones. The important point, however, is that both fictional and factual accounts are constructed in accordance with prevailing professional practices and embedded in an industry that is always impacted by economic imperatives.

News Depictions

Despite journalistic claims that they don't make the news, they just report it, news organizations have a well-documented history of being selective and biased in their choice of news topics. "The works of Epstein, Gans, Tuchman and others have made it axiomatic that what mainstream journalism offers as 'news' is a highly selective text and that what it portrays as reality is highly constructed" (Moritz, 1992a, p. 157)

News organizations, print and broadcast, never have been prohibited from writing and reporting on gays and lesbians. But unwritten news codes—those generally accepted definitions of what constitutes a story—for decades provided a powerful barrier to coverage of many minority groups, including gays and lesbians. Far from being independent, news codes flow out of the larger culture and reflect the attitudes and socioeconomic hierarchies in society at large. Given that system, it is hardly surprising that gays and lesbians were not considered worthy of coverage well into the 1980s (Moritz, 1992a). In 1987, to cite one notorious case, both *Time* and *Newsweek* ignored the gay rights march in Washington, D.C., the largest civil rights demonstration in the capitol since 1969 (Freiberg, 1993).

What coverage the incipient gay rights movement did get was often problematic. Before 1973, when the American Psychiatric Association removed homosexuality from its list of mental illnesses, the occasional news accounts that did exist often framed gayness as psychological sickness. Stories on gays and lesbians have a long history of being caste as "morality tales, with the homosexual being the negative reference point in a discourse that reaffirmed society's sense of what is normal" (Fejes & Petrich, 1993, p. 402). In the 1980s, media attention focused on the emergence of AIDS and reframed gays around their

> "promiscuous and abnormal" sexual behavior and lifestyle. . . . A common media frame was to distinguish between the "innocent" victims of AIDS, those who did not acquire the virus from gay sexual contact, and, implicitly, the "guilty" victims of AIDS, those who did. (Fejes & Petrich, 1993, pp. 403-404)

As AIDS became *the* gay story of the 1980s, gayness became equated with deadly disease. Yet at the same time the networks could point to their coverage of AIDS as satisfying gay advocates' demands for visibility; even in this instance, the coverage of the emerging epidemic was limited until the story of Rock Hudson's death from AIDS in 1985 sparked the first significant media response to reporting on the disease.

Ironically, the subtext of the Rock Hudson story was that AIDS might be infiltrating the straight world. "Now fears are growing that the AIDS epidemic may spread beyond gays and other high-risk groups to threaten the population at large," *Newsweek* reported ("AIDS: Special Report," 1985, p. 116). *Time* offered a similar narrative:

> For years it has been dismissed as the "gay plague," somebody else's problem. Now, as the number of cases in the US surpasses 12,000 and the fatal disease begins to strike the famous and the familiar, concern is growing that AIDS is a threat to everyone. ("The Frightening AIDS Epidemic," 1985, p. 116)

Lesbians, meantime, remained almost as invisible as ever. Yet, because the media had consistently used the word *gay* to refer to both men and women, lesbians were implicated in the AIDS crisis even though they are among the lowest risk sub-groups for the disease, a fact that rarely was reported.

Although coverage of AIDS no doubt has had its negative implications, in some real ways the epidemic also gave gays and (by implication and association) lesbians increased public visibility: "it was not until the AIDS crisis that stories about individual gay men and lesbians —and the issues that concerned them began to appear with regularity" (Freiberg, 1993, p. 55).[8] In the 1990s, that trend has accelerated into what the gay and lesbian newspaper, the *Washington Blade,* has described as an explosion of interest, a "radical departure" from news practices of even the late 1980s, a "sea change," like being on "a different planet" (Freiberg, 1993, p. 55). Even the formerly distant *New York Times* did an about face, increasing its coverage of the gay and lesbian community by "65% from 1990 to 1991 and the paper began using the word 'gay' instead of 'homosexual' " (Fejes & Petrich, 1993, p. 405). Because of its impact as the national paper of record, this change has created "what many activists and media watchdogs assert is a 'ripple effect' on other media" (Freiberg, 1993, p. 53). In addition, as of 1995, the newly organized National Gay and Lesbian Journalists Association had attracted 1,000 members in 14 chapters around the country. Among their goals is increased visibility in newsrooms and in news content.

Despite vast improvements in news coverage of gay and lesbian issues, heterosexism remains a prevailing norm. In 1990, the American Society of Newspaper Editors (ASNE) decided for the first time to examine the coverage of gays and lesbians as well as the working conditions for gay and lesbian newsroom personnel. Its national survey gave the nation's newspapers "a grade of mediocre" on the issue of coverage and said that antigay attitudes remain "the last acceptable basis for discrimination among so-called acceptable Americans, including editors." Though the study found newsrooms "largely hospitable" to gay and lesbian employees, it also noted "a palpable undercurrent of bias" (Aarons, 1990, p. 40).

In news coverage, that bias surfaces in a number of different ways. For example, contemporary news accounts increasingly are focused on issues of gay rights. But even as demands for equal protection are viewed as legitimate news, the "legitimacy" of those demands is still viewed as "questionable" (Fejes & Petrich, 1993). The on-going media debate over the appropriateness of outing offers another example. Outing, after all, rests on the homophobic assumption that being identified as gay or lesbian is still a stigma. If it were not, then it would not be problematic to reveal any person's sexual orientation (Fejes &

Petrich, 1993). News headlines in local papers still refer to "openly gay" individuals (Knopper, 1993). As recently as July 1993, well after the media flurry around gays in the military, the *Chicago Sun-Times,* a major metropolitan paper, felt the need to define "coming out" in an article about a gay newscaster (Williams, 1993, p. 1). And, though many newspapers have editorialized about lifting the ban on gays in the military, "they are often quick to point out that such support does not mean they 'endorse the gay lifestyle' " (Fejes & Petrich, 1993, p. 405).

The creation and selection of images to represent gays and lesbians represent another level of concern. In terms of mass media images, gay men have been limited to a few very stereotyped portrayals: hair dressers, floral designers, houseboys, men in black leather, men in baths, men in bars (often faceless, shown from the back or from an angle designed to obscure their faces), men in doctors' offices, in hospital beds, men with AIDS.

Lesbian images are far more rare on television and in print—just as images of women in general are far more rare than images of men in the media. The few lesbian images that have been featured over the years have relied on stereotypes that have included sadistic prison wardens, blood-sucking vampires, murderers, or, at the other ex- treme, asexual spinsters. Even today our collective imagery does not include visual vocabulary that defines gay or lesbian.

In news, both still photos in print and moving images in television have been a point of contention. In their early attempts to depict gays and lesbians, journalists often utilized the bizarre to illustrate the homosexual look. News editors showing gay pride parades, for exam- ple, typically selected 20 seconds of footage that featured whips, chains, and bare breasts. Gay watchdog groups in cities around the country pressured television newsrooms to change. The Gay and Lesbian Alliance Against Defamation (GLAAD) still instructs media personnel on the issue:

> Do not show or describe only the most unconventional members of our
> community. There is nothing wrong with unconventionality—many in
> our community quite properly celebrate it—but it is nevertheless unfair
> to reinforce misconceptions that all lesbians and gay men are into, say,

leather or drag. (Gay and Lesbian Alliance Against Defamation [GLAAD], 1993, Sec. 2, Pt. 1, p. 31)[9]

Television news practices did begin to change and images that reflected a more mainstream look became more common. But that technique has now led conservative critics to complain that the liberal media is sanitizing the gay issue in an effort to be politically correct. In essence, they argued for a reframing of gay images to illustrate not only perversion, but also danger. This is precisely the technique used so persuasively in their own video, *The Gay Agenda.*

The Gay Agenda: Production Strategies

Although a number of production strategies combine to give *The Gay Agenda* credibility, the selection and juxtaposition of visual images may be the most crucial and may raise the most significant questions with respect to naturalizing a hate message. The video is modeled on the formal news documentary and relies on videotape footage of actual events for most of its images. In the vocabulary of news, the still photograph and later the moving image has become synonymous with reality. A reporter's words may be disputed, but pictures are considered to be unmediated representations, a true rendering that is not subject to debate or interpretation. In short, news consumers have been conditioned to believe that pictures equal reality, that they are documentation that is irrefutable, and that news simply holds up a mirror to the real world.

This view, however, fails to account for the complexities of production and of reception both. Communication research has demonstrated that news pictures and copy ares not reality but a particular construction of reality (see, e.g., Epstein, 1973; Gans, 1979; Tuchman, 1978). In producing video images, the decisions of what picture to take and what picture to ignore, what picture to leave on the proverbial cutting room floor, become determining factors in shaping a particular reality. In addition, the ways in which pictures are juxtaposed and the ways in which they are combined with sound tracks during the editing process will also have an impact on the messages conveyed.

The Gay Agenda, for example, opens in black with only the sound of police whistles, chants, and ominous music to draw the viewer in. When the first images appear, they show a storefront window being shattered, a street fire burning, an angry crowd, jeering protesters confronting rows of police officers armed with shields and helmets—a quick succession of images that together convey the by-now familiar look of an urban riot. Added to the throbbing beat of the music is the so-called Voice-of-God narrator, a disembodied speaker who is never identified, the authorial voice of someone who is never seen but who speaks as if from on high, telling the viewer what these images are about: a protest over California Governor Pete Wilson's veto of Assembly Bill 101, legislation that "would have granted special minority rights" to gays and lesbians.

And thus begins the first of several references to one of the video's subtexts—that gays and lesbians want, and in some cases are getting, "special rights" that should not be "equated with the truly, morally neutral condition of a particular racial or national origin or other status." At the same time, this opening montage visually recalls images of race riots and thus indirectly suggests that just as angry blacks are to be feared, so too are angry gays and lesbians.

A second set of visuals follows shortly after this opening. In this sequence, there is no narration to compete with the visuals—only pictures and a pulsating soundtrack, a gay pride parade as music video. In this sequence, we see simulated sex acts; nudity; whips, chains, and other forms of sadomasochism; men in drag; men in nun's habits; and signs with messages such as "God is Gay" and "Fuck." Intercut with these images are shots of small children and presumably their gay and lesbian parents who also are participants in the parade. I have said the sequencing of images can create meaning, and this is precisely the case here. By juxtaposing children with sexually provocative paraders, the video effectively taps into the often repeated myth that gays and lesbians are pedophiles, that they recruit young people into homosexuality, and that they are unfit to be parents. Public opinion polls have demonstrated that for "the majority of Americans, the belief in homosexuals recruiting the young is still strong" (Fejes & Petrich, 1993, p. 409). Through its editing strategy, *The Gay Agenda* reinforces and extends that belief, especially to segments of the audience who are least familiar with pride parades and the role such events play in gay and lesbian culture.

Studies in audience reception show that there is no single reading of a text. Instead, there are multiple readings often linked to subcultural group membership. So readings may cluster around age, ethnicity, race, gender, religion, or sexual identity. In their review of the literature on gays, lesbians, and the media, Fejes and Petrich (1993) describe the phenomenon this way: "To cope with the overwhelming heterosexist and homophobic bias of media content, homosexuals, not surprisingly, develop complex interpretive strategies different from heterosexual viewers" (p. 410). They cite an audience study reported in *Outweek* in which African American gays and lesbians were questioned about their responses to the comedy skit "Men on Men," which is featured on Fox Television's *In Living Color.* Results showed a very complex reading with a number of individuals expressing

> great pleasure in their realistic and funny depiction, while at the same time voicing concern and even anger that these skits will be misread by heterosexual white viewers, who do not understand the source and meaning of gay camp. (Fejes & Petrich, 1993, pp. 409-410)

Certainly gay pride parade images will be read differently by straight, white, conservative audiences than they will be by gays and lesbians who are likely to view these events as queer performance, that is, an expression that may incorporate irony, camp, comedy, confrontation of mainstream sexual mores, exotica, erotica, and more. By showing only those gays and lesbians who most critically challenge conventional standards for public behavior and cultural expression, the video implies that they represent the entire group. As many have pointed out, this is the equivalent of showing pictures of drunks during Mardi Gras to illustrate the lifestyle of white, heterosexual men.

Use of Experts

In typical news documentary fashion, *The Gay Agenda* relies on several experts to add supporting evidence to the narration and thus develop a particular point of view. And here, too, the production strategy employed is highly effective in giving those who appear an aura of credibility, even though the content of their remarks is very much open to challenge.

In television news and in news documentaries, identifying a speaker can be accomplished in a variety of ways. Typically, the reporter or narrator will give a one-sentence identification designed to position the individual in a particular way in the viewer's mind. For example, "Mary Smith lost 20 pounds in two months," would position the speaker as a successful dieter. When a speaker is being utilized to lend expertise or credence to a report, it is common to have the identification line include pertinent details of employment, research credentials, or other aspects of experience. A scientist might be connected to a university, a laboratory, or a research project.

In *The Gay Agenda,* four reputed experts on homosexuals are used extensively to comment on various aspects of gay and lesbian life. In every case, the identification is done in the same way. The speaker's voice is heard, but the screen remains black until electronic lettering is inserted and the screen is filled with these words: Stanley Monteith, M.D., Author, "AIDS, The Unnecessary Epidemic." After several seconds, the titles fade out and the video of the speaker fades in, revealing Dr. Monteith.

The technique focuses the viewer's attention on the credentials of the speaker without the distraction of facial characteristics, mannerisms, gestures, or looks that might be conveyed in full video. Thus, the viewer in effect can underscore the fact that this is a medical doctor and author of a book on AIDS who is making these comments. And so we similarly are introduced to Joseph Nicolosi, Ph.D., Author, "Reparative Therapy of Male Homosexuals"; David Llewellyn, President, Western Center for Law and Religious Freedom; John Smid, Director, Love in Action. Nowhere is their connection to the Radical Right political agenda even hinted at; no one explains even briefly what, for example, the Western Center for Law and Religious Freedom is or who supports it. The full screen titles direct the viewer focus to labels we have been conditioned to accept and respect—M.D., Ph.D., author.

When the speakers are eventually shown, they are white males, well dressed and well spoken—the image of what an expert is expected to look like in traditional news terms. Their comments are direct, articulate, fact-based, which is to say they sound factual. These are not people who quote the Bible or say that homosexuality is an abomination. They are reasoned, calm, credible. The language is elevated, often invoking scientific evidence. So, even though their claims can be challenged or disproven, these so-called experts come across with a very high level of credibility. Even though their credentials are foregrounded, their more revealing political connections are never discussed. Monteith, for example, was the subject of a *Los Angeles Times* story that identified him as "not only a member of Pat Robertson's Christian Coalition, but also a member of the overtly theocratic Coalition on Revival" The statistics on gay male sexual practices that he quotes in *The Gay Agenda* are from a study that has been widely discredited for its lack of scientific rigor (Flanders, 1993a). Nicolosi's reparative therapy described in the tape as a viable option for gays and lesbians who want to change their lifestyle has been similarly discounted by the vast majority of psychologists and psychiatrists and officially rejected by the American Psychological Association. Yet this idea, that gays and lesbians choose to be homosexual and therefore can choose to change or to be cured, is another subtext prominent in the video.

You Decide

Another message that is carried by all of the expert testimony is that the mass media does not tell the public the truth about gay and lesbian life and politics. The following sound bites excerpted from the video illustrate the point: "Certainly our newspapers, our TV and our radio is not going to tell us." "I saw many things we don't see in the media today." "The gay agenda and the media today are trying to put out a message that these are a group of loving, caring people." The closing sequence of the video carries the subtext to its logical conclusion. A black screen is used once again. This time the words "YOU DECIDE" are superimposed on the screen. The implication is that now that the viewer has been given the facts that the mass media typically hides, he or she can decide where to stand on the issue of "special rights" for gays and lesbians. By turning the decision over to the viewer, the video reinforces a sense of neutrality and suggests that it has not advocated a point of view but has simply presented the otherwise unavailable facts.

Conclusion

The tactics employed in *The Gay Agenda* serve as a potent illustration of the future direction of the antigay movement. The message that invokes science, that relies on deeply embedded stereotypes, and that lets "you decide" the issues is far more difficult to combat, but its effect on the lives of gays and lesbians is no less devastating. The call for a rhetoric that can be more easily marketed to the mainstream is being applied directly to election campaigns. While Amendment Two's "no special rights" passed with 54% of the vote in Colorado, becoming the "first statewide constitutional amendment to limit civil rights in the history of the U.S.," the more harshly worded Oregon measure was defeated, 57% to 43%. Using the Colorado model, a variety of state and national organizations of the Right are preparing antigay legislation for upcoming elections in more than half of the 50 states (*When Hate Groups Come to Town,* Internet/Gaynet communication, 1994).[10]

These ballot initiatives are only part of the debate over gay and lesbian rights that will be carried out for years to come. Gays in the military, adoption rights, parental rights, depictions of gays and lesbians in the arts are just some of the issues that are starting to be confronted by the culture. Inevitably, the mass media will play a central role in framing these topics.

Indeed, the debates promise to be frequent; whether they will also be informed remains an open question. And it is here that media practitioners and media institutions have not only a role but a responsibility. I began by saying that the media is still deeply implicated in the perpetuation of homophobia and heterosexism and I would like to conclude by pointing to some of the specific ways in which this happens, the assumption being that the more frequently these practices are exposed the more likely they are to change.

The issue of civil rights for racial and ethnic minorities, for the aged, the disabled, and the disadvantaged is no longer a matter of debate in the media. Yet the issues of civil rights for gays and lesbians still triggers what the Gay and Lesbian Alliance Against Defamation (GLAAD) calls the Hitler response:

> Anti-gay zealots are in no sense "responsible spokespersons" about lesbian and gay issues, yet their hate often gets presented whenever any lesbian or gay topic is covered. A Ku Klux Klan member or neo-Nazi is not included to discuss "the other side" in every story about African Americans or Jews. (GLAAD, 1993, Sec. 2, Pt. 2, p. 42)

Not only is the Radical Right position given prominence, its spokespersons are rarely challenged on the accuracy of their claims. One news reporter explains the process this way:

> You have a lot of stuff getting into the paper and on TV from extremist bigots, and it goes unchallenged. . . . Somebody will say, "85% of homosexuals are pedophiles," and because this is a quote it gets in unchallenged, simply because the editor in charge has no idea whether that's real or not. (Freiberg, 1993, p. 57)

If the media have a role to play in terms of determining the credentials of nominated spokespersons, they are also responsible for explaining basic legal principles. The countless letters to the editor that appeared in Colorado papers after the passage of Amendment Two is a case in point. After the amendment passed, an immediate challenge to its constitutionality was launched in the courts. Letter writers by the score wrote to argue that such a challenge was wrong because the people had spoken and therefore the law must follow.

In our system of government, however, minority groups are in fact protected from discrimination by the will of the majority. As Charlene L. Smith writes in the *Washburn Law Journal,* "If the majority of the people had the power to decide who is, and who is not, worthy of equal protection, the Equal Protection Clause would be meaningless." This principle was explicitly stated by the Supreme Court in a 1943 decision that reads in part, "One's right to life, liberty and property . . . and other fundamental rights may not be submitted to vote; they depend on the outcome of no elections" (Smith, 1993, p. 377).[11]

The media, however, seem far more interested in the sensational than the instructional. So as recently as 1993, we see the NBC flagship station in New York carrying a three-part series on the man-boy love association. After protests from GLAAD, the station did respond with another series, this one looking at substantive issues such as domestic partnership (*GLAAD Newsletter,* 1993).

Story selection is one obvious place where the media's role is critical; use of language and selection of images are two others. In the case of language, the Radical Right has been highly successful in exerting its influence. Just as it succeeded in renaming and thus reframing its antiabortion stand into a "pro-life" position, just as it turned antifeminism into "pro-family," so has it successfully turned the issue of civil rights for gays and lesbians into one of "special rights." In the case of imagery, the Right has been less able to push its agenda, but here too its efforts have had some impact as was evident in the aftermath of the 1993 march on Washington.

Unlike the 1987 march, which got virtually no media coverage, the 1993 event was heavily covered by national and local newspapers and television stations. Much of the coverage emphasized the peaceful nature of the march and the everyday character of the participants. Immediately, the charge came from the Radical Right that liberal media had sanitized the parade. Soon thereafter media critics, reporters, and editors were questioning whether they had indeed been hiding, protecting their audiences from the real gay community, the one depicted so graphically in *The Gay Agenda.* Headlines such as these soon followed: "What the Gay Media Didn't Say About the Gay March—and Why" and "Did the Networks Sanitize the Gay Rights March?"

At this point the issue is shifted once again to the complex terrain of cultural conformity and morality. And it is in this very complexity that clarity is so sorely needed:

> The fight for equal rights for gays and lesbians is a myriad of complicated issues and emotions. Like abortion, the legal issues are often subordinated and confounded by religious and moral beliefs. The rights of gays and lesbians, however, are not moral or religious issues. They are legal issues —issues that define the new frontier of civil rights. (Smith, 1993, p. 374)

Perhaps there is much to be hoped for in the legal arena. The courts in Colorado thus far have rejected the constitutionality of Amendment

Two, and there is reason to hope that the Supreme Court will follow. But the legal debates and decisions take place within the culture. And changes in the law do not necessarily translate into changes in practices, beliefs, and attitudes. That struggle takes place in a variety of venues, not the least of which is represented every day in the morning paper and every night on the evening news. Let us hope it will be represented fully and fairly.

Notes

1. The Radical Right includes secular conservative political groups whose ties have been traced to the 1964 Presidential campaign of Barry Goldwater and to the 1968 third-party campaign of George Wallace, whose reactionary agenda attracted Southern whites and blue-collar and farm workers who had traditionally voted Democratic. The term *Radical Right* is used throughout additionally to refer to what is also called the Religious Right, fundamentalist Christian organizations that work in the political arena for a conservative, antiabortion, antigay agenda. The most prominent groups include Free Congress Foundation, Concerned Women of America, the Moral Majority, the Eagle Forum, the Family Research Institute, the Heritage Foundation, the Christian Coalition, the Traditional Families Coalition, and the American Family Association.

2. S. Nakagawa, 1994. "Introduction" to an Internet/Gaynet communication (National Gay and Lesbian Task Force, Washington, D.C.).

3. Reprinted from "Oregon Measure Asks State to Repress Homosexuality," by T. Egan, *New York Times,* August 16, 1992, p. 1. Copyright © 1992 by The New York Times Company. Reprinted by permission.

4. J. Mozzochi, G. Leichtling, & S. Gardiner, 1994. Communication titled "The New Right and the Christian Right" on the Internet/Gaynet (National Gay and Lesbian Task Force, Washington, D.C.).

5. From "The Fall of Our Discontent: The Battle Over Gays on TV," by M. J. Moritz, in D. Shimkin, H. Stolerman, & H. O'Connor (Eds.), *State of the Art: Issues in Contemporary Mass Communication* (1992) New York: St. Martin's. Reprinted by permission.

6. Excerpts reprinted from "Invisibility, Homophobia, and Heterosexism: Lesbians, Gays, and the Media," by F. Fejes & K. Petrich, *Critical Studies in Mass Communication,* 10(4), June 1993, pp. 396-422. Used by permission of the Speech Communication Association.

7. Reprinted from M. Moritz, "How U.S. Media Represent Sexual Minorities," in *Journalism and Popular Culture,* P. Dahlgren & C. Sparks (Eds.), © 1992, by permission of Sage Publications Ltd.

8. Reprinted from "Gays and the Media," by P. Freiberg, *Washington Blade,* 24, April 23, 1993, pp. 53-57. Used by permission of the publisher.

9. Reprinted from *Media Guide to the Lesbian and Gay Community,* by Gay and Lesbian Alliance Against Defamation [GLAAD] (1993). Used by permission of the publisher.

10. Center for Democratic Renewal, 1994. Communication titled "When Hate Groups Come to Town," on the Internet/Gaynet (National Gay and Lesbian Task Force, Washington, D.C.).

11. Reprinted from "Undo Two: An Essay Regarding Colorado's Anti-Lesbian and Gay Amendment 2," by C. L. Smith, *Washburn Law Journal, 32*, 1993, p. 377. Used by permission of the publisher.

References

Aarons, L. F. (1990, Summer). Alternatives: Gays and lesbians in the newsroom. *Newspaper Research Journal, 11*, 38-43.

AIDS: Special report. (1985, August 12). *Newsweek, 106*, pp. 20-29.

Bennetts, L. (1993, August). k.d. lang cuts it close. *Vanity Fair, 56*, pp. 94-98, 142-146.

Egan, T. (1991, August 16). Oregon measure asks state to repress homosexuality. *New York Times*, p. 1.

Epstein, E. J. (1973). *News from nowhere*. New York: Random House.

Fejes, F., & Petrich, K. (1993, June). Invisibility, homophobia, and heterosexism: Lesbians, gays, and the media. *Critical Studies in Mass Communication, 10*(4), 396-422.

Flanders, L. (1993a, June). Hate on tape: The video strategy of the religious right. *Extra!, 6, 5*.

Flanders, L. (1993b, June). Hidden agenda: Behind an anti-gay propaganda video. *Extra!, 6, 6*.

Freiberg, P. (1993, April 23). Gays and the media. *Washington Blade, 24*, 53-57.

The frightening AIDS epidemic comes out of the closet. (1985, August 12). *Time*, pp. 40-47.

Gans, H. (1979). *Deciding what's news*. New York: Vintage.

Gay and Lesbian Alliance Against Defamation [GLAAD]. (1993). *Media guide to the lesbian and gay community*. New York: GLAAD.

GLAAD Newsletter. (1993, July/August).

Hartley, J. (1982). *Understanding news*. New York: Methuen.

Kasindorf, J. R. (1993, May 10). Lesbian chic: The bold, brave new world of gay women. *New York Magazine, 26*, 30-37.

Knopper, S. (1993, November 21). Openly gay flirtations mix goofy fun with stirring solemnity. *Boulder Sunday Camera*, p. B4.

Levine, R. (1984, March). Family affair. *Esquire, 101*, 225-226.

Mansfield, S. (1993, May 1). Gays on campus. *Redbook, 181*, 124-127, 140-142.

Moritz, M. (1992a). The fall of our discontent: The battle over gays on TV. In D. Shimkin, H. Stolerman, & H. O'Connor (Eds.), *State of the art: Issues in contemporary mass communication* (pp. 262-268). New York: St. Martin's.

Moritz, M. (1992b). How U.S. media represent sexual minorities. In P. Dahlgren & C. Sparks (Eds.), *Journalism and popular culture* (pp. 154-170). London: Sage.

Peters, P. J. (1992). *Death penalty for homosexuals is prescribed in the Bible*. LaPorte, CO: Scriptures for America.

Russo, V. (1981). *The celluloid closet: Homosexuality in the movies*. New York: Harper & Row.

Salholz, E. (1993, June 21). Lesbians coming out strong: The power and the pride. *Newsweek,* pp. 54-60.

Smith, C. L. (1993). Undo two: An essay regarding Colorado's anti-lesbian and gay Amendment 2. *Washburn Law Journal, 32,* 377.

Straight talk about gays. (1993, July 5). *U.S. News & World Report,* pp. 42-48.

Tuchman, G. (1978). *Making news.* New York: Free Press.

Williams, S. (1993, July 27). Going out in public. *Chicago Sun-Times,* sec. 2, p. 1.

Work-Hate

Narratives About Mismanaged Transitions in
Times of Organizational Transformation and Change

H. L. Goodall, Jr.
University of North Carolina at Greensboro

Editor's Introduction

So far, our focus has been on elite discourse: the use of hate as a
stratagem to obtain power and the use of hate appeals to negate the
(potential) power of an opposing point of view. In this chapter,
Goodall examines hate in the context of individual empowerment.

AUTHOR'S NOTE: The author wishes to thank Eric Eisenberg for his many helpful
suggestions.

For Goodall, hate is not exclusively the province of the powerless; powerful people are capable of hating their situation in life, too. And each of them has a story to tell.

Goodall explores hate in the narrative language that describes the workplace. At times, the language used here is offensive and distasteful, but it is hate's substance and expression that Goodall analyzes. Moreover, he explores why the expression of hate is both necessary and satisfying as well as why it will continue to be an integral part of our internal processes.

Work-hate narratives, as Goodall describes them, help us understand how expressions of hate function to restore balance to an imbalanced world. Through language, rather than violence, people can express the depths of their dissatisfaction and emerge, in some linguistic paradise, more powerful and in control of their own lives.

I was watching the news on TV last night when they led with the report of that guy, some former postal worker who had been laid off, returning to his office and blowing away his former boss and several co-workers. And for a moment I thought to myself, "that could have been me. Yeah, I feel like that. I hate my boss. And I feel like murdering her a lot. (Pause) I just don't own a gun."

Female office worker, anonymity requested

I hate my job. And I can't sleep at night because I am scared to death of losing it.

Male office worker, anonymity requested

According to a recent survey of American workers, roughly 70% of all employees dislike the work they do. That same study finds that on the average, American workers characterize themselves as "being in a bad mood" approximately 110 days a year ("Harper's Index," 1993). In addition, the media "saturates" (Gergen, 1991) these already disgruntled selves with continuous stories about unemployment rates; competitive global pressures; planned layoffs in *Fortune* 500 corporations; open clashes of cultural values attributed to the "new" cultural diversity of the workplace; downsizing and restructuring of companies; the inability of most retirement or health care plans to provide adequately for contributors; weekly if not nightly investigative reports on government and private industry scandal, corruption, and waste; ongoing accounts of imminent environmental decay; plus feature movies, popular novels, newspaper stories, and even television sitcoms that collectively represent, and in some cases actually reproduce, the cultural conditions of an increasingly uncertain present leading to an increasingly unpleasant future.

These contexts shape and further contribute to "ordinary"—often daily—narratives[1] of personal or family worry, routine life stress, interpersonal or organizational envy, fear of change, feelings of alienation or despair caused by beliefs that one doesn't really have "a life" because of time commitments to a job and/or family, perceptions of personal or professional unfairness, and the experiencing of deep, empty wells of unhappiness that stretch across the boundaries between work and home life.

The world of work is changing, and in the view of many workers not for the better. Put simply, work is often perceived as a tiresome, thankless task done in an unhappy place where what is accomplished is "never enough" and they work harder just to keep up with the inevitable "not-enoughness." Under these conditions, employees feel "victimized" or "enslaved" by the jobs they have and by a real fear of losing them. Under these conditions, to work is to be subjected to real and imagined domination (Goodall, 1992); it is not only to be told what to do and to be held accountable for doing it better and better *regardless* of what goes wrong or gets in the way, it is also to perform one's job *without benefit of stability*.

For many employees, to go to work is to go to a place where the needs for security, safety, secrecy, and effective public relations have "crowded out" autonomy and freedom (Shorris, 1984). It is to give up many Constitutionally guaranteed freedoms and rights, including the freedom of speech and religion, the right to privacy, and protection from unwarranted searches and seizures (Seeger, 1986). We give up these freedoms and rights as "natural" consequences of living and working with uncertain Others with whom we must share the fast, maddening traffic of a postmodern world defined by global capitalism, and do not pause to consider that with these rights we are also surrendering our autonomy and quite possibly our democracy

(Deetz, 1992; Eisenberg & Goodall, 1993). Totalitarianism, Earl Shorris teaches us, "is the process of destroying autonomy" (1984, p. 69); and,

> In business, men [sic] do not arrive at totalitarian methods because they are evil, but because they wish to do the good in what seems to them the most efficient way, or because they wish merely to survive, or with no more evil intent than the desire to prosper. (Shorris, 1984, p. 16)

Beneath these often "innocent" searches for efficiency, survival, or prosperity lies the lived experiences of a workaday world of smaller but interconnected injustices. To simply "be at work" is to expose ourselves to petty acts of personal jealousy and professional envy; to sexual and political harassment; to moral, spiritual, and ethical consternation; and in many cases to toxic substances that shorten both the length and quality of our lives (Carlsson & Leger, 1990). And for many employees not fortunate enough to be involved in self-actualizing work, to "be employed" means simply to exchange lives, dreams, the health and welfare of bodies and minds—even pride—for the diminishing returns of a shrinking paycheck in a global economy that can no longer be adequately explained—much less planned for—by even the most astute of leading economists.

In times of great economic, social, and political change we tend to impose rigid constraints on our institutions. We use institutions to create the grammar for orderly conduct and new rhetorics for governance, wherein all around us, disorder, disunity, and chaos thrives, if not rules. With the national debt tearing a major hole in the monetary ozone layer, we decide to reform political campaigns, reinvent the government, and reorganize businesses, hoping—and I think rightly so—that these institutional changes will have an impact on the national debt before it destroys the ozone layer and leaves us monetarily naked before world markets. What we are really hoping for is that these changes to our institutions will create in us a new understanding of work that will transform life outside of it; an understanding that will reach the embattled streets of our embittered cities, that will take the moral lessons of our brave new workplace—with flatter hierarchies, empowered employees, cross-functional training, flexible scheduling, continuous quality improvement, and (of course) open, honest, equitable communication—into the dysfunctional hearts of our alienated communities, stale marriages, and tortured souls.

Paradoxically, the strong pulls within the institution of work these days —despite the positive spin often given to flatter hierarchies, continuous quality improvement, cross-functional training, and empowerment —is actually toward greater organizational control and personal constraint: increased bodily surveillance of what workers ingest in their off-hours: monitoring (and in some cases censoring the content of) employee computer networks; encouraging the use of computers, faxes, and phones in the home (and commuting car) at nights and on weekends; stricter guidelines for formal and informal communication to avoid politically incorrect situations or harassment; and a continuously increasing demand for improved "creativity" and "innovation" to compete globally.

As Anthony Giddens (1984) teaches us, when institutional constraints are tightened, individual resources for release from those constraints will be sought. So it is that when employees are at work they try to resist situations they believe force the issues of control. This is why, I think, most employees resist change of any kind, for change means a loss not just of routines and rituals, but also of control; it means that the stable center they have learned to perform but dislike— yet nevertheless rely on—no longer holds, not even to curse.

Yet even for a person sympathetic to the problematics suggested by these issues, the questions raised so far might be summed up this way: *So what?* So work is hard, change is difficult, and employees are increasingly dissatisfied; hasn't it *always* been this way? Given the horror stories about child labor, lack of safety or health concerns in factories, open discrimination practices, and the running bloodbath that defined the birth of the American labor movement at the turn of the century, surely the ills we suffer at this end aren't as wicked or torturous. Isn't this, after all, why we call what we don't like to do "work?"

But this chapter is not about what—in a bygone era—organizational scholars and managers called "worker dissatisfaction." Nor is it about what might be termed in our present era "employee unhappiness." Nor is it about the mighty influence of media on social constructions of work, or the obviously gendered, politically victimized, and complex readings we can give to working, even though no scholarly essay these days cannot at least nod respectfully in these general directions. This chapter is not about those powerful ideas, although it draws cultural and interpretive strength from them.

This chapter *is* about hate, what I am going to call *work-hate*. Specifically, it is about the stories people tell about hate at work, and hatred of work.[2] These are important stories because they tell another side of what is always a many-storied work story, and they are of scholarly interest because the views of work life from this other side teach us invaluable lessons about the symbolics of organizing, relating, communicating, and—most important—about the symbolic work of *speaking* hate. What we get from studying "work-hate" narratives are lessons about what happens when societal and institutional structures for democratic living are in transition, lessons that suggest we ought to work on those transitions more carefully.

Organizing Order (and Resistance) Through Change: Power, Offstage Performances, Liminality, Madness, and Institutional Control

Work-hate narratives are spoken as offstage, tactical responses to interpretations of power-laden situations by frustrated individuals and groups, often when their cultural rituals have been, or actively are being, interrupted and they perceive themselves as victims of domination, or when they feel their dignity or self-image has been insulted or threatened. These narratives (or anecdotes) are performed "offstage" —"beyond direct observation by powerholders" (Scott, 1990, p. 4)— for an audience of peers or sympathizers as a way of relieving stress, "getting back" at the powerholders, fantasizing revenge, and/or enacting carnivalesque counter-rituals that act out inversions of the power relationship.

It is important to understand from the outset that *powerholders can hate too;* work-hate narratives are not necessarily defined by an institutional lack of power or status, but by the perception that the changes being made in the company, the workplace, the office, or the shop floor, are threatening and/or wrong. For the CEO facing "rightsizing" (e.g., downsizing of employees) due to pressure from stockholders or competitors, the experience of sudden—and badly handled

—change may be as frustrating as it is for the employee facing a serious alteration in work routines and schedules. In the following passages, then, it is important to remember that power relations and work-hate narratives are found *throughout* organizational and social hierarchies, however tall or flat.

OFFSTAGE PERFORMANCES AS "HIDDEN TRANSCRIPTS" OF POWER RELATIONS

James Scott (1990) characterizes the expression of hatred as one form of what he terms "hidden transcripts" (p. 4), a "derivative" discourse performed offstage, "consist[ing] in those gestures and words that inflect, contradict, or confirm what appears in the public transcript" (p. 10). It is "derivative" in the sense that it is discourse *derived from* the presence of power relations, and performed in *analogical correspondence* to those aspects of the relationship that are most obvious, offensive, or threatening.

Expressed in Burkeian (see Burke, 1950) terms, the "lowly" office clerk may act "up," or the "up" office manager may act "lowly," as each person inverts the world he or she experiences to rhetorically restore what each perceives as the "appropriate" form of balance and dignity. The "hidden transcript" may be also expressed as the negative analog to Habermas's "ideal speech situation, because Habermas omits from any discussion of rational, consensus-seeking discourse all forms of strategic action or dominated speech (Scott, 1990, p. 38). This "hidden transcript" of work-hate narratives is, therefore, a way—and a place—to demonstrate how subordinates (and superiors) attain "voice" through wish-fulfillment (Scott, 1990, p. 38).

POWER RELATIONS AND CHANGE

Although a thorough articulation of "power-relations in organizing the interests of capital" is a major part of ongoing critical theory projects (Clegg, 1989; Conrad, 1993; Deetz, 1992; Mumby, 1988), in my experience most Americans—believing in the fundamental equity of a democratic society—do not readily accept power differences—or a power critique—as directly relevant to their experiences of work. Ironically, they respect power differences, but believe—like the boys in Horatio Alger stories—that through hard work, initiative, courage, and pluck (or marrying the boss's son or daughter) they can transcend those differences and attain power themselves, a fantasy theme still overwhelmingly popular in films, television shows, and novels.

Even less understood or accepted are stories or accounts of organizational change as instruments of transforming "old orders" into "new orders." With these changes, ritual processes are interrupted, altering forever the taken-for-granted ideological assumptions about work and power relations of employees, as well as forms of social control in the cultures producing and consuming them (Alvesson, 1993).

This chapter is, in part, an attempt at narrative recovery of a variety of "hidden transcripts" and its interpretation as it applies to particular narratives about power relations in times of change at work. As such, it extends current work done in critical theory traditions by framing— or reframing—some recent forms of organizational change designed to "empower" employees as problematic, and to use that problematic to explicate narratives that speak to—and about—those power relations. Because this is the path I am on, I begin not in what is typically considered the obvious or necessary "beginning" for critical studies— the ideological domination of global capitalism—but instead in the middles of change narratives rendered in the lived experiences of employees. I select this place to begin because (a) it allows me to locate the emotional metaphors and allegories of work-hate as *transitionally centered* figures and tropes, and because (b) this placement evokes relevant work by Victor Turner (1969) about "liminal" space in ritual processes, or, in this case, in ritual processes that have been interrupted.

CHANGE, LIMINALITY, AND CONSTRAINTS

Not yet quite in step with the new order being created (and in many cases unwilling to accept the legitimacy of that new order), and forever separated from the old order that was understood (even if disliked), employees in the midst of change are—to use Victor Turner's (1969) apt phrase—"liminals." They are "betwixt and between" cultures, in this case work cultures, and they tend to behave—when their behavior is evaluated from either end of the cultural orders—*irrationally:* They

say they "hate" what they do—and whom they do it for—but they
continue to do it anyway.

From a historical and cultural vantage, this form of irrational
behavior is common in times of great change. From the cooperative
organizing required to create and sustain world wars in which millions
of working people are slaughtered to achieve ends that are routinely
not their own; to the social, political, and religious organizing of
movements aimed at greater liberation, or even salvation, yet that
routinely oppress their most willing volunteers; even down to the most
fundamental and ordinary social constructions of language realities
that call new worlds into being, but then are appropriated by the
constructors themselves to imprison their own thoughts and control
their own choices of actions, the organization of change is always
accompanied by irrationality caused by fear of and yet obedience to
control.

Anthony Giddens views institutional and cultural change as a dual-
ity of structure best understood as the inevitable tension between a
desire to maintain *order* and a corresponding demand for *individuality*
(see Eisenberg & Goodall, 1993; Riley & Banks, 1993). The desire to
maintain order "plac[es] limits upon the range of options open to an
actor, or plurality of actors, in a given circumstance or type of
circumstance" (Giddens, 1984, p. 177). Thus, constraints can be
framed as the institutional conditions of *power,* where "power relations are often most profoundly embedded in modes of conduct which
are taken for granted by those who follow them, most especially in
routinized behaviour, which is only diffusely motivated" (Giddens,
1984, p. 176). Table 4.1 displays three forms of constraint.

In the narratives that are contained in this chapter, I will offer
evidence that both delineates and collapses situated interpretations of
these categories, and against which "hidden transcript" tactics for
individuality, creativity, and resistance are *structurally* formulated
and *communicatively* deployed. At the outset, however, I think it is
important to understand—as Giddens cautions us—that situated interpretations of constraints are historically variable, bounded by the
dominant "rationalities" of their time, place, and circumstances. Toward an explication of that principle, I offer the following historical
parallel.

Table 4.1   Three Modes of Constraint

Material Constraint	*(Negative) Sanction*	*Structural Constraint*
Constraint deriving from the character of the material world and from the physical qualities of the body	Constraint deriving from responses on the part of some agents toward others	Constraint deriving from the contextuality of action, i.e., from the "given" character of structural properties vis-à-vis situated actors

SOURCE: From *The Constitution of Society* by Anthony Giddens (Berkeley: University of California Press, 1984), p. 176.

MADWIVES AS MAD WORKERS

Constraints on actions are often taken for granted because they are so deeply embedded within the material, historical, and social standards of their time. Similarly, what constituted "rebellion"—irrational behavior—under one set of historical conditions can be understood simply as the expression of "individuality" in another. Put differently: One person's terrorist is another person's freedom fighter. What we call "irrational" is a *cultural* product, saturated with the institutional orders and prejudices of its time.

Consider, for example, what Carol A. B. Warren (1987) has termed the "madwives" of the 1950s. These were women, all diagnosed as schizophrenics, whose "irrational" behavior was to question the legitimacy and constraints placed upon them as institutional workers known as "housewives," behaviors that damned them to mental hospitals, electroshock therapy, and other forms of institutional restraint, control, and torture, mostly because the narratives they offered suggested they "hated" that institution which they had voluntarily joined—marriage—and, as Warren's study demonstrates, that they continued to return to. That these "madwives" of the 1950s were living liminally between times of great social, political, and institutional upheaval (the 1940s and the 1960s), that the questions they posed about the institution that oppressed them are now—following the gender-consciousness revolution—considered normal, or that even the narrative expression of their hatred was a vital and necessary part of their coming to terms with their contexts, was, at the time, never considered. Their constraint was material, grounded in the taken-for-granted assumptions about a form of rational order known as "marriage," and bodily grounded in the fact that they were female in a male-dominated world.

Madwives and mad workers share a lot of common ground. If we understand the family as the basis for how most of us learn the rules for living in hierarchies, organizing tasks and roles, communicating emotions, and even resisting the rules-and-roles of localized oppression, we can see a connection between the "old orders" and "new orders" that informed both the madwives' rebellions and the current state of work-hate narratives among men and women of the workplace. What Warren's study provides, viewed this way, is evidence that those workers who are historically, culturally, and institutionally out of power (e.g., those whose stories enjoy less status) construct hate narratives *out of the same material used to oppress or to enslave them.* Put differently, what they rail against are precisely the (negative) sanctions used to further constrain their activities. Liminal to begin with, their actions become paradoxical in narratives of their making. Why is this?

INTERNALIZING CONSTRAINT AND COMPLICIT RESISTANCE

Maurice Brinton's (1993) work suggests that our lifelong subjugation to authoritarian, hierarchical, and class-dominated institutions link the organization of families to the organization of workplaces in ways that *reinforce internalized patterns of repression and coercion* capable of explaining otherwise "irrational" acts in times of change. Viewed in this interpretive context, it is entirely possible to see the outward downsizing and restructuring of families (as well as the many and varied "right answers" non-nuclear families give to questions about the organization of their activities and meanings) in relation to the current demand to downsize and restructure organizations. As new families require more personal responsibility and accountability from children who are often left to determine their own schedule of activities, we also see employees encouraged to become partners in newly "empowered" workplaces where personal responsibility and accountability for decision making, and flexible scheduling of activities, spell the terms of the new order.

It is also possible to reframe work-hate narratives as the *complicit counterpart* to institutional constraints. By articulating the conditions of powerlessness, an actor *reifies* it; by resisting compliance, an actor *deepens* it. In the end, like a child screaming back at parents who have yelled at him or her, or as the madwife denouncing the marriage she wants desperately to return to, the expression of hate at—or of—work by the dominated party may be also an expression, and very often a passionate one, of *admiration* for conditions of one's domination or enslavement. Hence, the paradoxical nature of living—and communicating—liminally in work worlds interpretively structured by the dualities of necessary, necessarily permeable, and intricately complicit oppositions: order/individuality; domination/resistance; constraint/ creativity.

> They (e.g., managers) don't expect us to comply. In fact, they do it to us so we will argue about it, resist it, fuck it up any way we can. That way, they can do it to us harder the next time. That is why I fuckin' hate the managers, and . . . am in training to be one.

In the above narrative we see this tension precisely expressed. I am particularly taken by the last phrase following the ellipsis: "am in training to be one." It would seem that this worker's "training" has been in place for a long time. Perhaps since the cradle.

The Cultural Space of Transitional Narratives in Times of Organizational Change

Michel de Certeau (1984) tells us that culturally dominated or marginalized people learn quickly to appropriate "space" in areas where "use" has already been otherwise determined by the dominant class interests. Those in power have "place" against which marginalized or dominated people seek "space." They "poach" on public territories, develop "tactics" to protect themselves from the "strategies" deployed by the powerful and to gain control over what they have appropriated. In many ways, de Certeau's analysis applies analogically to the cultural space of work-hate narratives used by workers who feel increasingly marginalized, victimized, or enslaved by organizational changes and threatened—ironically—by the possible loss of their indentured servitude. Here is but one example:

> I see Larry coming down the hall and I crowd him. I am larger than he is, physically. He is larger than I am by virtue of his status in the company. So I let him know—by crowding him—that sometimes he has to move out of my way, that damn it, I am human too. Do I hate him? Yes. I hate him because of who he is and because of what I am not allowed to be.

The above employee feels that he can "move against" that which oppresses him by small, tactical steps. Yet it is also likely that Larry recognizes these steps as purposeful invasions of more than corridor space, but of his "place" in the organization. If he tolerates this small act of resistance to his power, he probably does so because he can so easily dismiss it. If he chooses to respond to it, he can do so with the legitimate authority and weight of the recognized order behind him. So here again, the expression of hate, even at a nonverbal level, is complicit with the given order and in fact serves to reify it *through* opposition.

Employees who strike back do so because they fear losing control, and yet, in the act of the striking back, they admit they have already lost it. (To continue the analogy to families, this, too, is often the struggle of adolescent separation.) Disempowered employees know this, even if they cannot articulate it. They know they are losing control over their lives and their work. They often don't want to be "empowered," because attempts by even well-intentioned companies are often perceived by employees as further evidence of their actually being "disempowered," of having to "do more with less." In some cases, these programs are seen as further proof of organizational or managerial "tyranny," particularly when these programs are instituted without benefit of adequate preparation, necessary training, or an influx of needed new resources (Eisenberg & Goodall, 1993).

> I went home on Friday as a manager, and learned only when I showed up for work on Monday morning that I was now "empowered" to be something called a "facilitator." I hate it. I hate the whole goddamned thing. I mean, I worked damned hard all my life to become a manager. I took pride in it. My kids told their friends their dad was a manager, and that meant something. Now that's all been taken away from me. I am now

something I don't even understand, much less know how to do. And the company doesn't give a shit. I was told that either I would get in step in teams, or find myself at the outplacement desk, which used to be called being fired.

Considered as an emblem of rhetorical structuring in these work-hate narratives, "transition" is the practical opposite of "order." It expresses the inherent uncertainties, the anxieties, and the rage that change visits on the newly (dis)empowered, and sets up the rhetorical and semiotic conditions for understanding the perception of change as equivalent to "anti-order" in a ritual process (Turner, 1969). Placed within organizational contexts newly defined by flattened hierarchies, team-based organizing, cross-functional training, and empowerment, those once "up" are not so much "down" as they are "in the middle" of what increasingly adds up, narratively, to be "nowhere." They are *liminoids*, transitional figures caught in webs of significance at once no longer of their own making and yet entirely determined by what they make of it. The rituals they had made, and did understand, have been displaced by new orders, new rituals, that they are invited to participate in (as novices), but that seriously interrupt the progression —in most cases, completely turning it around or upside down—they had expected from the old way of doing things.

The fundamental human response to finding oneself in liminal space is to find that one has suddenly become *inarticulate*. The desire for "voice," therefore, is a survival skill as well as a power-gaining narrative device. To speak the conditions of one's experiences—in this case the experiences of change, of transition, of liminality—is to gain a sense of narrative control over otherwise inexplicable situations and otherwise indescribable dealings with Others. It is to narratively order—or narratively construct—the events and persons in one's experiences of change, and to use that newly articulated order—the terms and progressions of that narrative order—to make sense of— and to explain to sympathetic offstage Others—what has happened, as well as what might be—or must be—done.

In the case of "wage-slaves" performing hidden transcripts of work-hate resistance narratives, the persistence of the need for defining the terms of the new order and one's place in it, increasingly can become a *preoccupation*. Interestingly, the forms of expressing their offstage resistance to dwelling in an occupied, dominated territory are usually articulated *poetically*.

The Poetics of Organizational Domination

> *Happiness*
> *is an*
> *inside*
> *job*
> *overthrows*
> *the system*
> *from time*
> *to time*
> *comes in*
> *torrents*
> *like an*
> *orgasm*
> *then once*
> *again*
> *subsides*
> *to an undercover*
> *agent dressed*
> *in gloom.*

—Ronald Edward Kittell
(in Carlsson & Leger, 1990, p. 64)

To work in society is to occupy yourself doing the everyday work of the ordinary (Goodall, 1995), to commit to the business of being ordinary (Sacks, 1970-1971), and either to become preoccupied—or to resist preoccupation—with the symbolic, hierarchical neuroses of institutional domination (Burke, 1965). As long as the terms of one's personal survival are dictated by those beyond one's control, doing the everyday business of being ordinary at work is symbolically tied to a *poetics* of occupation.

Back a few years ago we used to all work overtime to get the turbines out on schedule. The company paid us well for the overtime, and most of us got used to the extra pay. So we bought bigger homes, new cars and trucks, boats, sent our kids to private schools, whatever, you name it, because we assumed that the overtime was going to continue. Then, two months ago, we suddenly walk in one day and find out that there is going to be no more paid overtime. None. By going to teams we are supposed to streamline the production process, and if we have to work overtime we should learn that this means we need to find more innovative ways to do the work on schedule.

Well. All that good will built up over the years between the company and the employees went right out the window. I mean, you can't just suddenly change a person's whole life—we are talking about mortgages, loans, promises made to children—and expect to be well-liked. And that is putting it politely. Most guys and gals here hate this place, and a lot of us have taken jobs elsewhere already. The teams idea is pretty much in the toilet too, and I hear the company is thinking about moving this plant overseas.

Don't tell me about teams. That word in this company ruined my whole life. I've taken my kids out of the schools they were in, my wife has taken a second job, and I sold my bass boat last Saturday. If I wasn't a good Christian man, I know I'd kill somebody. I would. And you can bet there are some harder types working here that just might do that. You can tell the management is scared. None of them go to their cars in the dark, I can tell you that.

But you know, I see this whole mess as the same mess the whole country is in. We lived too high for too long, now we're payin' the price. Thing is, back when the overtime money was good, our turbines were the world standard. Everybody was happy. So I feel like we have been betrayed. I blame the managers, because I sure as hell can't blame the people I worked so hard and so long with. We did our jobs. And now we are suffering because of it.

OCCUPATION AND PREOCCUPATION

To go to work in a dominated space is, necessarily, to be "occupied" —controlled, bounded, directed, consumed—by one's "occupation." In *Permanence and Change,* Kenneth Burke (1965)—following Veblen —teaches us that to be "occupied" at the organizing level of symbolic forming means to use one's "interests" to develop an "orientation," which, in turn, articulates those interests as well as produces a "trained incapacity" to see alternatives and to accept other explanations; it is a "state of affairs whereby one's very abilities can function as blind- nesses" (p. 7). The orientation process at the level of symbolic forming and its overall "incapacitating" narrative result is, Burke tells us, very much akin to John Dewey's notion of "occupational psychosis," or "a way of seeing [that] is also a way of not seeing" (Burke, 1965, p. 49), or, for our purposes here, a way of telling that is also a way of not telling.

It is within this general discussion of orientation, occupation, and preoccupation as trained incapacity or occupational psychosis that Burke's (1950) oft-quoted dictum, "motives are shorthand terms for situations" (p. 29) is given. Framed within this description of doing the symbolic *business* of ordinary work, his discussion also offers us a way into the interpretation of the "motive-situations" for hate-work narratives. For what gets spoken within the occupied—bounded— rationality of hate-work narratives is, in fact, the *terms* of one's occupational consciousness, the symbolic forming of interests *as* trained— or controlled—incapacities, of a preoccupational psychosis that literally speaks motives as shorthand terms for defining and gaining narrative control over situations (see Table 4.2).

Burke uses this discussion to set-up the rhetorical importance of understanding the *style* of occupational speaking as a *poetic* communicative device. The primary stylistic form of being "occupied" Burke (1950) notes is *allegory*, a poetic speaking of what he terms "perspective by incongruity" (p. 69), which itself is a *transition* from the terms of an old order to a new order that bodies forth, through analogy and metaphor, both an image of the occupied self as *heroic* and the meanings of one's preoccupations as a form of *piety*.

THE POETICS OF DOMINATION AS NARRATIVE TERMS FOR ORDER AND THE PLACE OF RESISTANCE IN IT

Smadar Lavie (1990) offers the definitive study of the poetics of occupation in her account of the Mzeina tribe of Bedouins under Israeli and Egyptian military rule. She describes the experiences of seven types of Mzeina characters who daily enact their identities— their primary preoccupation in lands that are not their own—through *allegories*. For Lavie, allegories must be understood as the common narrative form of an everyday poetics of identity in an occupied territory:

> Allegories are texts telling an individual story to convey a lesson for the whole group, a private story that attempts to represent the collectivity as

Table 4.2

Futile

I will not be pushed, filed,
stamped, indexed, briefed,
debriefed, or numbered.

My life is my own;
I . . . I . . .
aye . . . aye . . .

SOURCE: "The Prisoner," from Carlsson & Leger, 1990, p. 174.

Maundy
maundering
hither & yan
bee stings
syringes
bleed pressures
from the head

Dewsday
wake to
a breath
damp burlap

Vannsday
gridlocked
circuitous
highways
a chest of
shipwrecks

Thirsty
seconds
sandpaper
dry lips

Fried Egg
glaze of the swollen
eyes false
teeth on anodized
steel links

SOURCE: Carlsson & Leger, 1990, p. 175.

TABLE 4.2 Continued

The Gene Farm

This little piggy will go into MARKETING
This little piggy will stay in the HOME
This little piggy will transform to ROASTBEEF
This little piggy's a CLONE
This little piggy will cry WeeWee Wee
They made me with NO BONES

SOURCE: Carlsson & Leger, 1990, p. 172.

a whole. . . . Allegory, therefore, is a fragmentary form of inscription simultaneously serving two purposes—poetic expression, and didactic-political lamentation of the heroic past, now almost disappeared but to be reincarnated at some point in the eternal future. (p. 29)

This allegorical form of poetic address corresponds to the daily enactment of identities encountered in some work-hate narratives. This should come as no surprise if we consider that the expression of a historically, materially, and politically constrained self at work is experientially contiguous, if not symbolically analogous, to the displacement and loss of control of workers whose job space is "occupied" —and whose voices are disregarded or whose value is diminished—by the actions of hierarchical superiors, particularly in times of organizational change. Allegory offers an account of "the way things ought to be" if the definition of the situation offered by the teller is shared. As Fredric Jameson puts it: "the story of the private individual destiny is always an allegory of the embattled situation of the public . . . culture and society" (Jameson, 1984, as quoted in Lavie, 1990, p. 69). Consider this example:

Let me tell you a story. Once upon a time we had a problem here in the South, and some very bright college-educated guy discovered that if we imported this Japanese plant and put it in our own soil we could solve all our problems. That plant was called Kudzu, and it did solve the problem, all right, but it also grew so damned fast everywhere that people had a hard time cutting it back. And then we found out that you couldn't kill it, either. So now the South is pretty much the Kingdom of Kudzu, and you can't drive very far in any direction without seeing how this supposed Japanese solution has damned near ruined everything in its path.

So now my company tells us that they have imported this great new Japanese business solution—Just in Time manufacturing—and it will surely solve all of our supply and warehousing problems. Yeah, right. Well I can tell you this: I am damned sick and tired of Japanese solutions for American problems. This is our country, by god, and I am not going to become Japanese. Don't get me wrong, I'm not anti-Jap, just pro-American. Also, when I hear about Japanese solutions all I see is Kudzu, all over again.

God, I hate Japanese solutions. And if you lived in my house and had to deal with my yard, you'd hate them too. But what can you do? The company tells us what's what and what will be, will be. So I'm just pissin' into the wind, if you know what I mean.

As Lavie (1990) puts it: "the narrator who tells the allegory, and the narrative that constitutes his or her story, artistically construct a portrait of a given reality, while at the same time culturally criticizing that reality as well as him- or herself" (p. 318). Narratively, this paradoxical representation of the critic in a dominated space as the wise sage who must submit to the occupation as well as to the change—but knows better than to believe in it—is culturally revealing. The work-hate narrative is not so much directed at the fact of being "occupied" by unwanted Others, but instead reveals a deep "preoccupation," the fact that much thought—and work—has gone into the personal and cultural interpretation of its meanings.

GEOGRAPHIES OF NARRATIVE RESISTANCE: THE CHANGING GLOBAL MAP OF OCCUPIED SPACE

Resistance narratives in space "occupied" by multinational corporations also serve as localized inscriptions of work-hate narratives. For example, recently South Carolina was chosen as the site for the construction of the first BMW auto plant to be built in America. Mercedes Benz also considered this location for the construction of its first American plant. Though the obvious economic benefits to the region captured media attention, there was a strong local resistance to the use of South Carolina auto workers as a cheap source of labor for German-based firms, particularly given the tax trade-offs and financial incentives not available to American companies, yet readily offered to the German firms to locate here. One local restaurant owner used the space of his advertising on two large billboards along a major highway to express his resistance: "Go Home Y'All"—expressed in regional dialect—was the core message of resistance couched between the dominant corporate logos for the German auto makers. Ironically, this message is contained within the advertising context of a "Pasta House" owned by the Japanese-American protester.

The cultural appropriation of space for this complex work-hate construction reflects a clear semiotic reflection of "our" land being "occupied" by a foreign concern, but it also suggests—within the localized context of its meaning—a sense of betrayal. The site chosen by the German auto makers and enabled by the state government, between Greenville and Spartanburg, was selected *over* the Anderson site, where this restaurant and sign were located.

This was clearly a sign about "hate" contained within corporate interests about "work." Therefore, as a work-hate narrative it captured the *economic envy* and the *passionate denial* of the complex transition of the organization of localized space to multinational interests in much the same way as street gangs appropriate territories —the outsides of businesses—for self-affirming and Other-denying graffiti (Conquergood, 1994). And like the semiotics of gang graffiti, the "voice" of this text—given its strong affirmation of a regional dialect (much like the strong affirmation of the local dialects constructed in and reinforced by gang symbols)—historically implicated the need for local knowledge to come into play in the resistance politics of a soon-to-be colonized people. Here is another example, taken from a different context:

> The company is owned by a huge Japanese firm, man, which means that the Japanese own us. When that buy-out happened last year, a lot of people here were very, very upset. Now I see our products advertised as "American-Made," but what they don't tell you is that the profits from our sweat go back to Japan. We are working *for them*. They are taking everything they can get out of this country. We are their Third-World. Can you believe it? My old man fought in the Pacific, and then worked his whole life for the same company I now work for. I know he is turning over in his grave. I hate it. I hate the Japanese for doing it. And I hate myself for putting up with it.

Masters and (Wage) Slaves: Work-Hate
Narratives as Colonized Performances

Albert Memmi (1965) authored the classic work on the psychopa-
thology of colonizer/colonized narratives, a work that has serious
implications for the study of work-hate accounts. He suggests that all
colonized people tend to go through two narrative stages—two per-
formative answers—to the condition: (a) assimilation and (b) revolt.

FROM LIMINAL TRANSITION TO CULTURAL ASSIMILATION

Assimilation occurs when the colonized person attempts to model
her or his performance of self on the colonizer. As Memmi (1965)
expresses it,

> The first ambition of the colonized is to become equal to that splendid
> model and to resemble him [sic] to the point of disappearing in him. . . .
> By this step, which actually presupposes admiration for the colonizer, one
> can infer approval of colonization. But by obvious logic, at the very
> moment when the colonized best adjusts himself to his fate, he rejects
> himself with most tenacity. . . . Rejection of self and love of another are
> common to all candidates for assimilation. (pp. 120-121)

Assimilation is an appropriate way to understand the psychological
basis of the tension felt—and the colonized condition of the self in the
narratives articulated—by the madwives in Carol Warren's (1987)
study, for whom the "occupied selves" of traditional marriage were at
first accepted and even successfully emulated. Assimilation seems also
to be an especially resourceful tool for comprehending how and why
appropriated cultural space can—as a first step out of liminality and
toward resistance—be narratively inscribed with a *poetics* of domination. Allegories are always about the necessities of assimilation; they
represent or evoke attempts to carve a narrative space for one's story
within the dominant frame of a colonizer's presence, perspective, and
gaze. As Memmi (1965) points out, however, "as soon as the colonized
adopts [the colonizer's] values, he [sic] similarly adopts his own
condemnation" (p. 121).

So when they opened this [foreign auto] plant I thought, well, hell, I might as well go along with it. Things are changin' everyday and in everyway, and if you can't change with the times, you'll be buried by them. I hated the idea of it, though. But, my family needed to eat. So I went to work there and you know, it wasn't half bad. They had different ways of doing things, and it worked. No wonder American cars can't compete, I remember thinkin'. Hell, I even traded-in my old Ford pickup for one of these [foreign trucks] built in my plant. I never had a truck so good. I learned some of the language, too. There was a lot to admire about these people, even though they were ruining the American auto industry.

Memmi (1965) suggests that once the colonized assimilates further into the colonizer's narrative, the colonized "negates" his or her previous existence, the previous self. But,

> It is not enough to leave one's group . . . one must enter another; now he [sic] meets with the colonizer's rejection . . . [and] acquires thereby an additional trait, that of being ridiculous. He can never succeed in becoming identified with the colonizer, nor even in copying his role correctly. In the best of circumstances, if he does not want to offend the colonized too much, the colonizer will use all his psychological theories. The national character of the peoples is incompatible; every gesture is subtended by the entire spirit, etc. If he is more rude, he will say that the colonized is an ape. The shrewder the ape, the better he imitates, and the more the colonizer becomes irritated. With the vigilance and a smell sharpened by malice, he will track down the telltale nuance in clothing or language, the "lack of good taste" which he always manages to discover. Indeed, a man straddling two cultures is rarely well seated, and the colonized does not always find the right pose. (p. 124)

One might pause here to consider how the above description implicates the colonizer as the master of more than the colonized, but a master also of the "hate" narrative. Memmi (1965) argues that the inevitable failure of colonized people to assimilate fully is not due to their inability to model their performances on the colonizer's, or of the colonizer's inability fully to accept those performances, but instead because of the inherent *colonial dialectic* of the colonizer/colonized relationship. By willingly submitting to subjugation the colonized can never be free, can never transcend the enslaved conditions of his or her own narratives of self. By openly agreeing to subjugate, the colonizer can never relinquish power, nor move totally away from the narrative of self that places him or her in the dominant role.

> And so I continued to work in that [foreign auto] plant for three years. I worked hard, so did my fellow Americans. But we noticed that none of us was gettin' promoted beyond supervisor, and all the big jobs in the company were controlled by the [foreigners]. I was a supervisor myself, and wanted to move up. I approached the boss and told him, and he just laughed at me. He never even gave me a answer. Just laughed. I realized that I was never going to get that promotion, no matter what I did, or how hard I worked. They had no intention of allowing Americans to join them as equals, as partners. No, we were the worker bees, and they ruled. It was that simple. I don't know why I didn't see it before. I didn't want to, I guess.
>
> That was about when I started to take a good look at myself. I didn't like what I saw. There was a time when I didn't even know who I was. And I didn't know who to hate worse, the person I had become or the people who were responsible for making me that way.

FROM TRANSITION THROUGH ASSIMILATION TO FINDING THE TERMS FOR REVOLUTION

Hate narratives are the cultural products of a colonial dialectic. This theme has been fully developed in Homi Bhabha's (1990) work about the cultural construction of "Others" and in the articulation of cultural narratives of "imperialism" by Edward Said (1978). These works share a great deal of narrative common ground and serve as extensions of Memmi's foundational argument about the move from assimilation to revolution.

In Memmi's account, hate narratives become the basis for the second step colonized people make under conditions of occupation, a move to "revolt." Memmi (1965) writes,

> The colonial situation, by its own internal inevitability, brings on revolt. For the colonial condition cannot be adjusted to; like an iron collar, it can only be broken.
>
> We then witness a reversal of terms. Assimilation being abandoned, the colonized's liberation must be carried out through a recovery of self and of autonomous dignity. Attempts at imitating the colonizer required self-denial; the colonizer's rejection is the indispensable prelude to self-

discovery. . . . Henceforth, the colonizer adopts a negative approach. (pp. 128-129)

From the felt need to revolt comes a "new" narrative—what Memmi terms a "countermythology" (p. 139)—in which "[e]verything is justified because everything can be explained" (p. 139). For it is never enough simply to "hate"; the colonized countermythology establishes narrative as action that calls for activities justified *by* the action. Here is an extreme example:

> So like this fuckin' company, you know, man? They treat us like shit. We are shit to them. Empower my fuckin' asshole! Butt-fuckers, that's what they are. Yeah, right. Well you know that movie *Revenge of the Teenage Mutant Ninja Turtles?* Fuck, man, I think we should stage a revolution here, call it "Revenge of the Middle-Aged Empowered Ninja Turds." Yeah, that's right.
>
> Empowered assholes shittin' all over the place. Green shit, orange shit, shit with eyeballs and fuckin' hair in it, shit from fuckin' Mars. Empowerment Program, my ass. Fuckin' company, I hate this fuckin' company!

In the above work-hate narrative, the scatological theme combined with sexual profanities reveals, perhaps only too vividly, the power relations embedded in this teller's perspective. His position—and self-definition—in the company is as an "asshole," which thematically and contextually represents a relatively passive, powerless sexual receptor that must accept unwanted intrusions (e.g., "butt-fuckers" inserting a new "empowerment program") that, in the teller's view, could only be overturned through a "revolution" in which "mutant turds" (the upside-down, carnivalesque inversion drawn from a film is especially masterful) nasty-up the workplace (and, by implication, dirtying-down the "butt-fuckers"), therefore restoring balance through the work-hate narrative.

Work-hate narratives such as these should be understood as passionate justifications of individuals-as-individuals in colonial systems constrained by a loss of personal power and the feeling of being totally subjugated to organizational controls. Given the cultural and colonial thickness of this daily workers' soup, it should come as no real surprise that many employees go to work full of malice and yet hungry for meaning (i.e., witness the "work" of creativity in the above narrative).

Nor should we be surprised that most employees go to work reluctantly, some angrily, and a few—now and then—even go armed.

NARRATIVE COUNTERMYTHOLOGY AND IRONIC COMPLICITY

Ironically, as I have discussed earlier, any resistance action taken by the powerless against the powerholder is *narratively complicit* with the conditions of maintaining—even tightening the institutional grip of—that relationship. Carol Warren's (1987) madwives moved from institutional domination in traditional marriages to institutional domination by physicians in mental hospitals; street gang members often find their acts of resistance lead them into prisons where the institutional domination continues as the same conditions sponsoring the narrative relationship are reproduced. And, in the "Ninja Employees" narrative above, the teller was identified as a "troublemaker," given a serious "talking to" by his superior, and told that if more complaints about his "language" were heard, he would face dismissal. Even dismissal is a complicit fate; employees who resist change in one organization may quit or lose their jobs only to seek employment in other places where they tend to encounter the same changes being instituted, the same face of colonial domination rigidly in place.

"Hate" narratives about work may be understood, therefore, as complicit, but destructive, poetic forms of employee resistance to domination. To speak "hate" is itself an act of violence as well as a possible aggressive precursor to it. To "hate" work but feel powerless to change the conditions of wage-enslavement, except by actively resisting the persons or forces that can be identified as complicit with the enslavement, is to position the subject/object of hate—the job, the change, the boss responsible for the change, a co-worker who will benefit from the change, or the company—in a tangible narrative form. The stories they offer, as well as the threats, the curses, the allegories, and the graffiti, are—again—their narrative attempts to gain *narrative control* over situations and Others.

Ultimately, the "iron collar" that Memmi (1965) suggests must be broken will not be broken simply through the telling of resistance narratives nor through the perpetration of resistance acts, for these actions serve mostly to reify the conditions of enslavement. The new order cannot be equitably assimilated into, nor can liminal status as a transitional figure in a dominated, occupied narrative be maintained. Offstage inversions temporarily alleviate some of the pain, but not all of it.

Narrative control gotten through varieties of work-hate narratives, when viewed this way, is more of sign of *desire* than of actual accomplishment. To move *beyond* the colonizer/colonized relationship is possible *only* through symbolically reconstituting the terms of that relationship, of moving from power dialectics of master/slave narratives to a partnership constructed out of authentic, democratic dialogue (Eisenberg, 1993). Put simply, "empowerment" programs must *actually* empower the work experiences of employees; team-based organizing must *actually* sponsor dialogue as well as productivity; flattened hierarchies must *actually* improve communication and flexibility; and the needs and fears of displaced—or outplaced—employees *actually* must be recognized and tended. Not only must these changes be experienced as actual and beneficial by employees, but the narratives spoken about those changes must be acknowledged as the localized site of constructions of meaning that will ultimately spell the success or failure of the change efforts.

Although a full articulation of that move is beyond the scope of this chapter, it does establish a vision by which attempts to release workers from the constraints of organizational domination may be productively understood. More important for the theme pursued here, it allows us to focus on the *constrained self* as the material and symbolic resource for understanding the terms of work-hate narratives as well as the substantive foundations for creating dialogue.

The Constrained Self: Work-Hate Narratives as the Narrative Work of an Overly Bureaucratized Self

Release from organizational constraints can be both real and productive; consider the many fine examples of company-sponsored change programs that actually give employees real voice and say-so in operations, or the many similar employee-led work-space redesign efforts that meet employee's needs while also improving productivity. In these cases the clear organizing locus that effectively produces benefits and improves productivity is a *transition to the change* han-

dled with *integrity*. In those examples what employees talked about—
the narratives for and against the change—were taken as the material
substance of the meanings employees had for what was going on
around them and happening within them. Put simply, *taking seriously
employee communication about change* and about the transitions to it
led directly toward proactive improvement and away from destructive
resistance.

The difference between success and failure in change efforts is in
how the *transition* to the new program, the new ownership, or the
new design is handled. *Transition* here refers not only to the actual
change of work processes, relationships, or sites, but more important
to the *narrative transition of the self* from conditions of known
occupational structures and communication to an unknown, often
unpredictable, future. This part of the change effort should be seen as
an opportunity for dialogue—and more important, that dialogue as
the real agent of change—where the work-hate narratives that surface
should be read and interpreted as clues to solving the organizational
drama.

> I don't really hate my job, or the company. I just hate what it is doing to
> me. If I could handle that, I could handle everything else.

When the narrative transition of the self isn't handled well, when
the change effort and its attendant alteration of one's organizational
identity is thrust upon employees without benefit of explanation,
preparation, or training, the result is predictable: *resistance* (to the
alteration of self); *anxiety* (about the required "new" self); *less time
spent performing work* and more time devoted to balancing the self's
fears with performances of offstage resistance narratives that feature
as a theme hatred about the company, the superiors, and/or the
change; and high turnover rates (turnover of often the most valuable,
and therefore most mobile, employees).

For employees whose narrative selves are expressed in terms that
define oppressed or colonized change states, release from uncertainties will be sought by perceiving, imagining, and enacting particular-
ized balancing acts against the injustices through a wide range of
"self-proclaiming" or "self-ish" resistance narratives and activities.
These activities include small acts of terrorism (the self "getting even")

that may become the substance of offstage performances, spreading of gossip and innuendo (the self "being bad"), trying to get co-workers or bosses in trouble with their new superiors or co-workers (the self "getting back"), defacing or rendering inoperable organizational property and materials (the self as "terrorist/freedom-fighter"), theft of organizational equipment or supplies (the heroic self restoring "equity"), deliberately slowing down or pulling down the amount or quality of work done (the self "in control"), and even well-planned and often elaborately executed forms of outright sabotage (the self having "a bad attitude") (Carlsson & Leger, 1990; Sprouse, 1992).

NARRATIVE SELF AS AN IDENTITY-SEEKING MESSAGE

One question that directs attention to the narratives of the constrained self and away from the material, structural, or even negative sanctions of organizational constraints is why do employees resist change when (a) complaints about the bureaucratic ordinary, the boring in everyday work rituals, and the inflexibility of the status quo saturate employee communication, and (b) the payoff for making the change effort could lead to increased autonomy and opportunities for self-expression?

When interpreted through the lens of Giddens's ideas about structural, material, and negative constraints *or* within the framework of Memmi's or Warren's psychopathologies of the institutionally colonized, it is again the transition of the self that requires attention. In both cases, Victor Turner's sense of "liminality" helps us to define a zone of change awareness that prescribes particular actions. In the case of Giddens, liminality leads the liminoid to seek *individual creative self-expressions;* in the case of the colonized self, entry into the liminal zone—from the oppressed comfort of assimilation into the resistance path of revolution—marks the beginning of a *change of one's self-identity.* Narratives of work-hate that emerge from this period of transition often feature distrust of superiors as a major motif; in the following excerpt, consider the underlying message to be a deeper critique of a failure to trust the self when conditions of control are lifted:

I don't understand empowerment. I mean, who am I supposed to go to when I have to complain? Who do I report to? Who will let me know how I am doing? I hate the whole thing, the whole damned idea. So now I'm supposed to take responsibility? I'm supposed to make all the decisions? What the hell does that mean?

NARRATIVE IDENTITY AND DEEP BUREAUCRACY

Both interpretive conditions as well as the above narrative assume—and in the case of the above narrative, embody—what elsewhere I have called an "overly *bureaucratized* self" (Goodall, 1991). The "overly bureaucratized self" is a narratively constructed one that accepts as its *natural condition* that life itself—as well as work—is (or should be) formally structured and thoroughly hierarchical, that what is "right" must be conspicuously well-tended, conservative, and neatly kept. Furthermore, it supposes that most everyday communication between or among persons is (or should be) phatic or ritualized; necessarily goal-directed, rule-bound, and overtly polite; mostly other-directed (to appear "social" and to become "well-liked") yet necessarily self-satisfying, self-monitoring, and self-protective. "Good" communication for the overly bureaucratized self combines the simple linearity and empirical representation of "information transfer" with the plausible deniability of "strategic control" (Eisenberg & Goodall, 1993). It is the communication of a self that uses talk to get what it wants, and if it doesn't get it, can deny that was what it wanted anyway.

For the overly bureaucratized self, communication at work should be compliant if not complicit with superiors' needs and requirements, socially pleasant—competent—among one's peers, self-effacing whenever possible but capable of demonstrating leadership through "answers" given to situations, respectfully unsettled in times of conflict but always willing to compromise, complacent about the "givenness" of "the ways things are," and thoroughly monitored within the known and accepted frameworks of institutional, social, and organizational authority. It is, simply, a self made for "being worked" (and for "being at work"), a self whose boundaries are made out of lifelong preoccupations with the relationship between one's identity, one's communication, and one's work. It is a self that unfailingly seeks to patrol, guard, and protect from interpenetration those narratively constructed boundaries, a self that denies itself the need to take risks (or that feels "guilty" when it does), the self that may see, for example, the telling of a mild joke or making an unkind comment as the absolute outer reaches of eccentricity.

The overly bureaucratized self tends also to be a suburban self (this is a metaphor as well as a source of lived experience) whose well-tended lawn and meticulously maintained automobile and home tend to reflect images of middle-class perfection and personal self-control, as does the wearing of "appropriate" business attire, as does the maintenance of unsatisfying relationships (intimate and social) for fear that the unknown world beyond those relationships would be even less satisfying and certainly more lonely and confusing. It is a self that is content to be *un*content but that is never *dis*contented, for the conditions of discontentedness would call into question the whole framing of the self-portrait, not just a narrative particular of its contents.

I'll go along with this new way of doing things because I have learned that is best. Change is inevitable anyway. Sure, I dislike it. Yes, I think the old way was better. But we'll see.

(Long pause). I mean, damn it, what else would you have me do? I have a wife, three kids, a mortgage, two cars, and parents who are probably going to move in with us pretty soon. If I say too much that is negative, or start acting up like some of the others, I'd be risking my job, my home, my life. So, no thank you, I'll stay in my place, even though I'm not sure where that exactly is anymore.

Between you and me—this is off the record, isn't it—I hate it. I just hate it. I got to keep my salary, but if any of my new team members knew how much I was making, they'd be jealous. Hell, I used to think I'd retire a Vice-President, but now there aren't any of those. So, yes, I hate it, what it does to me, to my ambitions. But I know that hating it won't make it go away. I work here. I have worked here for twenty years. I just want to stay here. That's all. Change my title, but let me keep my salary. I hate to admit it, but that really is enough for me.

BUREAUCRATIZED SELF AS THE HUMAN
PRODUCT OF AN OLD NARRATIVIZED ORDER

Earl Shorris (1984) sees this sort of person as the victim of what he terms "the politics of an oppressed middle." Shorris defines this "everyperson" as a mid-level manager or mid-level managerial aspirant (or college professor, or seminarian)—in many ways, the ideal construct for American workers (Whyte, 1956)—who is the human product of corporate bureaucracy, a living outcome of what Antonio Gramsci (1971) termed the "hegemony" of institutional controls. In Shorris's view, it is common business practices—keeping "secret" how much money employees make, allowing "higher-ups" to define "happiness" as equivalent to material and hierarchical advancement, engaging in untruths for the purpose of public relations, and so on—that conspire to produce the "totalitarian" state of corporations and agencies. It is a system of largely invisible bargains made with the vast machinery of capitalism that requires employees at every level, as a condition of their continued employment and promise of advancement, to exchange their already dwindling allowance for personal freedoms and choices for a thoroughly false sense of security.

> When I started out at this university I thought all I had to do was teach well and write maybe one article a year, and maybe later on a book. I spent a lot of time in my office, and most of that time interacting with students and colleagues. Those were the good old days. I got tenure, got promoted twice, became Chair.
>
> Then everything started to fall apart. First came "strategic planning," which defined academic units as "cost centers," and made us responsible for covering all of our salaries and operating expenses with student credit hours or income from grants. So we went to large enrollment courses, even though we knew that meant a decrease in the quality of what we would teach and what students would learn. Then came "TQM" and because it occurred in conjunction with the university's redefining of its mission, we learned that a lot of what we were doing had little to do with that mission, and unless we brought in more grants we would lose some positions. Quality was a word that really meant Money.
>
> So now most of our junior faculty members don't keep office hours, don't teach very well, and dedicate most of their time to finding grants. And me, well, I teach a course with 350 students in it and I never even learn their names. All my tests are computer-graded. And I spend a lot of time in meetings that I used to spend with students or even just reading a book.
>
> I hate being a college professor. I hate it because all of these changes have made what I got into this line of work for obsolete. I'm not a teacher anymore, just a salesman; I'm not a scholar, instead I am what my school calls an entrepreneur. My career isn't anything like I expected it to be,

even though I've always played by the rules and done fairly well. But at my age there aren't many options, and I'm mortgaged to the teeth. I sound like Willy Loman, don't I?

When change comes to the overly bureaucratized self, it threatens the terms of that bargain, that deal, that total and totalizing "arrangement" of self to Others, to contexts; most important, it threatens the narratives of self that have so well constructed its known domain. In colonial terms, having submitted so completely, surrendered so fully, to the conditions of an occupied, assimilated self—to an understanding of this construction of the narrativized world and what works narratively (if just allegorically) within it—the self confronted with organizational change—particularly change that flattens hierarchies, requires cross-functional training, or empowers employees to take control of situations they have so long been denied control over—is a self confronted with deep chaos, not just surface uncertainties. It may also be a self that is forced to confront its own complicity in the terms of its own enslavement; after all, there is no face uglier in one's own mirror than one's own face when its eyes cannot be looked into without wincing.

THE HARD WORK OF TRANSITIONAL NARRATIVES FOR THE OVERLY BUREAUCRATIZED SELF

So it is that the overly bureaucratized self comes to recognize its own liminality. In betwixt-and-between parallel worlds that do not share a common language code much less common values, understandings, or goals, is a narrative domain in which the *expression of emotions* passes for rational discourse. Because expressions of emotion occupy a cultural space mostly marginalized by highly developed and routinely organized rituals of civility, it is a space fit only for a primal self, a self pushed beyond the borders of civility and into a nether region reserved for outcry, for hatred, for tears. Turned wrong, the mismanagement of this transition can lead to self-loathing and self-destruction; moved through with a sense of guidance, acceptance, and coaching, it can lead to self-renewal and perhaps self-discovery.

This liminal space also figures as a prelude to entry into alternative constructions of a new world, the unknown territory of realized change, narrative realities for which one's self-preparations are aimed first at survival, then at mastery. Survival and mastery, as interpretive domains for situated individuals, can arrive through narrative destruction and/or physical violence just as they can arrive by democratic dialogue and/or physical transformation. The course of the outcome is largely determined by the decisions about how to manage the transition, the liminal zone. If these constructions seem extreme, consider what might happen in times of great upheaval and change as roughly akin to what might happen to a self-actualizing person who suddenly confronts the possibility that she or he—now having experienced the peak—has lost the net of safety that allowed the peak to be experienced and is facing the rude prospect of staring up at what was yesterday only safety as it now appears from the bottom of things, again.

I had it all. I was a Vice-President before 40, had the big house and perfect wife and fancy cars, you name it, I had it. I had it double. Triple. Then the company restructured and I was out of a job. Not just me, but me and about a thousand other guys who had pretty much the same resumes, just from different companies. I kept thinking things would turn around, I mean, they always had.

My wife left me, then I lost the house and cars and a bunch of other stuff in the divorce. She didn't want to be married to a loser, that's what she said. Another year went by and I still didn't have a job, and by that time I didn't have any money left, either. And it wasn't because I hadn't been looking for work, and it wasn't because I wasn't willing to take some position that might have been beneath me. There just weren't any jobs, not for someone like me. I was overqualified for most of what I applied for, but I was turned down just as hard anyway. I even tried being a consultant for awhile, but I never did have the speaking skills for that.

So here I am, a 43-year old assistant manager of a fast food restaurant, working about 60 hours a week for less money a year than I used to spend in a slow month. I'm hoping to get a new Visa card soon, if you can imagine that. My ex-wife married another guy like I used to be and lives well. And my boss is ten years younger than me.

But I have a plan. When my old company restructured, they didn't lose everybody at my level. I figure I was sold out, and I think I know who and I am sure I know why. He doesn't know it yet, but his days are fucking numbered. He comes in here to eat once in a while, but he doesn't recognize me. Nobody would. I'm going to either put shredded glass in his food or maybe just poison him. But one way or another he'll die, and his death will not be an easy one. I want to watch. Just like he watched me. I hate the son-of-a-bitch. And I will get back, even if I can't get even.

The above example is a hard one to read, even harder to discuss. Obviously this hate narrative transcends work, although it emerges from a loss of it and from a loss of self that went with it. But if we pay attention to the liminal zone—the narrative about the time that change in the company led to change within the self—we see clear evidence of a mismanaged transition. In this case, the company did not do a good job of dealing with displaced executives, this one in particular.

THE NEED TO MANAGE THE NARRATIVE TRANSITION: FROM BUREAUCRATIZED SELF TO EMPOWERED TEAM PLAYER

Even in the narratives that preceded this one—narratives less potentially violent but nonetheless full of work-hate—it is the transition from the overly bureaucratized, thoroughly incorporated self to a newly restructured, empowered, team-based or work-redesigned, or even foreign-national owned company self that must be most carefully managed, by which I mean most thoroughly invited into a democratic dialogue. Put differently, although the focus of most organizational change efforts are vested in the material and structural conditions of the workplace, what should be realized is that changes to these surfaces will be reflected in the discourse of those who must inhabit changed selves on, across, and within those surfaces. One *caveat:* If the decision frame for the change is predetermined and narrow, the pursuit of "dialogue" as a transition tool at best lacks integrity and at worst is entirely disingenuous. Once employees see through the rhetoric of promoting "dialogue" when, in fact, such a move is merely viewed as a "transition device" and not as an agent of promoting employee voice and participation in decisions about the change effort, any future attempts at establishing it in the same company will be seriously compromised.

When work-hate narratives appear, they are signs of something other than "worker dissatisfaction"; they should be interpreted as signs of selves in transition wherein the effective management of that transition depends largely on the construction of *genuine* dialogue. In the case of the former employee who is plotting revenge—an all-too frequent theme on nightly newscasts—perhaps we have evidence that the narratives that need management attention extend beyond the final day of pay.

Conclusion: Transitional Hate Narratives as Signs of Necessary Transitions

Why do people behave the way they do? The answer is, "Because they think they should." Regardless of the evaluative label we attach to everyday performances of social interaction, for the person or persons engaged in constructing and rendering meaningful the world they perceive, live within, or socially enact, their actions *always* represent reasoned interpretations of situations and Others. They act *because* they believe they must act; they act the way they do *because* in the world they inhabit, they feel that such actions are warranted.

Narratives of and about hatred, viewed this way, cannot wholly be understood as "destructive" or "demonic" or—to borrow argot from popular usage—"twisted" communication; they also represent or evoke —often passionately—a reasoned construction of the world, a world in transition. It is a world in which "hatred"—for the teller—is a rational, maybe even a necessary action. It is a world in which the identity of the hater must be understood as a complex social, political, economic, gendered, historical, and autobiographical quest for authenticity and meaning as well as—all too often—honor.

"Hate" makes for a organizationally common but ultimately *strange* narrative. These narratives are not so much "stories of hate" as they are contextual commentaries within which reside some sharp edge, and it is on that edge that one hears, locates, or experiences an unsettling point of view. The commentary supports—mostly justifies— the "righteousness" or "rightness" of the hate for the teller, and it doesn't so much reveal intentions as it conceals them in the communicative activity of telling of the tale. In most cases, that activity of saying the hate is enough of an action itself. But sometimes it isn't enough; sometimes it is just a warning.

Hate narratives become—in the mismanaged transitions of organizations whose mismanagement actually sponsors the narrative—a two-headed, tell-tale monster. One head points into those vast autobiographical and historical interiors, leading the teller to some tight space from which a simple utterance finally gets articulated. That utterance may be an offhanded remark, an allegory, an account of personal injustice, a cry, a scream, a long series of virtually inarticulate curses, or even the kind of "firing back" that bursts from the barrel of a semi-automatic weapon. The other head moves serpent-like around the office or plant floor, drifts out with the wind into the parking lot, and even permeates the dinner conversations in a wide assortment of homes, restaurants, private clubs. And when that head returns to the body it derives sustenance from—the organization mismanaging its own transition—the story continues to evolve and grow, and through its evolutions, the utterance of work-hate narratives escalates.

Perhaps this is why work-hate narratives seldom end. Once the hate is achieved in speech, it articulates a version of reality that the speaker then lives within. Whatever that reality is—however, and wherever, it is articulated—there is a holy place reserved for violence in it. From the perspective of the hater, that violence is legitimate, justified, rational, and ultimately *moral,* for as Earl Shorris (1984) puts it "most of the moral activity of the world is of searching for scapegoats and villains" (p. 49). It is also *empowering.* It acts *on* the world as well as *in* it.

Given this view, what then can be done? My conclusion is straight-forward: *Hate narratives are largely the work of mismanaged organizational transitions.* The narratives reveal patterns of institutionalized control in times of change that are lived by the haters as powerful sources of boundaryless domination, borderless occupation, and totalizing self-denial. Because the issue is clearly one of power, and because the seat of power—however structurally formalized—is located in speech, the solution to this organizational problem must also be located in speech. More to the point, in the *purpose* of speech.

Elsewhere (Goodall, 1993), I have argued that the current popularity of the spirituality metaphor for organizations encourages us to think differently about the purposes and meanings of work and communication for humans termed "employees." If we begin with the idea that humans are—first and foremost—*spiritual beings,* then our "work" is directly connected to issues of human and environmental ecologies, which makes the work and communication of each one of us *interconnected* to the work and communication of one another.

Ultimately, that bond—that inherent interconnectedness—that unity, is *sacred* (Bateson & Donaldson, 1991; Hawley, 1993; Spretnak, 1991).

Admittedly, we live—as Plato recognized—in the eternal shadows of this phenomenal world, and our work—as we all undoubtedly recognize—in organizations and for institutions is mostly defined by tasks, routines, and responsibilities that do not reward our spiritual values, or at least do not see them as relevant to the material concerns of productivity, efficiency, or corporate survival. Indeed, if these organizations and institutions did recognize that connection, we might very well have very different definitions for ideas such as productivity, efficiency, and survival.

Yet the current popularity of the spiritual metaphor does offer us a window of opportunity. It suggests, dramatically, that in our time of great upheavals and change, perhaps the greatest of all changes is yet to come. As we literally "come to terms" with new ways of organizing labor and empowering communication, as we broaden the operational articulation of "progress" to include human and environmental sustainability (Hawken, 1993), and as we increasingly act on the idea that our realities are, in fact, *socially* constructed, maybe we will learn that our "work"—wherever it is done—is first and foremost to care for each other and our blue planet.

In a very strange way, the study of work-hate narratives helps get us there. These are tales of organizations that cannot sustain us despite their material survival. They are accounts of a "presence of an absence," of something gone wrong or just missing, of something gone wrong or missing from their lives that is very important. The speaking of "hate" should not, therefore, be understood solely as a negative force, as yet another symbolic enemy in the occupied territories to be systematically hunted down and technologically slain. This would be only to further tighten the constraints that produced the narratives anyway, and to somehow rub out the symptom of a far deeper intercultural malaise in the interests of yet a larger form of global domination, control, and—ironically—*hate* that we pray to, fear, covet, and call "capitalism," would be a tragic error of interpretation. Instead, this symptom must be viewed as what it narratively is: a sign of a transition, albeit a highly mismanaged one.

To manage the transition requires more than simply talking the madwife back into the bad marriage, or narcotizing the suddenly unemployed with better letters of recommendation or the promise of a bigger welfare check. First, the fact that there *is* a transition going on must be acknowledged, and the persons experiencing it must be trusted to speak for the terms of its realities. There is a very good chance that what gets talked about will implicate more than just a job, or a company, or even a community. In times of crises—as these narratives show—persons tend to connect questions about the meanings of their suddenly interrupted lives to questions about the ritualized work they have always been doing. Probably we should learn to pay close attention to this: The absence of boundaries reveals the presence of opportunities to seriously redefine purposes.

Second, the terms of the spoken realities then must be used to construct an authentic dialogue that cuts across organizational and institutional boundaries, even national boundaries. This should become a dialogue that empowers us all to reenvision what we are doing here and to reconnect what counts as "work" to the work of life—and the sustainability of the planet—itself. In the academic world this sort of sentiment is too often seen, and too easily dismissed, as simplistic idealism; ironically, the true idealists are very much in the business world, already organizing "future search conferences" (Weisbord, 1993) to discover common ground capable of reshaping the world we live in *through dialogue.*

In the communication field we don't take dialogue seriously enough. After years of seeking social science "objectivity" and distance, we tend to observe, categorize, and analyze rather than *participate.* Our academic conventions—yearly transitions about which work-hate narratives abound—seldom even sponsor opportunities for us to take dialogue seriously by engaging in it. So, even though I would like to close this chapter about hate on a more positive note about the role of communication as a field in the social construction of dialogue, I don't think I can take that risk. At least not yet. We are, after all, a field very clearly in the throes of a largely mismanaged transition from social science/humanistic dualities to clever domination by empty pluralism posing as academic dialogue. How we learn to listen to the work-hate narratives in our own midst may well determine how we learn to connect the terms of *our* organizational future to the broader institutional and spiritual interests of our common *ecological* future.

Notes

1. Oral narratives and recalled anecdotes used in this chapter were collected between 1987 and 1995 in various locations in the American South. I make no claim that they "represent" a typology of work-hate accounts; they are at best a "convenience sample" used here to evoke the lived experiences—and interpretations of those experiences—of the individuals speaking them.

2. For this study, "work-hate" narratives are defined as accounts of and about "hate" of work, of workers, or of the conditions that surround or invade an employee's job, in which the term *hate* is used in the account by the speaker. There are several problems with this approach. First, studying "hate" narratives often requires the interpreter to rely on previous frameworks and understandings. Therefore, an employee may not have to speak the word *hate* to evoke it from previous contexts. Second, in our culture, the term *hate* is used rather loosely; many people regularly say they "hate" everything from the taste of food to the quality of their lives, without much distinction being made about the level or depth of the emotion. This study—relying primarily on ethnographic data—is based on the assumption that the ways in which individuals talk about their own lived experiences represent the best source of information about their own interpretations of the meanings of contexts. Third, because we associate the use of the term *hate* with extreme attitudes (e.g., racism) and behaviors (e.g., violence), ordinary expressions of it tend to be overlooked or are at least underexamined. The very "ordinariness" of the work-hate narratives used in this study are not as sensational as one might expect; however, their very ordinariness is—as this study will demonstrate—interpretively rich and—as far as our understanding of American work cultures is concerned—deeply meaningful.

References

Alvesson, M. (1993). Cultural-ideological modes of management control: A theory and case study of a professional service company. In S. Deetz (Ed.), *Communication yearbook 16* (pp. 3-42). Newbury Park, CA: Sage.

Bateson, G., & Donaldson, R. E. (1991). *Sacred unity: Further steps to an ecology of mind.* New York: HarperCollins.

Bhabha, H. (1990). *Nation and narration.* London: Routledge & Kegan Paul.

Brinton, M. (1993). *The irrational in politics: Sexual repression and authoritarian conditioning.* Tucson, AZ: See Sharp Press.

Burke, K. (1950). *A rhetoric of motives.* Englewood Cliffs, NJ: Prentice Hall.

Burke, K. (1965). *Permanence and change.* Indianapolis, IN: Bobbs-Merrill.

Carlsson, C., & Leger, M. (1990). *Bad attitude: The processed world anthology.* New York: Verso.

Clegg, S. R. (1989). *Frameworks of power*. Newbury Park, CA: Sage.

Conquergood, D. (1994). Homeboys and hoods: Gang communications and cultural space. In L. R. Frey (Ed.), *Group communication in context* (pp. 23-56). Hillsdale, NJ: Lawrence Erlbaum.

Conrad, C. (1993). Rhetorical/communication theory as an ontology for structuration research. In S. Deetz (Ed.), *Communication yearbook 16* (pp. 197-208). Newbury Park, CA: Sage.

de Certeau, M. (1984). *The practice of everyday life* (S. Rendall, Trans.). Berkeley: University of California Press.

Deetz, S. (1992). *Democracy in an age of corporate colonization*. Albany: SUNY Press.

Eisenberg, E. M. (1993, October). *From consensus to dialogue: Inter-organizational cooperation and inter-city education*. Paper presented at the Discourse Conference, Temple University, Philadelphia.

Eisenberg, E. M., & Goodall, H. L. (1993). *Organizational communication: Balancing creativity and constraint*. New York: St. Martin's.

Gergen, K. (1991). *The saturated self*. New York: HarperCollins.

Giddens, A. (1984). *The constitution of society*. Berkeley: University of California Press.

Goodall, H. L. (1991). *Living in the rock n roll mystery: Reading contexts, self, and others as clues*. Carbondale: Southern Illinois University Press.

Goodall, H. L. (1992). Empowerment, culture, and postmodern organizing. *Journal of Organizational Change Management, 5,* 25-30.

Goodall, H. L. (1993). Mysteries of the future told: Communication as the material manifestation of spirituality. *World Communication, 22,* 40-50.

Goodall, H. L. (1995). *Divine signs: Connecting spirit to community*. Carbondale: Southern Illinois University Press.

Gramsci, A. (1971). *Selections from the prison notebooks*. London: Lawrence & Wishart.

Harper's index. (1993, May). Harper's.

Hawken, P. (1993, September-October). A declaration of sustainability. *Utne Reader*, pp. 54-60.

Hawley, J. (1993). *Reawakening the spirit in work: The power of Dharmic management*. San Francisco: Barrett-Koehler.

Jameson, F. (1984, July/August). Postmodernism, or the cultural logic of late capitalism. *New Left Review, 146,* 53-92.

Lavie, S. (1990). *The poetics of military occupation*. Berkeley: University of California Press.

Memmi, A. (1965). *The colonizer and the colonized*. Boston: Beacon.

Mumby, D. (1988). *Communication and power in organizations*. Norwood, NJ: Ablex.

Riley, P., & Banks, S. P. (1993). Structuration theory as an ontology for communication research. In S. Deetz (Ed.), *Communication yearbook 16* (pp. 167-196). Newbury Park, CA: Sage.

Sacks, H. (1970-1971). *Doing the business of being ordinary*. Edited transcript of Lecture 1 (Spring 1970) with additional materials from Lecture 2 (Winter 1970), Lecture 4 (Spring 1970), and Lecture 1 (Spring 1971). University of California, Irvine.

Said, E. (1978). *Orientalism*. New York: Random House.

Scott, J. C. (1990). *Domination and the arts of resistance*. New Haven, CT: Yale University Press.

Seeger, M. (1986). *Free speech yearbook 6*. Carbondale: University of Illinois Press.

Shorris, E. (1984). *Scenes from corporate life: The politics of middle management.* New York: Penguin.

Spretnak, C. (1991). *States of grace: The recovery of meaning in the postmodern age.* New York: HarperCollins.

Sprouse, M. (Ed.). (1992). *Sabotage in the American workplace: Anecdotes of dissatisfaction, mischief, and revenge.* San Francisco: Pressure Drop Press.

Turner, V. (1969). *The ritual process.* Chicago: Aldine.

Warren, C.A.B. (1987). *Madwives: Schizophrenic women in the 1950s.* New Brunswick, NJ: Rutgers University Press.

Weisbord, M. E. (Ed.). (1993). *Discovering common ground.* San Francisco: Barrett-Koehler.

Whyte, W. (1956). *The organization man.* New York: Basic Books.

Symbolism and the Representation of Hate in Visual Discourse

David E. Whillock
Texas Christian University

Editor's Introduction

In an era of political correctness, overt expressions of hatred are diminishing. This does not mean that people have fewer feelings of hatred, but that public forums for its expression are becoming less tolerant. David Whillock argues that the repression of hate speech has led to the development of more sophisticated readings of signs and symbols: tools that are more difficult to censor.

In this chapter, Whillock explores the use of hate in symbolic expressions with the recent dress code controversy in the public schools over students wearing Doc Marten boots as the backdrop for his analysis. Although some students argue that Doc Martens are merely comfortable shoes dressed up with colorful laces as a matter of style, opponents contend that the shoes are symbols used by skin- heads and neo-Nazis to unify members and express an "unhealthy" quest for dominance over other groups. Frequently these debates center on whether symbols have specific meanings, their power, and the school's right to regulate them.

This chapter helps us better understand how symbols "talk." Using the appropriation and development of Nazi symbols as examples, Whillock demonstrates how symbolic codes are culturally and historically imbued with meaning. He then explains how these images can be used for persuasion or defense. Finally, Whillock argues that hate can be both symbolically expressed and experienced, and that developing the ability to read visual cues is critical to an understanding of text.

Man's Symbolic Nature

Their Doc Martens are laced with contrasting colors: white for the purity of the Aryan race, red for the spilt blood of their enemies—a symbolic way to emphasize their struggle for political and ethnic supremacy. The setting is a local high school where 16- to 18-year-old white, middle-income youths, feeling betrayed and threatened by the influx of other nationalities and genealogies, use verbal denigration, group intimidation, and visual symbols to frighten their perceived enemies: Blacks, Asians, and Jews. These tactics and symbolic codes mirror those used by the German Nazi party in the 1930s and 1940s. The grandparents of these teens grew to loathe and despise these images, justly regarding them as symbols of hate representing the worst humans can do to one another.

Some scholars argue that the resurgence of Nazi symbols and military dress should not be interpreted in a historical context. I argue, however, that historical context is precisely what imbues them with meaning. As school boards debate the appropriateness of dress codes to curtail the hostile environment created by neo-Nazis and Skinheads, the least that must be conceded is this: Symbols do convey specific meanings; and they do have specific cultural effects.

Kenneth Burke, a noted rhetorical theorist, based his work on the concept that humans are symbol-using animals. Indeed, he contends that we are defined by our symbols: "What is our reality for today (beyond the paper-thin line of our own particular lives) but this clutter of symbols" (Burke, 1993, p. 70). For Burke, symbols remind the receiver of specific cultural interpretations of significant events. They convey not only a point of view, but also a declaration of faith about the future.

Burke (1993) contends that, as a form of expression, symbols have specific contextual meanings. He paraphrases the Apostle Paul when he notes that descriptions are introduced through the spoken word: "Faith comes from hearing" (p. 72). Yet while faith statements may be introduced and reinforced by the verbal word, often this faith is integrated into our reality through visual media.

Consider the discussions and descriptions of Hitler's Final Solution. Words cannot adequately describe this terrible episode in Germany's history. It was Resnais's film *Night and Fog* that seared the images into our imagination and provided the visual specificities of time, place, and atrocity that gave names like Dachau, Treblinka, and Auschwitz new and horrible meanings. The visualization of bulldozers efficiently piling bodies into open graves with no regard to dignity or propriety will forever be associated with the Swastika, a symbol that had positive meanings in European religious tradition before its adaptation by the Nazis. The power of such visual images is what O'Shaughnessey (1990) addressed when he argued that "people identify with moving images more intensely than with printed words" (p. 22). In this sense, symbols are the threads in the fabric of our collective memory.

The Persuasive Use of Images

Once established, visual images may be used in a variety of ways. Roland Barthes (1977), in his seminal essay "The Rhetoric of the Image," discusses how icons and images go beyond supporting a reflected ideology propagated by state apparatuses. For Barthes, the rhetoric of the image appears as the "signifying aspect of ideology" (p. 36). Consequently, symbols are more than reflections of social conformity—they may also produce ideological beliefs.

Barthes's (1977) analysis of the image begins with a series of questions on the role of the image in our society and "how meaning gets into the image" (p. 37). In the opening question of Barthes's essay he asks, "Can analogical representation (the copy) produce true systems of signs . . . and not merely simple agglutinations of symbols?" (p. 36). Can an image do more than glue together symbols that are perceptually accepted as forms reflecting societal codes? Can the image, in effect, produce a semiological epistemology and indeed fuse perceptual and anthropological knowledge of ourselves?

To address these issues, Barthes (1977) analyzes advertising strategies to see how they create meaningful symbols that influence culture. He states that, "in advertising the signification of the image is undoubtedly intentional; the signifieds of the advertising message are formed *a priori* by certain attributes of the product and these signifieds have to be transmitted as clearly as possible" (p. 37). In the marketplace of ideas, product images must be positioned to convey significant information during a short time span in order to generate brand awareness and increase the desirability of the product. This is true also when positioning a message for political/ideological purposes. Symbols, once established, may be used to achieve immediate effects. Yet the construction of symbolic meaning must be carefully developed over a period of time, because understanding the symbol depends on a specific decoding by its reader.

How do people learn to decode symbols similarly? Barthes identifies three messages present in every mediated message: the linguistic message, the iconic message, and the non-iconic message. It is important to understand that although Barthes analyzes an image through three separate parts, the rhetorical impact is derived through the combination of all messages within the image/symbol. The "gestalt" of the images is what gives them ideological power. Barthes (1977) claims that the "viewer of the image receives at one and the same time the perceptual message and the cultural message" (p. 38). Yet, to understand this gestalt and how reading the separate messages within the image/symbol create ideological meaning, it would prove fruitful to break the image/symbol into its parts to examine them more closely and attempt to understand the image/symbol's overall structure.

The linguistic message "is indeed present in every image: as title, caption, . . . dialogue" (Barthes, 1977, p. 39). The linguistic message explains what it is that we are viewing. Barthes explains, "the text helps to identify purely and simply the elements of the scene and the scene itself; it is a matter of the denoted description of the image" (p. 39).

The denotative image is the anchor of all possible meanings. In this role, the linguistic message is ideological. As Barthes (1977) states, the anchorage function of the linguistic message "directs the reader through the signifieds of the image, causing [the reader] to avoid some and receive others" (p. 39). The impact of this is clear. If the linguistic message is a "road map" necessary for the understanding of the image/symbol, there is little room for interpretation. The creator of the image may lead the reader to decode the message with the intent perceived by them. As an example, the Skinheads' use of the swastika has historical anchoring. The message is clear for those who fear or loathe the representation of such icons. Thus, the explanation of the image becomes its meaning.

The second message given to the image/symbol is the iconic message. The iconic message is the connotative extreme of the image/symbol. In its relationship to the image, the iconic message transmits cultural meanings to symbols. In essence, the iconic message is a code recognized by members of a culture who assign commonly understood meanings to images/symbols. It relies on the combination of visual and aural cues to interpret correctly the culturally coded message. Through the iconic message, we begin to peel away the layers of cultural and symbolic meanings found in the image. Within this message we begin to "read" colors, visual framing, configurations, roles, locations, and a true investigation of the signifieds. The use of red and white shoelaces and the Doc Martens is encoded by their display to represent the purity of the race and the blood of their enemies.

The iconic message relies on the certainty that specific images have cultural significance in order for the image to resonate meaning. Without the "prearranged agreement" between creator and reader, the message would have no significance beyond its linguistic function. Because the message is interpreted by an unspoken yet prearranged agreement between an institution to which the image belongs and the members of that culture, the impact of the icon is significant within a society.

The third message, non-iconic, is simply its physical existence. In essence the non-iconic message "is what it is." The message is "not drawn from an institutional stock, is not coded . . . [it is] a message without a code" (Barthes, 1977, p. 35). While the non-iconic message is without coding, it still demands a reading. Thus, knowledge is needed to interpret the perception. Although the reader must know what the images/symbols are, there is for this message no meaning except its physical existence. The message is only what is connoted. The mixture of the colors red, white, and blue, for instance, is just that. There is no extrinsic message: It would not be, in this instance, the symbolic concept of "America." Nor would Doc Martens be construed as anything other than comfortable boots.

In all mediated messages, symbolism and cultural coding are essential to the successful relaying of a concept for cultural meaning. Whether the intent of the creator of the message is to sell the consumer an item, to support a societal ideology, or to create within the culture a tension based on hatred, the intent must be clear. The clarity of such messages can be found in the historical development of that image/symbol.

The Message of Hate as Historical Icon

Beginning with the inception of photography in the mid-1800s, the proliferation of visual images has placed an increased importance on our culture's ability to interpret them correctly. The effect of visual images on a culture cannot be understated. Indeed, some critics argue that visual images have become a major source of information about our society and culture (O'Connor, 1990). John O'Connor (1990) reminds us of Vachael Lindsay's characterization of the United States as a "hieroglyphic civilization," one in which "images-turned-icons" allow us "literally [to] see the fundamental tensions" in culture (p. 1). Understanding this "hieroglyphic civilization" permits us to identify and analyze our symbols of hate.

Many of our culture's symbols of hate emanate from images created by governments in the course of war. These propaganda efforts were designed to generate near-universal acceptance of the government's actions by its citizens. The population of a country will be used to generate the war effort through sacrifice of life, of work, and of ideology. Without this sacrifice, the war effort will fail. One of the more successful methods for gaining public acceptance of particular agendas is propaganda. Jacques Ellul's (1965) seminal work on propaganda discusses the importance of visual symbols and the importance of symbol manipulation. He states that we study "[t]he manipulation of symbols for three reasons. First, it persuades the individual to enter the framework of an organization. Second, it furnishes him with reasons, justifications, motivations for action. Third, it obtains his total allegiance" (p. 23). Never has this been more overt than the propaganda efforts attempted throughout World War II.

These efforts helped transform Germany from the disillusioned and depressed country preceding World War I to the powerful war machine of the Third Reich that led Germany into a total war for Aryan superiority in the late 1930s. This rise is documented in several books, including Joachim Remak's (1969) edited volume, *The Nazi Years: A Documentary History.* The use of symbols in various propaganda films to endorse and create hate and loyalty in the German population is very much at the heart of this chapter.

The Expressionist period that occurred after World War I in German cinema is considered one of the more important developmental periods of world cinema. The innovations developed in this era of film history are still used today. The Germans were creative and successful in using Expressionism's psychological and mythical methodologies to construct narratives of Teutonic greatness. Through symbolism, they were able to describe vividly the mental anguish and devastation that resulted from World War I (see, e.g., Kaucauer, 1947). Although many of the filmmakers of the Expressionist period left Germany when the Nazis came to power, the lessons learned from this period of film history were important to the propaganda machine constructed under Joseph Goebbels in 1933. The construction of symbolic codes was essential to the Nazi efforts. Although this construction evolved over time and used several vehicles for presentation, the 1934-1935 documentary film *Triumph of the Will,* directed by Hitler's chosen director, Leni Riefenstahl, is considered by most film and propaganda historians as a turning point in the use of symbols in motivating universal and unquestioning loyalty from the population.

This filmic document of the Nazi party rally at Nuremberg staged in September 1934 is "an emotional hymn of praise to Hitler" (Manheim, 1994, p. 54). This film resonates with lessons learned from Barthes's rhetoric of the image. The linguistic message is taken from Hitler's *Mein Kampf,* as speech after speech in this 3½-hour film describes the loss of German pride and economic free will after World War I and glorifies the Germanic past with emphasis on Teutonic military victories. Hitler borrowed from his favorite composer, Wagner, to carefully construct and stage this self-glorification to both himself and Germany's past. This is evidenced by the strong linguistic message given at the very opening of the film:

> On September 5
> 1934
>
> 20 years
> after the outbreak
> of the World War
>
> 16 years
> after the start
> of German suffering
>
> 19 months
> after the beginning
> of Germany's rebirth
>
> Adolf Hitler flew
> again to Nuremberg
> to review the columns of his faithful followers
>
> (As quoted in Barnouw, 1993, p. 105)

The linguistic message sets the tone for Hitler's agenda at the rally. It emphasizes Germany's loss in World War I, the cause of suffering, and the rebirth of the nation. Combining mythical strength with specific verbal assaults on the Jews and Bolsheviks for contributing to

Germany's failures, Hitler helped cultivate increased paranoia and feelings of hatred.

The linguistic message was clear and to the point. "Subhuman" groups would no longer be tolerated. Any verbal or physical assaults against them, then, would be justified and seen as defensive measures. Hitler made this position clear in *Mein Kampf;* it was echoed by Goebbels as early as 1928 (Remak, 1969, p. 145). Indeed, Hitler's speech to the Reichstag linked his anti-Semitic and anti-Bolshevik agenda together:

> I have often in my life been a prophet and usually people laughed at me. . . . Let me be a prophet again today: If international financial Jewry, in Europe and beyond, should succeed in plunging the nations into another world war, the result will not be the Bolshevization of the world and thus the victory of Jewry, but the destruction of the Jewish race in Europe. (quoted in Remak, 1969, p. 145)

As a linguistic sign, the anti-Semitism of the Nazi party was part of its creation.

The linguistic message of hate in *Triumph of the Will* is underscored by the iconic messages found throughout the careful and deliberate staging of events by Riefenstahl. In the opening of the film, Hitler in his tri-motor airplane descends onto the city like a mythical Teutonic god coming to save his people. Crowds of adoring followers await his arrival. Hitler's ascent symbolically represents Germany's reemergence from the ashes of World War I, the details of which are offered in Hitler's plan to become the 1,000-year Reich. Riefenstahl's task was to establish three elements in her films: First, to connect Hitler to Germany's history, both its mythical and too realistic past. Second, to establish the power of a new generation of Germans to rule the world. Third, to prove Hitler's overpowering support from the German population.

Iconic images that support these three elements include the camera angle on Hitler. Usually the camera shot Hitler from a position that placed him behind a large podium surrounded by his visually and numerically powerful Black- and Brown-shirt associates who would nod their heads in agreement. This visual representation created an acknowledged dress code of difference. Those who were connected and politically correct were identified by their uniforms. Or, using images of implied power, Riefenstahl would place her camera below Hitler so that the viewers looked up into the face of their leader, producing a height advantage that accented his position and command. Another, and more powerful, position of the camera gave the shots of the adoring crowds straining to get a glimpse of their leader and hero. Many times Riefenstahl's camera would find a child, a mother, or an elderly member of the crowd to emphasize that the nonmilitary citizens also held Hitler as their culture's best hope for survival.

The visual impact of the film is never so evident as in the scenes of the true followers, the youth of the German people. Scene after scene gives witness to the conformity and commitment of Hitler's youth brigade. The camera captures straight rows of thousands of uniformed youths carrying shovels like rifles and reciting lyrical oaths to their Führer and the German nation. Indeed, Riefenstahl's use of close-ups of these youths and their nonverbal agreements to Hitler's anti-Semitic and anti-Bolshevik plan emphasize visual iconic codes. The visual emphasis conveys the depth of their agreement as well as the unstated threats to those who would oppose them.

Symbols can represent what groups stand for as well as the objects of a culture's disdain. While Hitler used the swastika and eagle as signs of loyalty to the Nazi party, Germany, and his political agenda, he used the Star of David as an iconic image of directed hate. Remak uses as evidence documents of the Nazi party to show when certain laws, policies, and directives were placed in motion in Germany. By 1941, the Jewish population was required by law to wear the Star of David on their clothes to identify them as Jews. This iconic code directly identified those who were to be shunned, harassed, and later killed. Laws concerning Jews and their daily life began much earlier, however. The "Law for the Protection of German Blood and Honor" was passed as early as 1935. The Nazi hate crimes against the Jews, whether through the symbolic use of signs or through direct physical conflict, began in Germany the same year (see, e.g., Remak, 1969, pp. 145-160). The linguistic and iconic rhetoric of hate presented in the *Triumph of the Will* had found wide public support by the turn of the decade.

The creation of hate codes against ethnic groups is not restricted to Germany. During the 1930s and 1940s, Great Britain, France, the Soviet Union, and the United States also used film as a vehicle for the development of emotions of hate during the war. Employing the British methods of propaganda used in the social documentaries of the 1930s, the United States felt it had to counteract films such as *Triumph of the Will* to be successful in its own attempts to motivate an isolationist public to support its new foreign policy toward Germany, Italy, and Japan. Such an attempt can be found in the propaganda films in the "Why We Fight" series.

While Nazi propaganda focused on the construction of hate through the process of historical blame, the United States used more recent precipitating events to gain momentum for the war effort. Both the bombing of Pearl Harbor by Japan and the immediate declaration of war by Germany on the United States in 1941 gave rise to a collective response.

U.S. propaganda efforts reinforced the outrage and racial hatred created in response to Japan's attack. On the Western front, propaganda efforts fostered ideological hate by emphasizing differences between a Democracy (the United States) and Fascism, authoritarian regimes (Germany and Italy). Indeed, using footage from *Triumph of the Will* and captured German, Italian, and Japanese combat films, the American propagandists focused on the differences between *us* and *them:* the "free world and the slave world." Employing the talents of the already well-established all-American filmmaker Frank Capra, the efforts of the American propaganda machine proved successful.

The "Why We Fight" series was not only a required part of military training but a standard preview before every movie. Using stereotypes and linguistic and iconic messages created through ethnic fear (Japanese) and ideological differences (Germany and Italy), the films portrayed Hirohito, Hitler, and Mussolini as dictators of the slave world. Disney's animation depicted a world painted black. This animation portrayed the darkness spilling into what was once free France, Belgium, China, Indochina, and Northern Africa, threatening the last of the democratic countries, England and the United States.

The linguistic message was clear. In the series' film *Prelude to War,* the narration by John Forsythe reminds us to "Take a good look at this trio. Remember their faces . . . if you ever meet them, don't hesitate. . . ." The style of linguistic message favored aphorisms. In *Divide and Conquer* the narrator states, "For free men are like rubber balls. The harder they fall, the higher they bounce. . . ." The linguistic message had to build hatred upon the idea of fear and perseverance. The message focused on our difference, whether racial or ideological. Its concise presentation reminds the soldier and the population that if we are slow to act, we will not only lose our American heritage and freedoms, but will be directly responsible for a slave world of authoritarian control. Indeed, the use of stereotypes in the linguistic message was a successful element of the films. This success is underscored by Ellul's (1965) statement that, "the stereotype arises from feelings one has for one's own group, or against the 'out-group' " (p. 163). By splitting the world into stereotypical evil leaders of the "slave world" and good leaders of the "free world," the agenda of the propaganda was more clear and understandable by the groups for which the message was intended.[1]

The iconic messages of the "Why We Fight" series underscored the linguistic message. Not only did the filmmakers use the animation of dark versus light in their films, they used also a compilation of captured military and combat footage. There were scenes depicting the horrors of war and the dislocation and miseries of the populations of Europe, China, and Micronesia. Capra's directors, like Hitler's, used close-ups of children, the elderly, the disempowered. But unlike in Hitler's films, they were portrayed as victims. As victims of war, a myth was created teaching us that we, the Americans, were the only ones who could save them. The British were hanging on by sheer tenacity and we "Yanks" had to save these innocents. Using iconic codes, films focused on creating or reinforcing already existing feelings of hate and fear.[2] The iconic messages were clear in these films. The portrayal of Germans, Japanese, and to some extent Italians in their quest for control of all the world played upon the existing fears of foreigners by an isolationist population. Indeed, the films worked best in reinforcing fears of invasion more than in aiding our allies. This is evidenced in the iconic message found in 1942's *Prelude to War.*

The focus of *Prelude to War* is to explain why America had to fight a European and Asian war. Using fear tactics, the director superimposed marching armies of the Axis power over Pennsylvania Avenue. In *Divide and Conquer* (1943), the director used a similar "What if?" fear tactic by using combat footage of Japan and Germany to ask, "What if war came to America?" Visions of the apocalypse and the destruction of our very family fiber were prevalent in these films. The "Why We Fight" series built upon stereotypes and the prevailing myths and fears. They were successful in providing a call to arms for the American populous and in bringing an isolationist country into battle. Unfortunately, they also built a historical legacy of hate in the American psyche.

The linguistic and iconic images presented in the propaganda films of World War II established a standard for future propaganda films. The success of these images, with the historical facts of the atrocities of Hitler's Final Solution and the death march of Americans to Bataan, have been proven by the continued "remembrance" of the Holocaust and the racial distrust of the Japanese two generations later. The reason for this continuation of racial and ideological hate is evidence of the power of the image. As historical memory continues through visual images such as these, the swastika, the Rising Sun, and the facsimiles of the combat uniforms worn by the Axis powers will continue to have emotional and semiotic significance.

Hate as Symbolic Experience

Is it possible to hate ideas or specific groups of people without first-hand knowledge and experience of them? A review of the literature on hate suggests it is. Gordon Allport (1958), in his seminal work *The Nature of Prejudice,* discusses the differences between hate and anger. His point, taken from Freud, is that hate is a natural progression of the human psyche. According to Allport, hatred "must be classified as a sentiment—an enduring organization of aggressive impulses toward a person or toward a class of persons" (p. 341). Such sentiments, then, may be described as hateful when the natural internal aggressive nature of humankind is directed toward specific individuals or groups of people.

Fromm (1947) describes this kind of hatred as "character conditioned." That is, it "has little relation to reality, although it may be the product of a long series of bitter disappointments in life" (p. 214). Importantly, these disappointments may be directly experienced or only symbolically perceived. Yet either condition may provoke feelings of hate.

For example, more than 50 years ago Germans felt that a conspiracy by the Jews and the Bolsheviks ruined their social structure and created the poor economic conditions of the 1930s. As in other parts of the world, Germany suffered an economic depression during this period. Separating the Germans from other societies who had suffered similarly was the way the culture assigned blame for their problems. Ideologically, the German people were a defeated society after World War I. As with their military defeat, the economic depression could be more easily tolerated if their suffering could be attributed to some cause extrinsic to their culture. Through speeches, writings, and a carefully constructed visual campaign, Hitler and the Nazi party rekindled Germans' emotional response to the hardships of that period. Then they reinforced these emotions in ways that empowered the Nazi party and created support for military solutions. Hitler helped foster the dream of a better world, if only through symbols. But accepting the dream and working toward a restored Germany meant accounting for the distasteful reality of defeat. In an effort to assess blame, Germans were encouraged by Hitler and his party to define the enemy, stereotype their characteristics and then punish their crimes against the culture. This spiral of stereotypical labeling, blame, and hatred eventually led to war and the Holocaust.

Rhetors can make use of symbols to advance hatred. Hitler, for example, galvanized a movement through symbols. The swastika and the Star of David were used to perceptually polarize Germany into two camps with the intent of separating good from evil, and symbolically identifying those who caused Germany's destruction: the Jewish population. Similarly, after Britain's defiance of Germany, Hitler turned his country's hatred against the Bolsheviks to provoke war with the Soviet Union. When carefully manipulated, such symbols stir emotions, provide cultural interpretations of events, and direct aggression toward specific groups blamed for real or imagined injustices.

Hate as a Symbolic Defense

Hatred can be used effectively by individuals, organizations, and leaders to define, perpetuate, and even excuse a culture's acts of aggression and violence. At the heart of hate is the assessment of morality. Murphy and Hampton (1988) distinguish among four types of hate: simple, moral, malicious, and retributive hate. Their classification of these types is derived from their assessment of the causes of the hate. Simple hate is an aversion to an individual that is a state of nature. The authors argue that there is no offense to this hatred if there is no immoral reaction to the individual who is hated. Moral hatred is an aversion to an individual because of that person's connection with an immoral cause. This type of hate, like simple hate, has no immoral action because the hatred is justified. Malicious or spiteful hatred is immoral because at its very center is an attempt to diminish or hurt another to gain advantage over the person. Similarly, retributive hate is immoral because it is motivated by the feeling that the person's current level of well-being is undeserved or ill-gotten (Murphy & Hampton, 1988, pp. 88-89). According to Murphy and Hampton, if there is a just moral cause for the hatred, then it is justified. Thus, hate becomes a qualified defense.

In order to understand how hate symbolically conveys particular moral positions, we must understand how ideas are propagated. Jacques Ellul (1965), in his book *Propaganda: The Formation of Men's Attitudes,* explains both the processes and effects of state propaganda.

Ellul (1965) defines *propaganda* as "a set of methods employed by an organized group that wants to bring about the active or passive participation in its actions of a mass of individuals, psychologically unified through psychological manipulations and incorporated in an organization" (p. 61). Within the framework of this definition he identifies four elements. These include psychological action, psychological warfare, reeducation and brainwashing, and public and human relations (Ellul, 1965, p. xiii). For this discussion of symbols and their impact on the development and presentation of hate, Ellul's deliberations on psychological action and public and human relations are particularly relevant.

Ellul (1965) states that when using psychological action "[t]he propagandist seeks to modify opinions by purely psychological means;

most often he pursues a semi-educative objective and addresses himself to his fellow citizens" (p. xii). Politicians trying to gather supporters for a particular agenda may use such an option. As a "leader" and "educator," the politician may use this position to justify his or her position on important issues. Although this is common, the danger lies in which issues are presented and in what manner. History provides evidence of how politicians may use logical arguments to support an immoral agenda. Hitler, being one of the more obvious to use this method, blamed the Bolsheviks, intellectuals, and Jewish populations of Europe for controlling the economic and political strings that kept the hard-working Aryan population subservient. In order to succeed, Hitler had to develop his arguments carefully and educate potential followers skillfully. Yet we must also acknowledge that while Hitler used propaganda to promulgate his agenda, he was not the only leader to understand this method's impact on a population. Both Roosevelt and Churchill focused on "educating" their electorate concerning the issues and dangers at hand. Focusing on the acts of immorality committed by the German war machine, they kept the people of Britain vigilant when defeat seemed almost certain. Roosevelt, using the same method, readied American citizens for war by educating the American people on the necessity both of supplying the British war effort and of protecting American values from Nazi encroachment. Each of these leaders knew the impact of educating a populace.

More recently, we have witnessed the educational efforts of the U.S. government to prepare the country for military responses around the world. Americans were carefully prepared for an attack upon Iraq. They were morally certain of their role there. We saw the pictures and heard public testimony of babies thrown from their incubators and left to die on cold floors. We saw pictures of tortured Iraqis. Yet we would later learn that the very images and artifacts that provided the moral certainty and urgency for action were carefully constructed by Hill & Knowlton, an American public relations firm, whose job it was to educate the public and build war fever (see, e.g., Manheim, 1994). Similarly, the American invasion of Grenada was justified when the American public learned the strategic military threat posed by the Cuban airfield that was being constructed on this small resort island. The invasion of Cambodia was justified when we accepted the argument that invasion was necessary to stop the domino effect that would eventually spread communism through Thailand and Indonesia. Using symbolic language in conjunction with the iconography, the "education" of the public for political agendas, whether moral or immoral, will most certainly continue.

Equally compelling is the use of what Ellul (1965) describes as public and human relations methods to achieve results. These constitute "propaganda because they seek to adapt the individual to a society, to a living standard, to an activity. They serve to make him conform, which is the aim of all propaganda" (p. xiii). Using Ellul's area of public and human relations as a framework, a brief discussion of ideological and repressive state apparatuses may provide insight into the general process of conformity.

The establishment and reinforcement of language and symbols in the construction of hate is dependent upon what Louis Althusser (1971) calls Repressive State Apparatuses and Ideological Apparatuses. He identifies these apparatuses as two of the greatest pressures toward conformity upon a culture. For Althusser, a repressive state apparatus echoes what Marx identified as the organization of government that contains the police, military, courts, and prisons. Althusser (see especially pp. 121-173) continues with this identification by pointing out that the repressive state apparatus operates by violence and serves the public domain.

In contrast to a repressive state apparatus, the ideological apparatus is found in more "distinct and specialized institutions." These "institutions" have more of an impact on the everyday on each separate member of a culture (Althusser, 1971, pp. 121ff). Institutions such as religion, marriage, family, and education fall within the definitions of Althusser's ideological state apparatuses. The ideological state apparatus operates by ideology (belief system) and serves the private domain (Althusser, 1971, pp. 121ff). The impact of these apparatuses is due to their direct intervention in the thought and action processes of every citizen.

The importance of the apparatuses for this chapter is clear. The operation of each apparatus and the domain served accentuates the success or failure of a specific discourse. Indeed, government, education, and religion affects the impact and the acceptance of messages in any given culture. What is important to remember in this process is that while each specific ideological and repressive apparatus operates with the reinforcement of choice (i.e., violence and ideology), they interchange their methods of operation when it is deemed necessary. A church, for instance, may excommunicate its constituents; the government may support a certain "American ideological mythology"; and families may use types of "punishment" to have individuals of the family conform to the rules and operations of that household. Indeed, both apparatuses use levels of each method to assure conformity. Through cultural conformity, symbols reinforce the message of any propaganda. One of the strongest tools of conformity is the construction of meaning through the symbolic use of icons.

Conclusion

The use of symbols in what has been defined as "Postmodern" society still depends on the significance of the sign. The political and/or economic agenda of groups relies especially on the use of symbols and their historical significance to bring an agenda to the public. This is also true in the rhetoric of hate. The use of red and white colors by Skinheads and neo-Nazis reflects an iconic message that directs its roots back two generations. The boots, swastika, and Iron Cross are symbols of warning and superiority. The skinheads and neo-Nazis took their oaths and allegiance based on a political movement of the 1930s and the rhetorical message of Hitler's discourse of hate. This is emphasized in Clark Martell's call to arms to the American skinhead movement:

> Our heads are shaved for battle. Skinheads of America, like the dynamic skinheads in Europe, we are working-class Aryan youth. We oppose the capitalist and communist scum that are destroying our Aryan race. The Parasitic Jewish race is at the heart of our problem. (Hamm, 1993, p. 39)

The agenda of the neo-Nazis has not changed. Their symbolic artifacts remain those of their predecessors 60 years earlier. The importance of that connection lies in the creation of fear and the justification of their hate crimes.

The new linguistic message, the new discourse of hate, continues to emphasize historical blame as justification. The focus of their hate continues to be Jews, Communists, and now, capitalists. These groups give cause to violent actions in symbolic defense. The neo-Nazis view their actions as simple and moral hate that gives justification to these actions. Using the rhetoric and symbols of the past (e.g., the swastika) with the icons of the new (e.g., Doc Marten shoes and colored laces), this new group bridges the ideological agenda and time that separates them and the past generation.

The historical and cultural connection to the present use of symbols gives them power. As Gustave Le Bon (1982) writes in his study on crowd motivation and behavior, "Crowds being only capable of thinking in images are only to be impressed by images. It is only images that terrify or attract them and become motives of action" (p. 54). In a society that emphasizes the image and the power of manipulation based on the image, Le Bon's words underscore the importance of the iconic message in the representation of culture and call further attention to the central role played by the visual image in the production and development of the discourse of hate.

Notes

1. It is important to keep in mind that the "new" free world included Stalin's Soviet Union. The impact of the propaganda was dependent upon the audience's temporary removal of the distrust that the United States had for the Soviet Union. Many of the films focused primarily on the struggle of Britain and touched briefly upon the Soviet Union.

2. This is true specifically of the Japanese. The immediate internment of those Japanese American citizens of the Western United States emphasized the already distrustful racial tendencies that permeated the population and government of the United States.

References

Allport, G. W. (1958). *The nature of prejudice*. Garden City, NY: Doubleday.

Althusser, L. (1971). Ideology and ideological state apparatuses. In *Lenin and philosophy and other essays* (pp. 127-186). New York: Monthly Review.

Barthes, R. (1977). The rhetoric of the image. In S. Heath (Trans.), *Image music text* (pp. 191-205). New York: Hill & Wang.

Barnouw, E. (1993). *Documentary: A history of the non-fiction film*. New York: Oxford University Press.

Burke, K. (1993). Man is the symbol-using animal. In P. Kollock & J. O'Brien (Eds.), *The production of reality* (pp. 69-72). Thousand Oaks, CA: Pine Forge.

Ellul, J. (1965). *Propaganda: The formation of men's attitudes*. New York: Vintage.

Fromm, E. (1947). *Man for himself*. New York: Reinhart.

Hamm, M. S. (1993). *American skinheads: The criminology and control of hate crime*. London: Praeger.

Kaucauer, S. (1947). *From Caligari to Hitler: A psychological history of the German film*. Princeton, NJ: Princeton University Press.

Le Bon, G. (1982). *The crowd: A study of the popular mind* (2nd ed.). Atlanta, GA: Cherokee.

Manheim, J. (1994). *Strategic public diplomacy & American foreign policy*. New York: Oxford University Press.

Murphy, J., & Hampton, J. (1988). *Forgiveness and mercy*. Cambridge, UK: Cambridge University Press.

O'Connor, J. (1990). *Image as artifact: The historical analysis of film and television*. Malabar, FL: Robert Krieger.

O'Shaughnessy, N. J. (1990). *The phenomenon of political marketing*. New York: St. Martin's.

Remak, J. (1969). *The Nazi years: A documentary history*. New York: Simon & Schuster.

Acts of Power, Control, and Resistance

Narrative Accounts of Convicted Rapists

Peter M. Kellett
University of North Carolina-Greensboro

Editor's Introduction

In civilized society, the urge to censor expressions of hate as a means of limiting hate's power is a strong one; it is based on the presumption that talk can produce action. In this chapter about the narrative accounts of convicted rapists, Peter Kellett explores the relationship between hate acts and hate speech. Through this analysis we discover that hate may be used not only to perpetuate acts but also to defend action.

Can acts of hate be distinguished from expressions of hate? The line between expressive acts and expressive rhetoric is often too fine to distinguish, but—at some finite point on a continuum—some people move beyond words and symbols to action. Kellett helps us understand this linking between word and deed. In the rapists' narratives he recounts here, we learn that positions that appear hateful to society seem reasonable—even tolerant—to the person who commits such acts.

Reading the narratives of rapists is difficult, yet the resistance strategies Kellett identifies help us learn something about the way these marginalized members of a culture justify their acts by resisting the dominance of those in power.

Explicating Rapist Narratives as Hate

In this society, if you ever sit down and realize how manipulated you really are, it makes you pissed off, it makes you want to take control. And you've been manipulated by women, and they're a very easy target because they're out walking along the streets, so you can just grab one and say, "listen you're going to do what I want you to do" and it's an act of revenge against the way you've been manipulated . . .

A convicted rapist,
from Beneke, 1982, p. 44

Our responsibility is not to silence hateful speech, but to answer it.

Jensen, 1993, p. 11

Does the first man quoted above have a pathological hatred of women and therefore feel the need to oppress them actively and violently? Is it that he simply has hate in him and that women, as he says, are just very easy targets for that venting, convenient cultural objects for expressing hate? Is this the legitimate utterance of an oppressed person trying to reclaim his voice in the order of things, a perspective often favored by rapists? Or has this rapist learned (perhaps unconsciously), like a sort of rhetorically savvy terrorist, that to present rape as an act of resistance—an attempt to assert voice in the face of his own experience of devalued otherness—is probably the best way to have the act accepted as defensible and even reasonable? Each of these questions reflects a valid approach to studying hate, and particularly rape. This last question, however, is the most intriguing for it is based on a perspective grounded in the following assumptions about hate: First, hate is a rhetorically constructed phenomenon, a *name* rather than a definitive psychological state, gaining its meaning and forms of articulation in culturally mediated ways; second, rhetorical struggles exist in the process of defining acts as hateful or reasonable; third, this discursive struggle centers on the role of narrative in the struggle to define such acts as ones of resistance or domination.

People in academic, legal, and therapeutic institutions in our culture most likely view rape as an unacceptable act of hate, a practice through which broader issues in the politics of communication—power, control, gender, and subjectivity—are practiced in a particularly divisive, intolerant, and oppressive way (Finkelhor & Yllö, 1985; Lofles, 1991). Rape is regarded as an act of hate in that at the core of its meaning, for the rapist, exists a struggle to express a sense of self as a powerful subject through a violent negation of a victim's subjectivity. Rape makes the other into an object of hate. This antagonistic and intolerant struggle for power and control that gives the rapist his sense of self is usually articulated along gender lines: Men mostly rape women (Martin & Hummer, 1989).

Rapists often create narratives that give the act of rape a "particular sequence and meaning" (Fisher, 1984, p. 4), defending it as an act of resistance. The strategic goal of rapist narratives is to have the stories accepted as resistance narratives, as the voice of an oppressed and marginalized group (Scott, 1990) that has been victimized and left no alternative but to respond violently. These strategies rely on the selection and combination of various tactics (de Certeau, 1984) that rapists believe should persuade an audience that their choice to rape was a reasonable or even justified act of resistance against constraints imposed by another. Tactics used to achieve these strategies typically include assigning the responsibility for the act to the victim (Schult & Schneider, 1991), to the context or circumstances (Abbey, 1991; Lewis

& Johnson 1989), to the influence of past experiences (Harbridge & Furnham, 1991), to prevailing attitudes toward women (Muehlenhard & Falcon, 1990)—such as the belief in the right to consume the other, or the right or need to discipline and punish the other, and so on. These narrative tactics shift agency away from themselves and onto the victim and/or context. This narrative process, which may even for the narrator (Olsen, 1991) be just a typical way of telling such a story, is of great significance because it illustrates how stories are constructed to justify, rationalize, and even valorize acts of hate. At stake is not just the representation of extreme hate, such as rape, but also the politics of everyday communication. An array of tactical maneuvers is at work here: how other forms of hate are typically rationalized and storied; what expressions of hate are accepted and who's are marginalized; how narrative forms of representing hate—here as resistance narratives—are important in determining the seduction of audiences and society into hate; what counts as a resistance narrative and what counts as a dominance narrative; and, ultimately, how these narratives reify certain forms of power through hate, that is, how they "evolve from a structure of power relations, and simultaneously produce, maintain and reproduce that power structure" (Langellier, 1989, p. 267).

The following questions are more specifically related to this case study of rapist narratives and help us to work toward dealing with these broader issues. How do rapists construct narratives that attempt to both disguise and justify their hate? How do their narratives make sense as hateful if the hate is disguised? How can we learn to listen for these tactics in others' narratives and possibly in our own storytelling habits? Why do these narratives strike me as hateful, yet to the rapist seem perfectly reasonable—resistance narratives that prove his tolerance? Why might some be seduced into believing these stories? Why does the rhetoric fail for others, leaving them horrified by mental images that are the very embodiment of hate? Does this struggle have anything to do with the power of naming and renaming and preserving patriarchy? What does this struggle to accept or reject such narratives as resistance mean regarding the broader cultural attitudes toward hate, and what is held to be tolerable and reasonable in the United States? If tolerance (Lanigan, 1988, p. 61) is the ability to accept as a right another's capability to make choices that may be constraining and exclusionary, and intolerance is the negation of others' choice rights, how is their opposition at the core of these narratives? And how is this opposition significant in exploring alternative ways of storying rape that reduce or eliminate the desire to live it?

Methodology: A Phenomenology of Rapist Narratives

Five narrative examples from convicted rapists are explicated here. Although rapes vary on a surface level in terms of contextual details and characteristics such as level of acquaintance (relative, stranger, friend) and situation in which the rape takes place (marriage, random opportunity, date), the narratives cohere around certain core assumptions about power and gender. Such narrative consistency in structure and meaning is most significant to this study. The following narrative analysis is interpretive (Bockner, 1994), using the questions raised above to frame the analysis. Rapists may be, to some degree, unaware of the tactical constitution of their narratives and the rhetoric of their apparent motives. I use a phenomenological method to interpret their narrative intent. This methodology involves the steps of description, reduction, and interpretation (Giorgi, 1983; Ihde, 1977; Lanigan, 1988; Merleau-Ponty, 1962) in relation to the narrative as a "sign" or semiotic phenomenon. The structure of the sign involves (a) a Signifier: the narrated experience; (b) a Signified, or the consciousness of the rapist located in the tactical and strategic representation of his experience; and (c) the relationship between the signifier and signified that provides the *meaning* of the sign as a way of representing rape through narrative choices. The three main methodological steps of phenomenological description, reduction, and interpretation as schematized by Lanigan (1984, p. 19) are used to structure the analysis of these rapist narratives.

Case Description: The Lived Meaning of Rapist Narratives

The first stage of analysis is descriptive and locates the "signs" of conscious experience in the narration, explicating the tactical choices and combinations used to create the narratives. Specifically, the narrative representation of the practice of rape (signifier) is described and its relationship to its referent (signified), or lived meaning, is explicated.

EXEMPLAR 1: RAPE AS DEBT COLLECTION

I was raped at the age of nine by a woman. I believe she was in her mid twenties. . . . We were playing around in a park one day, and I got all dirty and muddy. Her name was Shirley. She wanted to spank me because I got so dirty. So I told her at that time, "You're not my mother. You have no right to spank me." . . . She sent me to my room, tied me down. . . . She got me all aroused and upset and *did her thing*. And that, I believe *I hate her to today for that*. Because if it wasn't for my bein' tied down, I probably would have enjoyed it all. *But she did what she wanted to do with me.* . . . She had me eat her which I don't like, *she used my body.* . . . She put something in me, in my rectum . . . I tried to fight it at that time. I tried to tear the ropes that she tied me down with. But *I couldn't get away.*

(Next sexual experience) I was eighteen. Yeah, that's when I enjoyed it. What I really enjoyed was when I tied them down. I tied this girl down in a position where she couldn't move. And *I just used her. I did everything I wanted to do to her, as Shirley did to me.* . . . She struggled because she didn't want to be tied down. *I used my masculinity to overpower her*—to tie her down secure—and I *did what I had to do.* I felt at that time it was *my rightful payment for what had been done to me.* This is why I took it out on her. . . . The pain part of it was the best part. Especially when I sodomized her. All six or seven of them. *had to get pain from entering them from behind.* Because I had been entered in that way. It hurt me, and I knew it was going to hurt them. . . . *After I was satisfied my revenge was satisfied.* . . . It felt good. Yeah, that's one of them. *I got one of them.* I thought, "I got you back Shirley. *I paid you back for what you did to me."* I'd be smiling. *I'd be happy that I used a woman.* I felt an overall happiness that she's still laying out there tied up on the bed, and she won't come around until half an hour or so—or until somebody finds her. I was a sodomizer—not a rapist. That was my specialty. (Abbreviated from Sussman & Bordwell, 1981, pp. 29-43, emphasis added)[1]

Analysis. The main semiotic connection in this example is between the action of "rape" as the signifier, and the concept of "usage" ("I just used her") as the signified. These are combined as a sign that represents the experience of a bodily freedom; a "power" to do "whatever he wanted," to "use" or "consume" the other as a means of experiencing this freedom.

The following main narrative combinations reveal the rhetorical choices by which the meaning of rape is represented. The signifier, the doing of "everything I wanted to do to her," takes on a narrative meaning through the structural relationship of a "rightful (signifier) payment" (signified). The action is rightful because it has a meaning as a (re)payment for something, a sort of outstanding debt incurred through "what she did (signifier) to me" (signified); that is, "she" had subjected the rapist to being an object. Rape is represented as the means of exchange, a rebalancing of "justice" through punishment legitimates the rape.

The narrative combines the concepts of "freedom-through-usage" and the "rightful payment for what she did to me." This relationship comes to mean a "satisfaction," because somebody was used to live out that "repayment" or *debt collection* process. Rape is made meaningful as a sort of bodily "money" exchange system that relies on a digital (either/or) distribution of bodily power. The strategic ambiguity over when this so-called debt is finally and fully repaid gives a rhetorical license to repeat the act within the same narrative frame.

EXEMPLAR 2: RAPE AS CONSUMER ADVOCACY

It was just going to be a burglary, and there was a person in there, the lady. . . . The victim. One thing led to another. I had a hunting knife. I told her to undress and what have you. She did so with no problem. Then the rape took place . . . I don't really know what made me rape her. . . . *It was just a thought, something I've never done before.* I said, *"Well, I'm going to try this.* It's probably nothing I'll ever do again, but I'm not sure. You know, women in general are all right. Some of them is kind, considerate. Some of them is bitches, you know? *These bitches are the types that need to be raped. They need to have it stuffed to them hard and heavy to straighten them out . . .* I mean these are the women that are *up on a high horse,* okay? They're stuck up. They think they're better than you.

They don't think you're worth throwing their legs up for. So these are the type of women that you have to take it from just to knock them down off that high horse . . .

Women also ask for it by these mini-micro skirts, these mini skirts, these hot pants and what have you, and them halter tops! Now they're just displaying their body. They're saying, "Hey!" Whether they realize it or not they're saying, "Hey, I've got a beautiful body and it's yours if you want it." Then when you take it from them, what do they do? They scream rape. . . . *Any woman that goes out and asks for it is going to get it.* It's all in the way a person conducts theirself. If they conduct theirself as a lady, clean cut and what have you, they don't have to worry about any of this. If they conduct theirself as a hussy, then they got it coming by *the law of the rapist—"get anybody that's asking for it."* (Abbreviated from Sussman & Bordwell, 1981, p. 147, emphasis added)

Analysis. The main narrative sign relies on a combination of the action of "taking" (signifier) that reduces the victim to a tolerable power position (signified). Thus, rape is represented as "helping the self" to "something I've never done before," *a sort of consumption choice* that is justified because the victim has apparently claimed a bodily exercise of freedom by not responding sexually (whether intentional or not), a way of behaving that is inappropriate for their legitimate status. To "take it from" (signifier) is to bring the victim into a spatial power relation that is tolerable. It is to "knock them down off their high horse" (signified).

This narrative, to "take it from" (signifier) relates to the apparent choice of the victim not to "throw their legs up" (signifier). Taking it is justified as a response to the victim's exercise of a bodily choice "not to" respond sexually. The rapist takes this to imply an attack on his personal sense of worth (signified). Subjectivity is inextricably linked to the power of choice to respond and not respond. Hence, her lack of response—*her silence*—is interpreted as "you're not worth it" (signified). This sign takes on a narrative relationship with the concept of power imbalance. Being up on a "high horse" (signifier) is an expression that means "they think they are better than you" (signified). An intolerable imbalance is represented as resulting from the woman's exercise of power.

The rapist's experience of restricted choice signals an illegitimate power claim. This is used to legitimate the "taking," as the assertion and advocacy of the right to consume. Rape *is* the rebalancing of power relations as it means the freedom from restriction on the exercise of choice. For the rapist, to force the victim to "throw their legs up" is sufficient bodily proof not only that "I am worth it," but also that the victim is not worthy of the choice that they *might* make.

EXEMPLAR 3: RAPE AS REASONABLE REVENGE

Let's say I see a woman and she looks really pretty and really clean and sexy, and she's giving off very feminine, sexy vibes. I think, "Wow, I would love to make love to her," but I know she's not really interested. It's a tease. A lot of times a woman knows that she's looking really good and she'll use that and flaunt it, and it makes me feel like she's laughing at me and *I feel degraded.*

I also *feel dehumanized,* because *when I'm being teased I just turn off, I cease to be human.* Because if I go with my human emotions I'm going to want to put my arms around her and kiss her, and to do that would be unacceptable. *I don't like the feeling that I'm supposed to stand there and take it,* and not be able to hug and kiss her; so I just turn off my emotions. *It's a feeling of humiliation,* because *the woman has forced me to turn off my feelings* and react in a way that I really don't want to.

If I were actually desperate enough to rape somebody, it would be from wanting the person, but also it would be a *very spiteful thing, just being able to say, "I have power over you and I can do anything I want with you,"* because really I feel that *they have power over me just by their presence.* Just the fact that *they can come up to me and just melt me and make me feel like a dummy makes me want revenge. They have power over me so I want power over them . . .*

Society says that you have to have a lot of sex with a lot of different women to be a real man. Well, what happens if you don't? Then what are you? Are you half a man? Are you still a boy? It's ridiculous. You see a whiskey ad with a guy and two women on his arm. The implication is that *real men don't have any trouble getting women.*

In this society, if you ever sit down and realize how manipulated you really are it makes you pissed off—it makes you want to take control. And you've been manipulated by women, and they're a very easy target because they're out walking along the streets, so you can just grab one and say, *"listen, you're going to do what I want you to do,"* and it's an *act of revenge against the way you've been manipulated.* (Abbreviated from Beneke, 1982, pp. 43-44, emphasis added)[2]

Analysis. The main sign involves the opposition of bodily power as it is exercised *on* the rapist and *by* the rapist. Victims are perceived as exercising a bodily power. By their *presence* they subject the rapist to an experience of a lack of power, hence, "they have power over me by their presence." Experiencing a lack of power to consume or control is sufficient grounds to exercise revenge by forcing the victims in turn to experience a lack of subjectivity as a negation of their bodily choice capability. To rape is to steal or loot when one does not have the means to "buy."

The power of "presence" (signifier) is reduced to the experience of being "melted" (signified). This subjection to the presence of the other takes on a meaning as feeling like a "dummy" (signified); that is, the exercise of power relegates the subject (rapist) and legitimates a desire to exercise bodily power. The victim's action of "melting" forces the choice of wanting revenge; it "makes me want (signifier) revenge" (signified). "Wanting" to rebalance power becomes a reasonable revenge for the perceived "attack" on the rapist.

This narrative represents a power struggle to reassert the self through revenge. The rapist becomes not the acted upon (subjection to), but rather the agent who defines how power is practiced. The other's capability for choice becomes an act of aggression; a restriction of the rapist's freedom to consume that, in turn, creates a need for rape. Rape becomes a reasonable revenge.

EXEMPLAR 4: RAPE AS RECLAIMING VOICE

All my life I felt I was being controlled, particularly by my parents, that people used me without any regard for my feelings, for my needs, and in my rapes the important point was not the sexual part, but *putting someone else in the position* in which they were *totally helpless.* I bound and gagged and tied up my victims and *made them do something they didn't want to do,* which was exactly the way I felt in my life. I felt helpless, very helpless in that I couldn't do anything about the satisfaction I wanted. Well, I decided, I'm going to *put them in a position where they can't do anything about what I want to do.* They can't refuse me. They can't reject me. They're going to have *no say* in the matter. *I'm in charge now.* (Groth, 1979, p. 30, emphasis added)[3]

Analysis. Rape is the action of "putting someone else in a position" (signifier) of being "totally helpless" (signified) so that the rapist determines the boundaries of use and restriction of bodily choices. "Putting into a position" takes on a meaning as a physical/psychic "binding," as the exclusion/negation of freedom. To bind and gag and tie ("I bound and gagged and tied my victims . . .") (signifier) signifies making the other do something that they did not want to do ("put them in a position where they can't do anything about what I want to do") (signified). The position is one where the absence of choice for the victim signals the presence of choice (freedom) for the rapist. This sign is combined with the meaning of helplessness, which is to have "no say" (signifier). This denial of voice excludes the possibility of rejection (signified) as has been the case before ("can't refuse me or reject me"). The subjectivity of the rapist relies on the subjection of the victim. To create a lack of choice possibility for the other means that the rapist is "in charge," in that he now has a reclaimed voice in the everyday order of people and things. Being in charge means making the other helpless, such that he cannot be refused.

EXEMPLAR 5: RAPE AS JUSTIFIABLE HOMICIDE

I got married when I was 18 and that was okay at first; but then I found out my wife was bedding down with family members. I would get into bed with her; she'd just lay there and I'd get pissed off and go out and get drunk. One night I came home and caught my wife in bed with my cousin. I almost beat that boy to death. If it weren't for a black friend that was with me, I'd have killed him.

I started hating all women. *I started seein' all women the same way as users.* I couldn't express my feelings to nobody. I'd go to work, clock in and be by myself. . . . I'd thought about murder and other *ways of getting even with women* and everyone who'd hurt me. *I was just waiting to explode.*

Then one night about a year after I'd split from my wife, I was out partyin' and drinking and smokin' pot. I'd shot up some heroin and done some downers and I went to a porno bookstore, put a quarter in a slot and saw this porno movie. It was just a guy coming up from behind a girl and attacking her and raping her. That's when I started having rape fantasies. When I see that movie, it was like *somebody lit a fuse from my childhood on up.* When that fuse got to the porno movie, I exploded. I just went for it, went out and raped. It was like a little voice saying, "It's alright, it's alright, go ahead and *rape and get your revenge;* you'll never get caught. *Go out and rip off some girls* . . . I tried to talk to this girl and she gave me some off-the-wall story. I chased her into a bathroom and grabbed her and told her that if she screamed, I'd kill her. I had sex with her that lasted about five minutes. When I first attacked her I wasn't even turned on; *I wanted to dominate her.* When I saw her get scared and hurt, then I got turned on. I wanted her to feel a lot of pain and not enjoy none of it. *The more pain she felt, the higher I felt.* As I did it to her, my head was back one night where my wife just lay there like a bump on a log and didn't show any pleasure. That's the one thing that was in my head. She was just laying there doin' nothin.' *It wasn't a victim no more; it was my wife.*

I pulled out of her when I was about to come and I shot in her face and came all over her. *It was like I pulled a gun and blew her brains out.* That was my fantasy. She was the blonde that reminded me of my wife. In my head it was like poppin' caps off. I said, "later," and just walked off and said, "Bye, Jane." That was my wife's name. *The orgasm was a great thrill. In my head I blew Jane's brains out and that made it more of a thrill. I not only raped a girl or raped Jane in my head but I killed Jane.* (Beneke, 1982, p. 74, emphasis added)

Analysis. The fact that "I did it to her" (signifier) has the existential meaning of "killing" his wife (signified) ("I killed Jane"). The punishment of raping means living out a justifiable homicide, a sort of exercising of the death penalty for the intolerable crime of choosing not to respond sexually. This personal meaning takes on a public meaning as a "punishment," whereby the pain of the other, an expression of a lack of choice, is related to the pleasure of the rapist, an expression of an increasing control over choices. The more the rapist restricts the choices of the other, the more he edifies himself as the mediator of power relations. The orgasm as the point of highest pleasure becomes a way of referring to the death of his wife; at orgasm (signifier) he "blew Jane's [wife] brains out" (signified). The sexual release is an expression of the personal release from the power of the other to subvert his masculinity with a lack of pleasure.

The rape is justified as a physically painful revenge for the perceived choice not to experience sexual pleasure. The rapist is reconstituted as a powerful sexual subject. That is, to force someone not to "lay there like a bump on a log" is taken as a recovery of the rapist as a powerful subject. Denying the choices of the other constitutes the self. The narrative represents this as a meaningful choice, as a bodily exercise of power that is a reasonable response to the victim's exercise of bodily power.

Reduction: Living Hate as Freedom Through Constraint

The second stage of analysis involves explicating meaningful themes that constitute the structure of the narrative as a coherent text (Lanigan,

1988) to discover what Giorgi (1983) calls "the essence of the phenomenon" (pp. 143-144).

The structure of each of the above narratives embodies the following themes that define how rape is rationalized and justified. First, there is the expression of a *bodily freedom* that the rapist achieves through the rape. To "use" the other, to do "everything I wanted to do to her" (Exemplar 1), to "take it" from them (Exemplar 2), to have "power over them" (Exemplar 3), to make them "helpless" (Exemplar 4), to symbolically "kill" the other (Exemplar 5), are all expressions that mean a freedom to exercise bodily power over another. This exercise of bodily freedom is edifying for the rapist as it signals an existential assertion of the self; a reconstitution of subjectivity; an experience of self as a choosing subject without the possibility of becoming subject to the other.

Second, the bodily freedom of rape relies on the radical constraining of the field of the freedom of the other. A victim must be created. Either the other has power and "I" am subject to the other (and therefore I am a victim), or "I" have power and they are subject to me (therefore I am not a victim). This thinking typically underlies rapists' narratives. Rape means the negation of the other's capability to make such choices as: ignoring, resisting, invading, limiting, restricting, challenging, teasing, and so on. Rapists ascribe these particular intents to the actions of the other that are inherently ambiguous (such as walking or dressing a certain way). This creates a point of resistance and struggle for control and dominance that is used to justify its violent "resolution." Hence, to do "everything I wanted" necessarily entails the "use" of the other; to "take it from" means to "knock them down off that high horse"; the wanting of power "over them" entails a negation of their power "over me"; "making someone feel what I felt" means making the other "helpless"; and ultimately in the final exemplar, to rape is to symbolically "kill," absolutely denying the lived embodiment of the other. These signifieds of "usage," "bringing the other down, "wanting power," "making the other helpless," and symbolically "killing," are all meaningful as paradigmatic exemplars, as possible ways of expressing the negation of the other's choices. The power of rape is meaningful because the other is made powerless. The rapist negates his status as a "victim" of the choices of others (women) by making the other into a victim. In fact, the very subjectivity of the victim takes on a meaning as a discursive rupture that sets in motion a power struggle (Foucault, 1980, p. 56). This is the field of struggle that rapists use to make sense of and articulate their freedom.

Third, this demeaning of the other is narratively "justified" because of the nonlegitimate power of the other. The choices of the victim are represented as intolerant and therefore intolerable. To achieve this goal, these narratives integrate typified "voices" from various other institutionalized social and cultural practices that help to represent the victim as adversary and the rapist as resisting that domination strategy. Hence, "relations of power include, by definition, the adversary role; they are inconceivable without the points of resistance everywhere in the power network" (Bersani, 1977, p. 5). For example, there is the "voice" of *justice* in representing rape as an act of discipline or punishment and as debt collection, and so on. There is the "voice" of *consumption* in the representation of rape as the restoration of the consumer's choice. Thus, for example, rape takes on a narrative meaning as a "rightful payment" for "what she has done to me" (a nonlegitimate choice/exercise of power). To "ignore" the rapist takes on a meaning as a conscious choice to negate the "worth" of the rapist as a consuming subject; to "not respond" becomes the denial of their presence as a consumer, intentional demeaning warranting an act of hateful revenge. Similarly, to "melt" the rapist by being co-present is to deny their power as consumers, as the controllers of choices. This point of possible power reversal (Foucault, 1982, p. 225) warrants revenge, to negate that power and restore order.

To impose a control over the apparent/actual choices that the female makes by raping her is to claim a right of control over the *possible choices that they might make,* that is, over their very subjectivity. That they *might* reject, ignore, or demean the rapist is taken as sufficient grounds for physically and symbolically negating that possibility through rape. For example, to impose "pain" and to enjoy that process of imposing is legitimate because of the pain that the other caused by not enjoying sex; the woman's act of "not enjoying" makes sense as a conscious act/choice not to respond appropriately. The woman's "act" of not enjoying becomes a "refusal," part of a power struggle that has to be "rightfully" and violently resolved. Thus, the rhetorical justification of rape rests on the injustice of the other's capability. For example, having the ability not to respond, not to enjoy, not to acknowledge the power of the other, not to be consumed, is to demean. This injustice is intolerable because it limits the power of consumption and requires the restoration of justice through physical/psychic punishment (Ivie, 1982, 1986). The female's apparent or possible attempt to make the rapist a "victim" is grounds for making her a "victim" (Corcoran, 1983). Rape becomes the minimization of resistance to power relations and is legitimate because of that (Griffin, 1981; TePaske, 1982). The other's "intolerance" is grounds for reasserting a different version of tolerance. Thus, a particular version of tolerance, a gender "order" centered on a particular version of freedom (self) and constraint (other) between the self and other, is symbolically restored for the rapist.

Rape becomes the bodily and symbolic achievement of a successful act of resistance, a "rebalance" of a rightful power relation (King, 1976), a reassertion of the self as part of and representative/mediator of that order through the physical and psychic negation of choice of the other and the imposing of a choice (to become an object—a "victim"). For the rapist, to experience subjectivity is to govern (Foucault, 1982, p. 221). This involves the activity of violently denying the others' choice capabilities. For the rapist, freedom makes sense only as the complete constraint of the other (Eisenberg & Goodall, 1993). These narrative themes of (a) freedom through (b) constraint of the other that is (c) justified as an act of resistance form the syntagmatic structure by which the meaning of all the various rape narratives are semiotically consistent.

Interpretation: Rapist Narratives as Hateful Resistance

The third methodological step of interpretation involves locating the lived meaning of the narratives (Merleau-Ponty, 1962). This is done by interpreting the phenomenon of rapist narratives in the everyday lived world in which it has a meaning. This interpretive step is achieved by understanding the narratives within the broader cultural context of hate, specifically the relationship of acts of hate to issues of power, control, and resistance. A large number of questions were used to frame this analysis. Here in the interpretation, these are embodied by three main questions. First, how do rapists construct narratives that attempt to both disguise and justify their acts of hate? Second, why do these narratives count as hate? Finally, what can we learn from this case about how hate works in American discourse? This final question is taken up in the conclusion.

Resistance narratives are most often seen as the strategies of the oppressed in their negotiation for discursive space and cultural power (de Certeau, 1984; Scott, 1990). This study illustrates how cultural groups, here rapists, engage this dominance-oppression dialectic to legitimate acts of hateful dominance. The rapist narratives analyzed illustrate how a dominant male voice colonizes and acquires the narrative strategies and tactics of typically subordinate and oppressed "voices" and how those strategies are used back on those least able to resist, here women, to attempt to justify and legitimate rape. We see that rape is not just an act of anger. Rather, it is part of a complex discursive struggle over key cultural concepts such as justice and freedom, and these concepts are used in the expression of particular power relationships. The dominant voice in these narratives reflects other typified cultural sites of struggle, such as justice and freedom. The narrative voices speak of rightfully collecting outstanding debts, of protecting the right to make consumer choices when others are trying to take such liberties away, of taking reasonable revenge when wronged, of reclaiming a voice in how things get done when others ignore that voice, of killing only in self defense, and so on. Each of these cultural typifications represent a "making do," a *bricolage* (de Certeau, 1984, p. xv) of borrowed tactics that are reused here in the specific case of rape to express a demeaning, a de-subjection, an oppression that must be righted in order that our culture reflects the principles of justice, freedom, rights of the subject, and so on.

The struggle, of course, is to have justice and freedom instantiated from a particular strategic power position, specifically one that legitimates the dominance action and talk of the rapist. This positional strategy involves the demeaning of the female victim. The female becomes the oppressor who limits choices, abuses power, subverts justice; she becomes the voice of domination that must be resisted, overthrown, and silenced. To achieve this silence and the return to order that the silence represents, she must become an object of hate.

The struggle is also about disguise. The ruse of legitimating rape involves disguising the domination strategy of rape by taking on the voice of the oppressed. This amounts to a sort of ironic doubling over of de Certeau's *la parruque* (de Certeau, 1984, p. 25), as the dominator steals discursive space to justify even more dominance. The disguise here is as righter of wrongs, protector of choice, right arm of the law, executor of justice, and so on. The ruse works on the premises that domination can be disguised as resistance, and vice versa, and that the colonization of these voices of the oppressed can perform the disguise.

These dominance-oppression narrative strategies are fundamentally tied to the struggle for the cultural power to name and rename. Naming is the "fundamental symbolic act" (Wood, 1992, p. 352) by which narratives, and the acts they represent, might be named "reasonable defense" or "tolerant act" rather than "hateful intolerance" and "resistance narrative" rather than "dominance narrative." In fact these narratives, and the rapes they represent, can be seen as "conserving moves," that is, tactics that ultimately hold a "dominant patriarchal order in tact" (Strine, 1992, p. 395) through their disguise as a response to the conserving moves of women. The dominance-oppression dialectic by which resistance narratives emerge and acts get named as hate or tolerance, and objects/subjects get named as legitimate objects for expressing hate is a complex rhetorical struggle. In the case of rapists, this struggle involves the colonization of culturally typical oppressed voices in order to legitimate further cultural space to perform further acts of domination and hate. Understanding these narrative strategies and tactics, within the context of a broader discursive power struggle, is the first step to realizing Jensen's goal of "answering" this kind of hateful speech.

If these rapist narratives are part of a fluid and dialectical struggle to define and name particular acts, here rape, as "hate" or as "justice," can we make a definitive argument that these *narratives* are hateful? After all, they do not appear to be profane or violently performed as one might think hateful *speech* would be. This, itself, could be seen as a repressive and conserving interpretive strategy. The definitive key to understanding these narratives as hate is that hate is not necessarily evident in surface performance, or even in the metaphors and images used in the narratives, though they are often quite gruesome and obviously hateful. Rather, such surfaces are indicative of a more fundamental intolerance that is intimately tied to the emergence and expression of hate. The hate lies in the intolerant representations of the relationship of others.

Tolerance is based on the understanding of others' "capability for choosing" (Lanigan, 1988, p. 61). That is, tolerance is based on the practice of allowing others the freedom to express their subjectivity, to have a voice even when that voice opposes our own. Rapists' narratives rely on the negation of others. As such, they are the embodiment of intolerance, the denial of others' capability for choosing. For the rapist, when a woman ignores, teases, or does not respond appropriately, these are intolerable constraints. Thus, while rapists claim to be reclaiming voice for themselves, they are simultaneously violently denying the voice of the other. This intolerant denial of the other in order to constitute self is at the essence of all the rapist narratives studied. The narrative strategies are all aimed ultimately at justifying and mystifying this intolerance. Thus intolerance, the perception (and related practices) that others must be negated and repressed for whatever reason, is integral to hate, how hate gets expressed, and how hate either attracts or horrifies people. Rapist narratives turn some people on because they find a resonance with the practice of reifying self through the negation of women. For others, such intolerance is abhorrent, and its mystification through narrative transparently hateful. When a fundamental intolerance is embodied by narratives and those narratives are performed with the intent of reifying that intolerance, then we have a case of hateful speech. As is the case with rape, when dominance is being disguised as resistance, there is a good chance that intolerance is being disguised as tolerance.

How might the analysis and understanding of how intolerance gets coded into hateful narratives be significant to actualizing Jensen's (1993) goal of "answering hateful speech?" Fundamental to current therapeutic strategies aimed at developing more positive or altruistic attitudes toward women (Lowenstein, 1989), resolving gender stereotypes (Abbey, 1991), and role expectations (Lofles, 1991), and understanding the relationship of gender and power (Martin & Hummer, 1989) should be discussion of how tolerance and intolerance are articulated as hateful practices such as rape within particular cultural contexts. Such narrative analysis may at least foster the "critical self awareness" (Fisher, 1985, p. 349) necessary for all of us to examine our own and others' narratives for deep-rooted and culturally accepted forms of intolerance and for alternative, more tolerant ways to live and narrate experiences—that is, without hate.

Conclusion

The objects and expressions of hate are part of a complex dialectical process in American discourse that relates to the contested relationship of power and narrative between particular groups, individuals, and social strata. This case analysis of rapists' narratives illustrates the following aspects of this broader discursive struggle. First, groups strategically borrow "voices" from other social and cultural practices and sites to create stories that justify and rationalize acts of hate just as readily as they might be used to rationalize acts of love or tolerance. Second, these narratives are strategically built around the realization that, in our culture, those who manage to present their experience or ideology within a resistance narrative frame may acquire for themselves the cultural power to name practices as, for example, "hate" or "tolerance." Simply, how well groups with power construct resistance narratives may be related to how much they are able to dominate through that power. How hate gets culturally valued is intimately tied to this ability to structure the naming process. Hate is always itself a political name. Third, in terms of the cultural politics of everyday communication, this study shows that this expression of hate as rape may be quite typical of how other forms of hate may be storied, because they too are part of the same dialectical struggle for culturally legitimate forms of intolerance through narrative. Typified cultural "voices" are constantly borrowed and melded into resistance narratives to justify actions, including the most heinous acts of hate. The study suggests a further analysis of other forms of hate, besides gender terrorism discussed here, using a similar dominance-resistance narrative interpretive frame. Also suggested is a more in-depth study of the relationship of intolerance and hate.

Notes

1. From *The Rapist File*, by L. Sussman & S. Bordwell. © 1981 by Chelsea House, New York. Reprinted by permission.
2. From *Men on Rape* by T. Beneke. © 1982 by Timothy Beneke. Reprinted by permission.
3. From *Men Who Rape: The Psychology of the Offender*, by A. N. Groth. © 1979 by Plenum Press, New York. Reprinted by permission.

References

Abbey, A. (1991). Acquaintance rape and alcohol consumption on college campuses: How are they linked? *Journal of American College Health, 39*, 165-169.
Beneke, T. (1982). *Men on rape.* New York: St. Martin's.
Bersani, L. (1977). The subject of power. *Diacritics, 7*, 2-21.
Bockner, A. P. (1994). Perspectives on inquiry: II. Theories and stories. In M. Knapp & G. R. Miller (Eds.), *Handbook of interpersonal communication* (2nd ed.) (pp. 21-41). Thousand Oaks, CA: Sage.
Corcoran, F. (1983). The bear in the backyard: Myth, ideology and victimage ritual in Soviet funerals. *Communication Monographs, 50*, 305-320.
de Certeau, M. (1984). *The practice of everyday life* (S. Rendall, Trans.). Berkeley: University of California Press.
Eisenberg, E., & Goodall, H. L. (1993). *Organizational communication: Balancing creativity and constraint.* New York: St. Martin's.
Finkelhor, D., & Yllö, K. (1985). *License to rape: Sexual abuse of wives.* New York: Holt, Rinehart & Winston.
Fisher, W. R. (1984). Narration as a human communication paradigm: The case of public moral argument. *Communication Monographs, 5*, 1-22.
Fisher, W. R. (1985). The narrative paradigm: An elaboration. *Communication Monographs, 52*, 347-367.
Foucault, M. (1980). *Power/Knowledge: Selected interviews and other writings 1972-1977* (C. Gordon, Ed.; C. Gordon, L. Marshall, J. Mepham, & K. Soper, Trans.). New York: Pantheon.
Foucault, M. (1982). Afterword: The subject and power. In H. L. Dreyfus & P. Rabinow (Eds.), *Michel Foucault: Beyond structuralism and hermeneutics* (L. Sawyer, Trans.) (pp. 208-226). Chicago: University of Chicago Press.
Giorgi, A. (1983). Concerning the possibility of phenomenological psychological research. *Journal of Phenomenological Psychology, 14*, 129-170.
Griffin, S. (1981). *Pornography and silence.* New York: Praeger.
Groth, A. N. (1979). *Men who rape: The psychology of the offender.* New York: Plenum.
Harbridge, J., & Furnham, A. (1991). Lay theories of rape. *Counselling Psychology Quarterly, 4*, 3-25.
Ihde, D. (1977). *Experimental phenomenology: An introduction.* New York: Capricorn Books.

Ivie, R. L. (1982). The metaphor of force in prowar discourse: The case of 1812. *The Quarterly Journal of Speech, 68,* 240-253.

Ivie, R. L. (1986). Literalizing the metaphor of Soviet savagery: President Truman's plain style. *The Southern States Communication Journal, 5,* 91-105.

Jensen, M. (1993). Developing ways to confront hateful speech. *The Speech Communication Teacher, 8,* 1-3.

King, A. A. (1976). The rhetoric of power maintenance: Elites at the precipice. *The Quarterly Journal of Speech, 6,* 127-134.

Langellier, K. M. (1989). Personal narratives: Perspectives on theory and research. *Text and Performance Quarterly, 9,* 243-276.

Lanigan, R. L. (1984). *Semiotic phenomenology of rhetoric: Eidetic practice in Henry Grattan's discourse on tolerance.* Washington, DC: Centre for Advanced Research in Phenomenology, and University Press of America.

Lanigan, R. L. (1988). *Phenomenology of communication: Merleau-Ponty's thematics in communicology and semiology.* Pittsburgh, PA: Duquesne University Press.

Lewis, L., & Johnson, K. K. (1989). Effects of dress, cosmetics, sex of subject, and causal inference on attribution of victim responsibility. *Clothing and Textile Research Journal, 8,* 22-27.

Lofles, I. L. (1991). Belief systems: Sexuality and rape. *Journal of Psychology and Human Sexuality, 4,* 37-59.

Lowenstein, L. F. (1989). Understanding and treating the rapist. *Criminologist, 13,* 196-205.

Martin, P. Y., & Hummer, R. A. (1989). Fraternities and rape on campus. *Gender & Society, 3,* 457-473.

Merleau-Ponty, M. (1962). *Phenomenology of perception* (C. Smith, Trans.). London: Routledge & Kegan Paul. (Revised by F. Williams & D. Guerriere, 1979)

Muehlenhard, C. L., & Falcon, P. L. (1990). Mens heterosocial skill and attitude toward women as predictors of verbal sexual coercion and forceful rape. *Sex Roles, 23,* 241-259.

Olsen, J. (1991). *Predator: Rape, madness, and injustice in Seattle.* New York: Delacorte.

Schult, D. G., & Schneider, L. J. (1991). The role of sexual provocativeness, rape history, and observer gender in perceptions of blame in sexual assault. *Journal of Interpersonal Violence, 6,* 94-101.

Scott, J. C. (1990). *Dominance and the arts of resistance: Hidden transcripts.* New Haven, CT: Yale University Press.

Strine, M. S. (1992). Understanding "how things work": Sexual harassment and academic culture. *Journal of Applied Communication Research, 20,* 391-400.

Sussman, L., & Bordwell, S. (1981). *The rapist file.* New York: Chelsea House.

TePaske, B. A. (1982). *Rape and ritual: A psychological study.* Toronto: Inner City Books.

Wood, J. T. (1992). Telling our stories: Narratives as a basis for theorizing sexual harassment. *Journal of Applied Communication Research, 20,* 349-362.

Hating for Life

Rhetorical Extremism and Abortion Clinic Violence

Janette Kenner Muir
George Mason University

Editor's Introduction

We often assume that hate is immoral. As a result, we forget that
people often believe they hate for good, moral reasons. This is the case
in Janette Muir's treatment of the abortion rescue movement in the
United States. Analyzing the rhetorical tactics and strategies of a
radical segment of the pro-life movement, Muir considers hate within
the context of morality.

Whereas politics is about the art of compromise, religious beliefs are often expressed in absolute terms. Muir suggests that when absolute values conflict with political solutions to problems, the ground for persuasion and compromise is limited. Yet hard lines are often difficult to maintain. Muir contends that in such cases, hatred can be used to sustain a movement by rallying members around core doctrines and focusing their efforts against a common enemy.

This analysis reminds us that hate is not something that will go away. There are certain divisive issues that arouse conflict over fundamental and compelling beliefs. As long as hate retains the power to propel people to do what they believe is right, we may assume that people will continue to hate for what they believe.

═══════════════

Let the resistance begin. Our worst political nightmare has come upon us a pro-baby killing, pro-sodomite, pass-out-condoms-in-school President.

Randall Terry (1992), Operation Rescue

I don't picket. I don't rescue. I kill baby killers . . . I am stalking you.

Anonymous Letter to Planned Parenthood Clinics
Milwaukee, Wisconsin

A woman's right to an abortion in the case of an unwanted pregnancy has been an issue in American society for decades. In campaign years, the abortion debate has become the single defining issue for many candidates. Both Capitol Hill and the Supreme Court are now arenas for furthering both sides of the cause. As the political pendulum swings slightly to the left, the United States now finds a pro-choice president in office. Bill Clinton's presence, along with a record number of pro-choice women senators and representatives, sends a clear message that those people against abortion rights must now fight harder to get their message across.

This fight has been loudest and strongest in front of abortion clinics throughout the United States. Right-to-life protesters have blockaded and bombed clinics; physicians who perform abortions have been terrorized and, in extreme cases, murdered. Seeing little room for dialogue, members of the "rescue movement"—right-to-lifers who engage in almost any tactic to save women from "abortion mills"— have adopted numerous strategies to get attention and keep their message at the forefront of abortion discussions. Actions taken by these groups have been compared to activities of the Ku Klux Klan, identified as domestic terrorism, and referred to as American vigilantism.

The overarching goal of the rescue movement is to save millions of unborn children from murder at the hands of abortionists (Faux, 1990). The movement's actions are grounded in and justified by hatred toward those agencies and clinics that perform these abortions, and its rhetoric is aimed toward the eventual dissolution of clinics around the United States. Using the love of God as a justification for hatred toward those who would murder the unborn, strategies are directed toward saving potential lives and toward keeping the abortion issue at the forefront of national news.

In an effort to better understand antiabortion rhetoric, particularly the expressions of hatred toward those who perform and provide abortions, this chapter will look at the rhetorical strategies used by those involved in the rescue movement. The purpose here is not to reconstruct or deconstruct the discussion that has already taken place about the pro-life[1] movement. The intention is, however, to focus specifically on those members of the pro-life movement who have turned attention to that which they define as the source of the problem—the abortion clinics, and the practitioners themselves. Hence, this chapter looks at the groups who define themselves as the "rescuers"—those who physically try to save women from the act of abortion. By considering the rhetorical expressions and strategies for hate employed by members of the movement, implications will be drawn regarding the difficulty of reaching a middle ground and engaging in dialogue that may one day ease the abortion controversy in the United States.

The Rescue Movement

The history and stages of the abortion debate have been explored by a variety of rhetorical scholars. Celeste Michelle Condit's focus on public discourse about abortion provides one of the most complete discussions of the controversy, revealing significant patterns for arguments presented by both pro-life and pro-choice movements between 1960 and 1985 in the United States (see Condit, 1990; Railsback, 1984). Randall Lake's research about antiabortion rhetoric employs Burke's theory of order and disorder to suggest important moral grounding for the movement (see Lake, 1982, 1984). Marsha L. Vanderford's work on the abortion controversy in Minnesota between 1973 and 1980 suggests that vilification strategies serve ultimately to sustain commitment for members of the movements in that state (Vanderford, 1989). All of these efforts have focused on early stages of the pro-life movement, offering rationales for the various activities the movement engages in, as well as an understanding of the rhetorical processes taking place.

Condit's (1990) description of the violent actions of antiabortionists in the early 1980s is of particular importance to rhetorical scholars. In *Decoding Abortion Rhetoric,* Condit writes a compelling description of abortion clinic bombings noting the societal frustration that led to this form of coercive action:

> The more the mass consensus accepting abortion seemed to solidify, the more frustrated and active became the minority of those who accepted the unalloyed pro-Life discourse. For them, the image of the unborn child continued to dominate the meaning of abortion. Gradually, throughout the eighties increasing percentages of these pro-Life activists began to shift away from the sanctioned American method of adjudicating disputes through persuasion toward the methods of coercion, law-breaking, and violence. (p. 151)

The picketing of abortion clinics and legal buildings such as the Supreme Court quickly evolved into more coercive and illegal activities, which included trespassing and bombing. For example, on December 25, 1984, four bombs exploded at abortion clinics in Pensacola, Florida. No one was hurt, but thousands of dollars of damage occurred to the facilities (see Condit, 1990, pp. 155-163).

Rescue Organizations

As with any large social movement, numerous groups fall under the umbrella of the larger movement's goals. Although many organizations within the pro-life movement advocate education and information against abortion activities, those organizations that focus on the rescue of unborn children are among the most vocal of the larger movement.

One of the oldest groups within the rescue movement is the Pro-Life Action League headquartered in Chicago and led by Joseph M. Scheidler. Professing to work through legal, nonviolent direct action, this group claims responsibility for the closing of numerous abortion clinics. In 1985 the House of Representatives Subcommittee on Civil and Constitutional Rights of the Committee on the Judiciary held sessions to consider abortion clinic violence. The committee's purpose was to consider whether or not unlawful activities against abortion clinics infringed upon the constitutional rights of reproductive freedom. Acting in response to reports about the blocking of clinic entrances, property damage, telephone threats, and other actions, the subcommittee listened to testimony from abortion clinic workers and doctors, women who had sought abortions and were harassed in the process, and representatives from the FBI and the Bureau of Alcohol, Tobacco and Firearms.

Speaking on behalf of the pro-lifers, Scheidler's prepared statement, followed by exchanges with Representatives on the committee, summarized the perspective of many protesters and the undaunted attitude that prevailed:

> The pro-life community has moved ahead to restore protection to the unborn. We have taken to the streets to bear witness to their humanity. We have no intention of being intimidated by threats to our rights of free speech, assembly and redress of grievance. We will return again and again to the abortuaries to talk women out of abortion, to try to convert medical personnel who have turned their healing profession into a killing profession. We will confront in the courts and on the streets, every false arrest, every malicious prosecution and every unconstitutional injunction attacking our First Amendment rights. . . . As activists, we caution the abortionists, and those defending their lethal trade, to cease their campaign to deny us our constitutional rights. Non-violent direct action

to end abortion is preferable to bombing abortion chambers. But if access to free speech, assembly and redress of grievances are denied, the
violence of abortion will inevitably be opposed by other means.
(Scheidler, 1985, pp. 56, 59)

Scheidler's testimony about "abortuaries" and the "killing profession"
was grounded in hatred toward the clinics and a woman's right to
choose an abortion. His 1985 publication, *Closed: 99 Ways to Stop
Abortion,* suggested many nonviolent activities, but also reinforced the
idea that abortion should end by "any means necessary," which moved
from general intimidation tactics to coercive action. In 1993, Scheidler
continued to run a hotline that provided a central data bank for
abortion protesters in the Midwest (Cobb, 1993).

One of the most significant forces in the rescue movement is
Operation Rescue, founded by Randall Terry. Terry became actively
involved in the pro-life movement in 1986 when his organization,
"Project Life," staged its first "rescue"—the goal was to save the unborn from being "murdered" by "abortionists." The success of this
initial effort led to a renaming of the organization to "Operation
Rescue" (see Panetta, 1993).

It was in 1988, however, that Operation Rescue gained national
prominence. In May of that year, the group organized 800 people to
stage a sit-in at abortion clinics around New York City and Long
Island. Demonstrations followed at the Democratic National Convention in Atlanta, where more than 100 arrests occurred for blocking
access to a midtown abortion clinic. By the end of the year, Operation
Rescue was responsible for rescues in at least 32 cities around the
country (see Bowers, Ochs, & Jensen, 1993; Sherman, 1988).
Wichita, Kansas, was the center of activity for Operation Rescue forces
during the summer of 1991. For 46 days, a series of vigils and protests
were staged against abortion clinics in this city. Although nonviolent
tactics were mostly used, there was some escalation and confrontation
between protesters, leading to the arrests of the three major leaders
of Operation Rescue: Randall Terry, Reverend Pat Mahoney, and Jim
Evans (Bowers et al., 1993).

By 1993, Operation Rescue had expanded its influence among
antiabortion groups by establishing a national training camp for pro-
lifers willing to practice aggressive tactics against abortion clinics.

A 3-month training course titled IMPACT (Institute of Mobilized Prophetic Activated Christian Training) was held in Melbourne, Florida, to teach abortion opponents how to use scripture to persuade women to keep their babies, how to investigate the personal and professional backgrounds of clinic doctors, how to find addresses and phone numbers of patients and clinic workers, and how to get arrested in efforts to stop abortion (Chandler, 1993). The training camp drew 22 students, ranging in age from 16 to 67. Referring to these students as future soldiers, Terry commenced to train them for abortion clinic protesting (Chandler, 1993, p. 1A).

Graduation for the pro-lifers culminated with a protest in front of the Aware Woman Health Center in Melbourne. With picket signs saying "Death Sold Here" and enlarged photographs of mangled fetuses, the students occupied the driveway into the parking lot and heckled clinic workers and women seeking abortions. By the end of the protest, 51 arrests had been made (Chandler, 1993).

Following the training camp, Operation Rescue planned a week-long, seven-city siege on abortion clinics called the "Cities of Refuge" campaign. Clinics around the country prepared for the worst, expecting major protests and potential violence, however, most of the cities found little confrontation and relatively low turnouts ("Operation Rescue," 1993).

Operation Rescue, and Randall Terry in particular, have continued to play a major role in the rescue movement. Protests are staged around the country to gain media coverage, and Terry has emerged as a major spokesperson at most Congressional hearings regarding the abortion issue. As one of the most vociferous speakers, he regularly attracts attention.

In addition to organizations guided by Scheidler and Terry, there are numerous other groups around the country that identify themselves as part of the rescue movement. Rescue America, led by Donald Treshman, is much smaller than Operation Rescue, and has been occasionally considered a rival of the organization. Treshman gained national prominence when someone who was not a member of his group but participating in a protest outside of a Pensacola abortion clinic shot Dr. David Gunn. Rescue America is primarily known for its "lock and block" technique of chaining protesters to doors and barricading examining rooms.

Other organizations that make up the rescue movement include Lambs of Christ—a small nomadic group of Catholics who have the reputation as the most aggressive of the rescue groups. This group has offered to pay women not to have abortions; nine "lambs" were arrested in El Paso after barricading themselves inside the examining rooms of an abortion clinic (Cobb, 1993). Another group called Missionaries to the Pre-Born claims to use nonviolent tactics such as obstructing entrances to clinics in order to prevent the occurrence of abortions. Young protesters also get involved in the rescue movement. A Minneapolis-based group called TRUTH—Teens Rescuing Unborn Tiny Humans—has held vigils at the Robbindale clinic, and its 24-year old leader, Michelle Cramer, has been arrested several times (Chandler, 1993).

Expressions of Hate

Whether identified as acts of domestic terrorism or vigilantism, the escalation of violence against abortion clinics is predicated on hatred toward the act of abortion and toward those clinics that offer this service. Hatred runs deep within the philosophy of the movement, therefore tactics employed often reflect this emotion. The most powerful expressions of hate have been directed toward the physicians who perform abortions.

TERRORIZING DOCTORS

In a rally in Washington, D.C., Randall Terry best exemplified the hostility felt when he suggested major tactics for antiabortionists to use in harassing abortion providers: "Do everything we can to torment these people . . . to expose them for the vile, blood-sucking hyenas that they are" (Boodman, 1993a, p. A17).[2] Scheidler details specific actions that should be taken to harass abortion providers and their families, suggesting that harassing does not stop with the physician— families, and spouses in particular, should also be harassed. Scheidler notes, "if you've tried to deal with the wife and she's for abortion, well, she's part of the team" (Boodman, 1993a, p. A17).

Harassment techniques include following spouses at grocery stores, damaging automobiles, making threatening phone calls, taunting the children of providers, and direct confrontation at the doctors' homes. Obstetrician-gynecologist Dr. Frank Snydle described the phone call received by his 80-year-old mother at 3:00 in the morning:

> Whoever it was told her that he was a trooper with the Florida Highway Patrol and that I'd been killed in a car accident. My mother has a heart condition. By the time she found me several hours later, she was hysterical. (Boodman, 1993a, p. A1)

Snydle has also seen "Wanted" posters that have offered $1,000 to anyone who can provide information leading to his arrest or the loss of his license. The posters contain his mother's address and phone number and the license plate numbers of two ex-girlfriends.

Dallas physician Norman Thompkins told a Congressional Subcommittee investigating abortion clinic violence that he had "endured death threats, terrorism, an extortion attempt and six months of continual harassment by abortion opponents" (Feeney, 1993, p. 27A).[3] Thompkins has filed a lawsuit against pro-life organizations in Dallas, claiming that "I have become a prisoner in my own home because I believe the woman has the right to choose" (Franken, 1993).[4] Noting the doctor as the "weak link" in continued abortions, Terry argues that the movement's current goal is to make "targeted doctors a liability to everyone they encounter" (Boodman, 1993a, p. A1), subjecting them to pressure from patients, employees, other doctors, members of their church, landlords, and families. These tactics have proved to be successful on several occasions. In Melbourne, for example, two doctors stopped working at an abortion clinic, claiming that they feared for their lives, and in Dallas at least three physicians have stopped practicing abortions for similar reasons (Boodman, 1993a, p. A1).

In their "John the Baptist" campaign, the Dallas Pro-Life Action Network (PLAN) in conjunction with Rescue America, attempted to persuade doctors to stop performing abortions. The organization spent months doing surveillance and gathering information about doctors who perform abortions in the Dallas area. One of the doctors who stopped was Dallas obstetrician Clay Alexander who signed a statement declaring that he would never perform another abortion. This statement, along with his photograph, was provided to PLAN after a series of incidents occurred involving harassment of his wife and 2-year-old toddler.

MURDER AS THE ULTIMATE TERRORIST ACTIVITY

The killing of Dr. David Gunn was seen by many abortion-rights activists as the culmination of years of violence and harassment against clinics around the United States. Gunn, a physician who traveled to women's clinics in Georgia, Alabama, and northern Florida, performing abortions, had been harassed on several occasions prior to the shooting. On March 10, 1993, Gunn was shot three times in the back and killed by Michael Griffin, an antiabortion activist.

Prior to his shooting, Gunn had regularly received hate mail and telephoned death threats. As was the case with other doctors, antiabortionists had printed up "Wanted" posters bearing Gunn's picture and his address and telephone number. The poster declared "We Need Your Help to Stop Dr. David Gunn." It ended with "REWARD: Babies' Lives Will Be Saved If He Stops!!!" (see Booth, 1993, p. A1).[5] Gunn was murdered as he arrived at the Pensacola clinic, using the back door to dodge protesters from Rescue America. Though Griffin had been with this group for previous demonstrations, the police concluded that he acted alone, that Rescue America was not responsible for the killing (Laurence, 1993).

Gunn's murder prompted a number of responses from antiabortionists. Although many pro-life organizations condemned the actions of Griffin, the more extremist groups justified the actions on the basis of saving hundreds of lives of unborn children. It was in their responses to the murder that some of the most vehement positions surfaced against the abortion clinics. Randall Terry called Gunn a "mass murderer" saying that "while we grieve for him and for his widow and for his children, we must also grieve for the thousands of children that he has murdered." Treshman claimed that "while Gunn's death is unfortunate, it's also true that quite a number of babies' lives will be saved" (see Olson, 1993, p. 9).[6] A protester declared, "I think the man that was killed—and it was unfortunate—he should be glad he was not killed the same way that he has killed other people, which is limb by limb" (Olson, 1993, p. 9).

These responses, and others, reiterated the position that killing one life to save hundreds of others was a justified action. In following with these beliefs, a fund for the family of Michael Griffin was established by Rescue America. A CNN interview with Treshman best summarized Rescue America's efforts to dissociate itself from Michael Griffin yet underscore the positive affect the murder might have on subsequent actions:

> I think most people will realize this is certainly not an action orchestrated by any organization, now. This is a lone individual's response, and it's something that we all regret, and that's certainly a negative side. There will be some fallout and that there [sic] will be people not wanting to associate with the activist role because of this. But on the same token, too, it will have a chilling effect on those who ply their grisly trade at abortion clinics elsewhere. It's getting harder and harder to find people willing to commit aborticide, and the National Abortion Rights Action League admits that it is harder to find professionals willing to turn their back on their oath of office and kill children. (Attkisson, 1993)[7]

Hence, even though Griffin's actions were condemned by many pro-lifers, he could also be forgiven because of the murder's chilling effect on other doctors who performed abortions.

On March 5, 1994, Michael E. Griffin was convicted of first-degree murder and sentenced to life in prison for shooting David Gunn. The prosecution had agreed not to seek the death penalty for the slaying. Florida Assistant State Attorney General James Murray read from a letter Griffin sent to other antiabortion activists that said if one baby is saved, it would be worth losing his life ("Antiabortion Activist," 1994, p. A22).

In following the pattern of the Gunn shooting, other protesters face charges for shooting or stalking doctors. On March 31, 1993, Charleston police arrested Cathy Ann Rider, a leader of the South Carolina Missionaries to the Unborn. Rider was accused of stalking Lorraine Maguire, director of the Charleston Women's Medical Clinic. The arrest warrant claimed that Rider made strong references to the murder of David Gunn and advised Maguire to get more security protection. In addition, the warrant stated that Rider informed the doctor that "she knows the layout of furniture in the Maguire home, has referred to Maguire's daughter, and encouraged others to 'rip her arms off' so that Maguire would know how aborted fetuses feel" (Boodman, 1993a, p. A17).

Shortly after Gunn's murder, Shelley Shannon shot Dr. George Tiller, a physician at the Women's Health Care Services clinic in Wichita, Kansas. With a handgun in her purse, Shannon walked into the clinic, made an appointment to see the doctor for an abortion, walked around the facility, then returned later to shoot him. Shannon was also the prime suspect in several firebombings of abortion clinics in both Ohio and Oregon ("Oregon," 1993). In October, 1994, Rachelle Shannon was charged in 10 arson and acid attacks at abortion clinics. Federal grand juries returned indictments totaling 30 counts, charging her for attacks in Oregon, California, Nevada, and Idaho in 1992-1993. Currently, Shannon is serving a 10-year sentence for the attempted murder and shooting of Tiller ("Antiabortion Extremist," 1994).

These convictions, however, provided little deterrence to Paul Hill, a former Presbyterian minister accused of killing abortion doctor John B. Britton and his escort, James H. Barrett, on July 29, 1994. Both men were shot outside The Ladies Center in Pensacola, Florida. According to a special report in the *Washington Post,* Hill was galvanized by the Gunn shooting. Within months he appeared on the Phil Donahue show, ABC's *Nightline,* and CNN's *Sonya Live.* Declaring himself as "the new national spokesman for abortionist killers," he told Donahue on national television, "I'm advocating the consistent theology of the Bible, and that is that we must protect innocent life" (Hill, quoted in Sawyer, 1994, p. A9).[8] Equating killing an abortionist with killing Hitler, Hill claimed that a woman who has an abortion is "an accessory to murder" (Hill, quoted in Sawyer, 1994, p. A9).

On October 5, 1994, Paul Hill was found guilty on three counts of violating the abortion clinic access law (discussed in the following section). He was also found guilty of a federal firearm charge ("Hill Guilty," 1994). In preparing for the murder trial, Hill attempted to argue that his action was justifiable because killing a doctor who performed abortions protected the lives of unborn children. Such a defense would excuse otherwise criminal conduct committed for the purpose of preventing an even greater harm. Florida Judge Frank Bell granted the state's motion that Hill could not use this argument as his defense.

Paul Hill was found guilty on both counts of murder and, in a 12-0 decision, the jury recommended that he be executed in the electric chair. Although he agreed to defend himself during the trial, Hill had no opening or closing statements, did not cross-examine witnesses, and mainly sat silent throughout the trial. Before the sentencing, Hill broke his silence and read a statement to the court:

> You have a responsibility to protect your neighbor's life, to use force if necessary to do so. In an effort to suppress this truth, you may mix my blood with the blood of the unborn and those who have fought to defend the oppressed. However, truth and righteousness will prevail. May God help you protect the unborn as you would want to be protected. (Hill, quoted in Booth, 1994, p. A1)[9]

Many pro-choice activists fear that Hill's execution will make him a martyr, encouraging more violent protests against abortionists and clinics. Certainly, statistics indicate the propensity for escalating violence, so the fears are well founded.

INCREASING VIOLENCE

Despite claims by Operation Rescue and other antiabortion groups that they are currently engaging in nonviolent protest to change the political landscape, recent statistics indicate that abortion clinic violence continues to be pervasive. In a nationwide survey conducted by the Fund for the Feminist Majority, 281 abortion clinics responded to questions concerning the nature of antiabortion violence. According to researchers Colleen Dermody and Jeanne Clark, the survey represents "one of the most comprehensive studies ever conducted of anti-abortion violence directed at clinics, patients, and health care workers" (Dermody & Clark, 1993, p. 1).

Of the clinics participating in the survey, 50.2% experienced severe antiabortion violence in the first half of 1993. These violent acts included death threats, stalking, chemical attacks, arson, bomb threats, invasions, and blockades. Death threats, the most frequently reported form of antiabortion violence, have caused health care workers to fear for their safety and their lives on a daily basis. The work of many clinics—which often includes other health services besides abortion—has been disrupted by damage to facilities and by invasions. Some clinics have had to cease operation because facilities were destroyed by fire or bombings (Dermody & Clark, 1993).

The study concludes that antiabortion violence is pervasive across the country. Clinics and health care workers in California, Florida, Illinois, Massachusetts, Michigan, Montana, New York, and Texas were among those who faced the most acute violence. The violence has been most devastating in small and rural states where abortion facilities are limited and where women have to travel long distances to obtain abortions (Dermody & Clark, 1993). Those who are affected the most by abortion clinic violence appear to be poor, often minority, women. In all the cases of violence there appears to be little that local law enforcement can do to prevent the violent attacks. Given the inability to act, or in some cases, the inherent hostility many law enforcement officers feel toward abortion clinics, doctors in particular find it difficult to receive adequate protection against the antiabortionists. Thus, more than one third of the clinics in the survey have been forced to ask the courts to intervene on behalf of their patients and health care workers. Some have sought restraining orders, others have obtained injunctions against antiabortion violence (Dermody & Clark, 1993).

Government Intervention

Treading a fine line between taking away the rescue movement's right to free speech and working toward stopping the violence at abortion clinics, the issue has been brought to the forefront of governmental decision making both on Capitol Hill and in the Supreme Court. Recognizing that the antiabortionists' tactics need to be addressed, on November 17, 1993, Capitol Hill voted for stiff fines and ns for people who attack clinic workers and patients. The of Access to Clinic Entrances Act, authored by Representative Charles Schumer (D-NY), makes it a federal crime to use threaten force against anyone using or working in abortion clinics. It also prohibits physically obstructing the entrance to abortion clinics and the destruction of clinic buildings.

Again, the issue of free expression of ideas entered the debate. In an earlier subcommittee hearing for this bill, Terry argued that "the very introduction of this legislation strikes at the core of what it means to live in political freedom—the right to vigorously disagree, and to non-violently express that dissent—without fear of crushing reprisals from an oppressive government" and compared the antiabortion group tactics with "civil disobedience in the tradition of Rev. Dr. King and Mahatma Gandhi" (Orman, 1993, p. A1).[10] Antiabortion legislators claimed that their cause was being singled out for punishment because of the extremists of the movement. Under the Freedom of Access Act it is argued, someone who prays in front of an abortion clinic will be subject to the same kinds of penalties as some who use coercive force (Orman, 1993). According to antiabortionists, civil disobedience, seen as the fabric of American life, is threatened. The Act was passed by both the House and Senate in the final days of the first session of the 103rd Congress.

Those involved on both sides of the abortion controversy are finding their cause debated more frequently in the Supreme Court. One of the most recent court cases involving abortion clinic violence was *National Organization for Women, Inc. v. Scheidler* (December 1993). Abortion rights advocates urged the court to let them use a law directed at the mob to fight "violent conduct" and "terrorism" aimed at putting abortion clinics out of business. NOW and abortion clinics sought to use the Racketeer Influenced and Corrupt Organizations Act (RICO) to obtain damages and injunctions against antiabortion groups' efforts to close down their facilities. Section 1962 (c) of RICO provides,

> It shall be unlawful for any person employed by or associated with any enterprise engaged in, or the activities of which affect, interstate or foreign commerce, to conduct or participate, directly or indirectly, in the conduct of such enterprises' affairs through a pattern of racketeering activity or collection of unlawful debt. ("Health Care," 1993, p. 3403)

Two appeals courts have ruled against NOW and RICO in favor of Scheidler and his claims to freedom of expression. Under the RICO act the intention is to attack organized crime syndicates, though in recent years the act has been used in numerous business disputes. In the case of NOW's appeal, the question lies in the motive for the attacks and whether, for example, pro-life protesters have a profit motive in trying to shut down the clinics. Although pro-choice advocates argue that the attacks threaten legitimate businesses and services, the Supreme Court determined if this appeal outweighed the groups' free speech activities.

On January 24, 1994, the Supreme Court, by a unanimous vote, ruled that abortion clinics may use the federal racketeering law to sue protesters who conspire to shut them down. The Justice Department played down the abortion rights connection and stressed that an expansive reading of the racketeering act was necessary to protect the government's ability to prosecute politically, or religiously, motivated violence. The ruling specifically reinstates a lawsuit brought by the National Organization for Women on behalf of abortion clinics nationwide, targeting the masterminds of criminal conspiracy rather than only the suspects at the scene of the crime (Biskupic, 1994).

The Rhetoric of Hate

Although many of the tactics of antiabortionists have already been discussed in context with the major events that have recently occurred, specific rhetorical strategies include powerful uses of naming, analogies, and metaphors to convey the force of the pro-life worldview. The simplest statements used by antiabortionists are rife with the language of violence. Protesters shout "murderer" at doctors; women are told "don't kill your baby." Filled with hatred, this language helps to create a climate of violence for all involved in the abortion controversy.

THE NAMING PROCESS

One only needs to consider the names of some of the antiabortion groups to realize the important power of naming for these individuals. "Missionaries to the Preborn" and "Lambs of Christ" aptly entitle the spectives of many of those who protest against abortion clinics.

Their goal is to save the innocent, to protect those who cannot protect themselves.

One of the major naming processes that takes place evolves around the "murder of children." Any action that prevents the endless murder of the unborn, according to Terry, is ultimately justified. Doctors who "murder innocent children" at "abortion mills" must be humiliated, embarrassed, shamed, and exposed; Terry tells activists, "they are like human rats, and they hate the light" (Bumpus-Hooper, 1993, p. A16).[11] He underscores the process of murder when he contrasts the name "rescue movement" with what he calls the "child-killing movement." Those who favor choice for women are described as "pro-abortion" and "pro-killing" with the notion of "choice" completely dismissed from the equation.

Terry's unidimensional way of viewing abortion was reiterated in an exchange with Kate Michelman, President of the National Abortion Rights Action League, on CBS *This Morning* immediately following the death of David Gunn:

Q: Randall Terry, let me ask you, what was your reaction to what happened yesterday?

Terry: Well, I was shocked and I was repulsed. This is an absolutely inappropriate, repulsive act that Michael Griffin has done to David Gunn. But we need to remember that this man, David Gunn, has single-handedly killed thousands and thousands of children throughout Florida, Mississippi and Georgia. So while we grieve for him and for his widow and for his children, we must also grieve for the thousands of children he has murdered.

Q: You condemn what happened yesterday?

Terry: Oh absolutely, absolutely. But we equally condemn what Kate Michelman stands for and what David Gunn stood for—the murder of innocent children. I mean, yesterday one abortionist was murdered, which is horrifying, and that's the first time in this century that we know of that's happened, but also yesterday 4,500 children were murdered in cold blood, and I don't see very much grief coming from Kate about that.

Michelman: What Randall Terry has just said appalls me—to use the murder of a doctor as an opportunity to again inflame rhetoric and to create again the climate that causes this man to go off whatever, in whatever way . . .

The fact is, the kind of climate Randall Terry and Operation Rescue have created in this country, a climate of intolerance and harassment and terrorism, that has led to Griffin murdering, gunning down a doctor, a hero.

Terry: We make no bones about it. We do not tolerate child-killing. We despise child-killing. . . . What happened yesterday was an aberration.

Michelman: It is not an aberration.

Terry: Excuse me, Kate. Kate should be thankful for the leadership of Operation Rescue because we insist that people commit to nonviolence. We are committed to nonviolence. We will continue to be committed to nonviolence. And if she and her cohorts, her feminist cohorts up in Washington, D.C., get their way, they are going to be responsible and the Clinton administration for driving the fringe people that are out there to acts of extremism. If you take away the right of people to have peaceful protest, like they're trying to do, and make it a felony to be involved in pro-life activism, then they are the ones that are responsible for what fringe people do out of frustration, not us.

Michelman: That's just complete nonsense. Randall Terry represents the extremist wing of his party, of his movement. He has created a climate where this could happen. Congress must move quickly to pass legislation that will protect women and doctors and personnel at the clinics and to establish a fundamental—

Terry: The murder of children has created this climate.

Michelman: —and establish a fundamental—

Terry: The murder of children, Kate, is what has created this climate.

Michelman: Excuse me, Randall.

Terry: 35 million babies are dead. (Ginsburg, 1993)[12]

This exchange illustrates Terry's fixation on the number of babies murdered, his penchant for hyperbole, and the shift of blame for the extremist behavior to the current political climate. It is the action of those who favor pro-choice, Terry claims, that will ultimately lead to more mayhem and murder.

This narrowing of the abortion debate is also reinforced by other pro-life leaders. Scheidler provided similar sentiment during Congressional Subcommittee hearings (*Abortion Clinic Violence,* 1985). Treshman also issued numerous statements about the "killing of the unborn." Condit (1990) identifies this strategy as one of "overweighing" that occurs when "one's values outweigh those of the opposition and so necessitate a complete sacrifice of the opposing values" (p. 159). In the case of pro-life activists, the right to life of an unborn child is more important than the choice a woman makes about her body, because the value of "life" is greater than the value of "choice." Condit explains,

> Those who choose to over-weigh, rather than to seek compromise, write off any competing claims and move in a uni-dimensional understanding of the world unbounded by other restraining principles, terms, and factors. Once a set of activists decides that the opposition's values are outweighed by its own, *and can therefore be totally ignored,* they can depict opponents as devil figures and supporters as saints. One's own grounds become the sole values; therefore, any means are justified to secure those ends. The dominance of the over-weighing strategy was thus the necessary rhetorical component which led pro-Life activists away from the sanctioned method of persuasion and toward coercion, law-breaking and violence. (p. 162)

The strategy of over-weighing becomes more evident in 1993 when many members of the rescue movement argued that, ultimately, the actions against Gunn were, ultimately, justified. By over-weighing values, pro-lifers argue that abortion doctors are devil figures or, for some, direct soldiers of Satan himself. Rather than focusing on the society that spawns abortion activity, and hence the underlying problems that perpetuate the need for abortions, attention turns to the doctor/devil who performs the unlawful act.

This naming process provides two important identification strategies for those involved in the rescue movement. First, members identify together against a common enemy. Burke (1965) argues that an important rhetorical advantage can be gained when a scapegoat is used to establish connections in terms of a commonly shared enemy, or identification by antithesis. In the case of the pro-life movement, even though there may be internal disagreements about the best strategies to use, the most vehement position is framed against the provider of abortions; hence, the one who performs the abortion is the scapegoat for all other actions. Second, the over-weighing strategy suggested by Condit serves as an important means of identification for antiabortionists, providing a means for consubstantiality—a way of acting together and sharing common ideas and attitudes (Burke, 1969b). Rescue movement participants join together because they identify with a higher principle—that life outweighs all other concerns. It is this overarching concept of life and the power of scapegoating that serve to keep members of the movement joined together for a common cause.

The Use of Analogies

The use of an analogy involves the transfer of meaning from one theme to another; its effect is to provide a comparative perspective. "Analogies," according to Perelman and Olbrechts-Tyteca, "are important in invention and argumentation fundamentally because they facilitate the development and extension of thought" (Perelman & Olbrechts-Tyteca, 1969, p. 385). Two major analogies are drawn by members of the rescue movement in justifying the actions taken against abortionists. Pro-life advocates invoke images of Hitler and Nazism, and images of the Civil Rights Movement in their appeals against abortion clinics.

COMPARISONS TO NAZISM

Expressions of hatred are predominant as the abortion process is compared with the Nazi annihilation of Jews. The comparison of abortion clinics to "Nazi ovens" is a recurring analogy used by the pro-life movement. Condit notes that in the case of pro-life rhetoric in the 1970s and 1980s,

The fundamental link was made through the theme of "the sanctity of human life." Since the Nazis did not value human life, they killed innocent humans. The abortionist was similarly accused of failing to value the "sanctity" of human life and therefore killing innocent humans. . . . This analogy was compelling because the American audience most powerfully dreaded another Nazi era. Moreover, the key discursive links were made directly through the acts of destruction. Nazis conducted mass executions, and abortions could be metaphorically identified as mass executions—both supposedly "executed" for purposes of "convenience" or "utility." The full force of the horrors of the Third Reich were thus brought down against abortion. (Condit, 1990, p. 51)

This analogy continues to be pervasive in current antiabortion rhetoric. Operation Rescue organizer and spokeswoman for the "impact training center," Wendy Wright, best exemplifies this analogy by claiming that "the abortion clinics are death camps. It's exactly what they did in Nazi Germany. . . . Abortion doctors should be put on trial and punished, like at Nuremberg. Yes, I do mean hanged" (Tisdall, 1993, p. 23).[13] Michelle Cramer, one of the participants of IMPACT, underscores the hatred inherent in the rhetoric:

We have to expose the baby-killers, humiliate them, bring them down. Jesus commanded us to love the sinner. So I don't hate them. I just hate what they do. They're murderers . . . I've been "Mace-d," spat at, abused, knocked down by anti-life men, arrested. It doesn't matter. We're fighting genocide. (Tisdall, 1993, p. 23)

Even Rep. Henry Hyde (R-IL) drew a similar analogy when advocating the free speech rights of protesters during the Freedom of Access debate on Capitol Hill:

If these groups . . . were in front of another killing place—let's say Auschwitz—you'd be honoring them, you wouldn't be making them felons. . . . We don't single out . . . environmental demonstrators, civil rights demonstrators—only the people who are concerned about people being exterminated in someone's womb. (Lawsky, 1993)[14]

Drawing an analogy between Nazism and abortion clinic activities has the capacity to strike fear in the hearts of many average Americans who are aware of the horrors of the Third Reich. The strategy serves to invoke hostility against those who engage in abortion activities, and once again, magnifies the enemy that the movement is fighting against. At the same time, the analogy serves to gain moral grounding because most people agree that Hitler's annihilation of Jews was a morally repugnant act. To draw the analogy to children being killed provides an important way to link members of the movement together.

COMPARISONS TO CIVIL RIGHTS

Another analogy drawn by members of the rescue movement occurs when arguing for maintaining First Amendment rights to protest. Much of Randall Terry's rhetoric is premised on upholding Operation Rescue's Free Speech rights because the group's work is no different from that of Martin Luther King's work in the Civil Rights movement. In response to the Supreme Court case and RICO, Terry declares,

> If we are tried as racketeers, then Dr. King and all of his followers should have been tried as racketeers. It's absurd. It's an insult to intelligence to say that a 65-year-old grandmother who's saying a rosary, or a 42-year-old Evangelical minister are racketeers. They're trying to save babies from murder, and when Dr. King and all of his followers did sit-ins to promote the higher good and higher justice, they weren't being challenged with being racketeers. No one would have even thought of that. (Totenberg, 1993)[15]

Terry continually attempts to draw a parallel between the antiabortion movement and the civil rights movement, and between himself and Dr. Martin Luther King, Jr. (Faux, 1990).

Many pro-choice advocates, however, take offense with the civil rights analogy because the intent of the antiabortion movement—to deny women their right to choose an abortion—is the antithesis of the goals inherent in the civil rights movement—to expand the rights of women and minorities. Panetta's critique of Operation Rescue's attempt to compare its Atlanta campaign to the effort of the Southern Christian Leadership Conference in Selma, Alabama, concludes that the movement's techniques actually served to "ghettoize" women and infringe on their rights (Panetta, 1993).

Despite Terry's attempts to draw comparisons to other movements such as the Civil Rights, many pro-choice advocates have compared the rescue movement's actions to that of the KKK. In *Bray v. Alexandria Women's Health Clinic* 113 S.Ct. 753 (1993) the court upheld that federal courts could not use the conspiracy section of the Ku Klux Klan Act, 42 U.S.C., Sec. 1983(3), to protect abortion clinics from illegal and often violent activities (Shatz, 1993). In the Bray litigation, a District Court had found that Operation Rescue's tactic of gathering around abortion clinics in attempts to disrupt activities and destroy property was similar to Klan attacks during Reconstruction. The Court therefore determined that Operation Rescue violated Sec. 1985(3) and state trespass and public-nuisance laws. A 5-4 ruling from the Supreme Court reversed that decision, because the Court interpreted that the Act did not apply to antiabortion protests (Shatz, 1993).

Although opponents of antiabortionists may vehemently argue against these analogies used by members of the rescue movement, they do have power in shaping world views. Perelman and Olbrechts-Tyteca (1969) note that in an analogy the substitution consists of the replacement of one structure by another that emphasizes characteristics regarded as more essential. The analogy's acceptance "is often equivalent to a judgment as to the importance of the characteristics that the analogy brings to the fore" (Perelman & Olbrechts-Tyteca, 1969, p. 390). For those who accept the comparison of killing the unborn to the practice of Nazism, or believe their actions are similar to those used in the civil rights movement, their worldview is dominated and shaped by this transference.

Rescue Movement Metaphors

Burke argues that there is an important relationship between metaphor and perspective. As an extended type of analogy, or comparison, metaphor involves "incongruity," or "the seeing of something in terms of something else," a "carrying-over" of terms from one often dissimilar realm to another (Burke, 1969a). By drawing relationships between objects that one might not normally connect, metaphors can serve to shift entire perspectives and, in turn, create new ways of seeing the world. Two dominant metaphors in antiabortion rhetoric—war and industry—each provide powerful rationales for why people should involve themselves in pro-life activities.

THE RHETORIC OF WAR

The rhetoric of war has long been a pervasive metaphor for American society. Whether it is the war against poverty, the war against drugs, or the war against the budget deficit, this metaphor serves to define groups and, in turn, enemies. The abortion controversy has been referred to as the Abortion War, the Cultural War, a Civil War, and of course, a Holy War. Martin Wishnatsky, a former Wall Street consultant and a current member of Lambs of Christ, claims he is involved in the antiabortion movement because it is a holy war against sin. In an interview with *Washington Post* reporter Sandra G. Boodman, Wishnatsky faults "unbridled lust" and the sexual immorality spawned by rock and roll music originating in the "fornication fifties" as reasons why America is on the decline (Boodman, 1993b).[16] Drawing from the Nazi analogy previously discussed, Wishnatsky equates abortion with the Holocaust and himself with members of the Resistance during World War II. "How many Jews were killed just for who they were?" he asks, "And how many babies have been killed for what they are?" (Boodman, 1993b, p. A18).

Randall Terry has used the term *cultural civil war* to suggest activities for Operation Rescue and remind people that in war there is only one victor (Saunders, 1993). Terry's reference to Green Berets in antiabortion training camps, and his talks about the "religious crusade" underscore the importance of the war metaphor in maintaining the group's identity. Terry's training manual for Operation Rescue members has clear instructions about their mission: "Warriors take orders and carry them out to the end. Warriors know if they don't defeat the enemy the enemy will defeat them. There is no stalemate, no middle ground. Warriors don't run into conflict; they run to it. Warriors are prepared to die" (Faux, 1990, p. 141). The metaphor of war justifies murder—in order to win a war, lives must be lost—as well as the necessity to carry on regardless of what happens to the "warriors" in the movement.

David Zarefsky's (1986) discussion of the rhetoric of war in relation to President Johnson's war on poverty is particularly instructive in understanding the potential power of this metaphor. Zarefsky identifies three important elements of the war metaphor: It defines the objective and encourages enlistment in the effort; it identifies the enemy against whom the campaign is directed; and it dictates the choice of weapons and tactics for fighting the struggle. These elements underscore the significance of the war metaphor for the antiabortionists, and offer two insights into the rhetorical extremism of the antiabortionists.

First, it is important to remember that most people involved in the rescue movement are fundamental, born-again Christians. They take as their dictum the Holy Bible and believe ultimately that Jesus Christ guides and supports their actions. The Bible is rife with references to the soldiers of Christ, to those who willingly sacrifice their lives for a Higher Being. To believe in God, however, also requires a belief in Satan, or the anti-Christ, who is set to destroy the world. Thus, actions taken against the evil enemy are authoritatively and morally grounded in the larger framework of their beliefs.

Second, by viewing this activity as a war certain actions are required to live up to the metaphor. Terrorist activities such as firebombs and attempts to takeover clinics are in line with the expectations that come with the naming of a war. One would not expect peaceful forms of demonstration to be part of the way to engage in warfare. The metaphor of war perpetuates images of hate and provides a powerful identifying means of mobilizing extreme words and actions.

THE METAPHOR OF THE MACHINE

Lakoff and Johnson (1980) explain the metaphor of the machine as it relates to the understandings of the human mind. "The Machine metaphor," they write, "gives us a conception of the mind as having an on-off state, a level of efficiency, a productive capacity, an internal mechanism, a source of energy, and an operating condition" (p. 156). Discussions of negative machine images and the alienation inherent in a technological society are useful for understanding antiabortion rhetoric. Writers such as Ellul, Mumford, and Roszak have offered severe criticism about technology and its impact on society and individuals. For example, Ellul (1964) argues that technological society, and "the machine" in particular, has created an inhuman atmosphere, evidenced by dehumanized factories and less connection with nature. "Life in such an environment," Ellul notes, "has no meaning" (pp. 4-5).

Given the estrangement often felt when one considers the dangers of a mechanistic, technological society, it is easy to see how persuasive the machine metaphor can be when connected to abortion clinics. Antiabortionists draw references to "abortion mills," "factories," and the "abortion industry." Efforts to squelch abortion clinic activities are often argued in terms of the business of abortion, the amount of money made by the abortionists, and the numbers of women seeking abortions who daily enter clinics. As antiabortionists claim, those who perform abortions are motivated by money and are absent any kind of feeling for unborn children. Thus, abortion clinics are viewed in a mechanistic manner, devoid of emotion and humanity.

This view of the abortion act and those clinics that offer this service transforms the perspective of health clinics as places where one is "healed" to places where one is "destroyed" and "alienated." To view an abortion clinic as a factory imbues it with the negative, alienating qualities of technology run amuck. Given the negative connotations that follow, it is easy to see how this metaphor would draw a powerful connection for antiabortionists.

The power of metaphors lies in their ability to create realities for those who use them. Lakoff and Johnson (1980) note that a metaphor may "be a guide for future action. Such actions will, of course, fit the metaphor. This will, in turn, reinforce the power of the metaphor to make experience coherent. In this sense metaphors can be self-fulfilling prophecies" (p. 156). Whether one considers the abortion controversy as a war that must be fought to the bitter end or identifies abortion clinics as part of an alienating, profit-motivated industry, it is easy to understand the formative power of the metaphors. Seeing the abortion clinics "in terms of" these metaphors defines the actions to be taken, and reinforces the power of such moral extremism.

Implications

This chapter has intentionally avoided entering into the abortion debate, choosing to focus instead on the hatred expressed by the extremist factions of the rescue movement toward those who practice abortion. Pro-life rhetoric is rife with appeals to hate the enemy, to save children from being murdered, to win the war at whatever cost. These appeals, grounded in powerful emotion, can be instructive in understanding social movements and in assessing the broader rhetorical manifestations of hate.

First, it is important to remember the difficulties in sustaining long-term commitment and identification with a social movement. In *A True Believer*, Hoffer (1951) argues that hatred is the most accessible and comprehensible of all unifying agents for a mass movement. As hatred unifies, however, it also can become the product of the unification:

> When we renounce the self and become part of a compact whole, we not only renounce personal advantage but are also rid of personal responsibility. There is no telling to what extremes of cruelty and ruthlessness a man will go when he is freed from the fears, hesitations, doubts and the vague stirrings of decency that go with individual judgment. When we lose our individual independence in the corporateness of a mass movement, we find a new freedom—freedom to hate, bully, lie, torture, murder and betray without shame or remorse. (Hoffer, 1951, p. 93)

Unifying efforts in the rescue movement are grounded in hate against the common enemy. This hatred, in turn, justifies extremist acts of terrorism and vigilantism because of the perceived nature of the greater cause.

As with many movements, the extremists are the ones who receive the most media attention and hence come to encapsulate the entire movement's perspective. Polarization naturally occurs between those who will stop at nothing to achieve success and those who wish to approach the controversy in a more moderate manner.

In the case of the abortion controversy, it is interesting to note that the blame for extremist activity is shifted to the present Administration. Both Scheidler and Terry argue that the political climate of pro-choice will serve to foster future extremist activities because the war must continue to be fought. Thus, it will not be the fault of the rescue movement organizations should more murders and terrorism occur, but rather the fault of a permissive society that allows abortions to continue.

This kind of extremist behavior also impacts the entire pro-life movement. The presence of an extreme element may increase the credibility of more moderate factions of the movement. In a discussion of the extremist environmental organization Earth First!, Jonathan Lange (1990) describes the impact that extremist "ecotage" has had on the environmental movement as a whole. The existence of Earth First!, he argues, has moved the "leftist" environmental movement closer to the middle, enhancing the ethos of more mainstream organizations. Similar movement has been seen in antiabortion organizations. Following the murder of David Gunn many pro-lifers denounced the terrorist activities that had come to symbolize much of the movement's efforts. Attendance at rallies staged during Operation Rescue's "Cities of Refuge" campaign in July 1993 attested to the fact that support for extremist rescue movement organizations was starting to dwindle (Saunders, 1993). One positive outcome, therefore, of the extremist activity and the decreased credibility of such extremism, may be a movement toward a more positive dialectical process, toward a more thoughtful exchange of ideas and a moderation of attitudes.

A second implication for understanding expressions of hate lies in the ability to objectify that which is hated. Hate speech has traditionally objectified people into labels and stereotypes. Typical examples of "name-calling" such as "gooks," "kikes," and even "yuppies," are efforts to strip away elements of the individual persona and focus on the underlying ideology one may be against. Thus, the focus turns to some thing (idea, philosophy, act) to hate, rather than the individual. Viktor Frankl (1978) explains that "hating something is more meaningful than hating someone (the creator, or 'owner' of what I hate), because if I do not hate him personally, I may help him to overcome what I hate in him. I may even love him, in spite of what I hate in him" (p. 70). In the case of antiabortionists, Operation Rescue and other groups succeeded in drawing together both personal and objectifying rhetoric. Cramer's comment above that she does not hate the doctor, but hates what he does is an example of focusing on the doctor as an instrument of death rather than the one who causes it. Doctors, in this sense, become instrumental, rather than personal. Such objectification may be a fundamental aspect of hate rhetoric, in as much as it is hard to hate individual people and much easier to vilify something inhuman.

There is, however, some tension in the contradiction between personalizing the individual while at the same time engaging in objectification. Wanted posters describing the details of doctors' lives, including addresses of parents, phone numbers, and so on, put faces on the abortion issue, by showing the "murderer" and entreating direct action against the physician. At the same time, however, the physicians are objectified as baby killers and murderers, as cogs in factories and mills of death. This tension, which should be further explored as an element of hate rhetoric, may reflect on special requirements of identification by antithesis: The object of hatred must be human enough to identify with, but inhuman enough to identify against.

A final implication worth noting is the integral relationship between the emotions of love and hate. Jane Goldberg (1993) argues that,

> Hate developed side by side with love because in order to have friends, you need to have enemies. . . . Although it may seem paradoxical, it is nevertheless true that if there is not enough hate, there is not enough love. If there is not enough hate, it must be conjured up in order to stimulate cooperation. (p. 50)

Hate, then, is a necessary component for bringing people together against the common enemy.

Much of the action of antiabortionists is predicated on the ideology of Christianity. In essence, the love of God sanctions hatred toward those who murder the innocent. Condit (1990) argues that the Christians who bombed the Pensacola abortion clinic operated from a "closed ideological discourse," concerned more with enforcing their beliefs rather than attempting to convince other that their beliefs were true. "That discursive closure, that rejection of persuasion as the fundamental mode of human influence," Condit notes, "was the crucial link in the move to violence" (p. 159).

Where much of the literature on the relationship of love and hate focuses on the close proximity of these powerful emotions toward the same object or person, in this instance there is a transference of the power of love for the unborn to hatred for the clinics and the doctors. This transference, Hoffer writes, may be among the most powerful forces guiding human action in the tragedy of life:

> When we see the bloodshed, terror and destruction born of such generous enthusiasms as the love of God, love of Christ, love of a nation, compassion for the oppressed and so on, we usually blame this shameful perversion on a cynical, power-hungry leadership. Actually, it is the unification set in motion by these enthusiasms, rather than the manipulations of a scheming leadership, that transmutes noble impulses into a reality of hatred and violence. (Hoffer, 1951, p. 94)

Notes

1. The term *pro-life* seems to be used interchangeably with the term *antiabortion* and will be treated as such in this chapter. Many people who protest against abortion clinics will define themselves as both "pro-life" and "antiabortion." As with the opposition term *pro-choice,* the proactive nature of the naming process suggests a more positive association to be made with being "pro" rather than "against." Although there are certainly people within the rescue movement preferring one term over another (as many who are in favor of abortion rights will argue the importance of being pro-choice), both terms will be used in the chapter.

2. From "Abortion Foes Strike at Doctors' Home Lives," by Sandra G. Boodman, *Washington Post,* April 8, 1993. Reprinted by permission.

3. From "Doctor Tells of Threats; Congressional Panel Hears From Dallas Obstetrician; and Representatives of Both Sides in Abortion Debate," by Susan Feeney. *Dallas Morning News,* April 1, 1993. Reprinted by permission.

4. From "Congress Hears Testimony Regarding Protests," by Bob Franken (April 1, 1993). © Cable News Network, Inc. All rights reserved. Reprinted by permission.

5. From "At Abortion Clinic, a Collision of Causes; Doctor, Accused Killer Both Impassioned," by William Booth. *Washington Post,* March 12, 1993. Reprinted by permission.

6. From "Crossing the Line: Distasteful, Even Dangerous, Speech Is Protected by the First Amendment, But Not Solicitation to Murder," by Karl Olson. [San Francisco] *Recorder,* March 23, 1993. Used by permission of *The Recorder*/American Lawyer Media and Karl Olson.

7. From "Doctor Killed Outside Abortion Clinic," by Sharyl Attkisson (March 10, 1993). © Cable News Network, Inc. All rights reserved. Reprinted by permission.

8. From "Turning From 'Weapon of the Spirit' to the Shotgun," by Kathy Sawyer. *Washington Post,* August 7, 1994. Reprinted by permission.

9. From "Jury Urges Death Sentence in Abortion Clinic Murders," by William Booth. *Washington Post,* November 4, 1994. Reprinted by permission.

10. From "My Father Was Murdered: Slain Physician's Son Accuses Abortion Foes of Terror Tactics," by Neil Orman. *Houston Chronicle,* April 2, 1993. Reprinted by permission.

11. From "Newest Strategy in a Passionate War: Harassment; Protestors Have Shifted From Blockading Clinics to Pestering Patients and Workers," by Lynne Bumpus-Hooper. *Orlando Sentinel Tribune,* March 14, 1993. Reprinted by permission.

12. *CBS This Morning interview with Kate Michelman and Randall Terry by Harry Smith,* Steve Ginsburg (Ed.). (1993, March 11). Reuters Transcript Report. Used by permission of Reuters and CBS News.

13. From "Storm Troopers of the Burning Red Line," by Simon Tisdall. *The Guardian,* April 3, 1993. Copyright held by *The Guardian* ©. Reprinted by permission.

14. From "House Gets Tough Against Abortion Clinic Violence," by David Lawsky. *The Reuter Library Report,* November 18, 1993. Reprinted by permission.

15. © Copyright National Public Radio ® 1993. The News report by NPR's Nina Totenberg was originally broadcast on National Public Radio's *Morning Edition* on December 8, 1993, and is used with the permission of National Public Radio. Any unauthorized duplication is strictly prohibited.

16. From "For Former Stockbroker, a Holy War Against Sin," by Sandra G. Boodman. *Washington Post,* April 8, 1993. Reprinted by permission.

References

Abortion clinic violence: Hearings before the Subcommittee on Civil and Constitutional Rights, of the House Committee on the Judiciary, 99th Cong., 1st and 2d Sess. (Serial 115) (1985) (testimony prepared by Joseph M. Scheidler).

Antiabortion activist is convicted, sentenced to life in killing at clinic. (1994, March 6). *Washington Post,* p. A22.

Antiabortion extremist indicted in attacks on clinics in West. (1994, October 25). *Washington Post,* p. A15.

Attkisson, S. (1993, March 10). Doctor killed outside abortion clinic. *CNN News* (Transcript #330-3). Atlanta: CNN.

Biskupic, J. (1994, January 25). Abortion clinics can use racketeer law on protests. *Washington Post,* pp. A1, A9.

Boodman, S. G. (1993a, April 8). Abortion foes strike at doctors' home lives. *Washington Post,* pp. A1, A17.

Boodman, S. G. (1993b, April 8). For former stockbroker, a holy war against sin. *Washington Post,* p. A18.

Booth, W. (1993, March 12). At abortion clinic, a collision of causes; Doctor, accused killer both impassioned. *Washington Post,* p. A1.

Booth, W. (1994, November 4). Jury urges death sentence in abortion clinic murders. *Washington Post,* p. A1.

Bowers, J. W., Ochs, D. J., & Jensen, R. J. (1993). *The rhetoric of agitation and control* (2nd ed.). Prospect Heights, IL: Waveland.

Bumpus-Hooper, L. (1993, March 14). Newest strategy in a passionate war: Harassment; Protestors have shifted from blockading clinics to pestering patients and workers. *Orlando Sentinel Tribune,* 3 Star Edition, p. A16.

Burke, K. (1965). Dramatism. In D. L. Sills (Ed.), *International encyclopedia of the social sciences* (Vol. 7, pp. 450-451). New York: Macmillan.

Burke, K. (1969a). *A grammar of motives.* Berkeley: University of California Press.

Burke, K. (1969b). *A rhetoric of motives.* Berkeley: University of California Press.

Chandler, K. (1993, April 18). Operation rescue boot camp. [Minneapolis] *Star Tribune,* p. 1A.

Cobb, K. (1993, March 28). How to grow a revolution. *Houston Chronicle,* p. 16.

Condit, C. M. (1990). *Decoding abortion rhetoric: Communicating social change.* Chicago: University of Illinois Press.

Dermody, C., & Clark, J. (1993, November). *Feminist majority 1993 clinic violence survey* [Press release]. Feminist Majority Foundation, Washington, DC.

Ellul, J. (1964). *The technological society* (J. Wilkinson, Trans.). New York: Vantage.

Faux, M. (1990). *Crusaders: Voices from the abortion front.* New York: Carol Publishing Group.

Feeney, S. (1993, April 2). Doctor tells of threats; Congressional panel hears from Dallas obstetrician; and Representatives of both sides in abortion debate. *Dallas Morning News,* p. 27A.

Franken, B. (1993, April 1). Congress hears testimony regarding protests. *CNN News* (Transcript #352-3). Atlanta, GA: CNN.

Frankl, V. (1978). *The unheard cry for meaning.* New York: Simon & Schuster.

Ginsburg, S. (Ed.). (1993, March 11). *CBS This Morning interview with Kate Michelman and Randall Terry by Harry Smith.* Reuters Transcript Report.

Goldberg, J. G. (1993). *The dark side of love: The positive role of our negative feelings—anger, jealousy, and hate.* New York: G. P. Putnam.

Health care: Abortion—Federal relief from campaign to close clinics. (1993, December 14). *The United States Law Week, 62,* U.S.L.W. 3403.

Hill guilty in clinic access case. (1994, October 6). *Washington Post,* p. A3.

Hoffer, E. (1951). *The true believer.* New York: Harper & Row.

Lake, R. (1982). *The ethics of rhetoric and the rhetoric of ethics in the abortion controversy.* Doctoral dissertation, University of Kansas.

Lake, R. (1984, November). Order and disorder in anti-abortion rhetoric: A logological view. *The Quarterly Journal of Speech, 70,* 425-443.

Lakoff, G., & Johnson, M. (1980). *Metaphors we live by.* Chicago: University of Chicago Press.

Lange, J. I. (1990, Fall). Refusal to compromise: The case of Earth First! *Western Journal of Speech Communication, 54,* 473-494.

Laurence, C. (1993, March 19). Florida doctor's killing marks new phase in the abortion wars. *Daily Telegraph,* p. 12.

Lawsky, D. (1993, November 18). House gets tough against abortion clinic violence. *The Reuter Library Report.*

Olson, K. (1993, March). Crossing the line: Distasteful, even dangerous, speech is protected by the First Amendment, but not solicitation to murder. [San Francisco] *Recorder,* p. 9.

Operation Rescue: What to make of cities of refuge. (1993, July 20). *The Abortion Report* [newsletter].

Oregon I: Shannon a suspect in Ashville clinic bombing. (1993, December 9). *The Abortion Report* [newsletter].

Orman, N. (1993, April 2). My father was murdered: Slain physician's son accuses abortion foes of terror tactics. *Houston Chronicle,* p. A1.

Panetta, E. M. (1993). The constitution of a pro-life public through non-violent civil disobedience: Operation Rescue marches on Atlanta. *Argument and the postmodern challenge: Proceedings of the Eighth SCA/AFA Conference on Argumentation* (pp. 358-363). Annandale, VA: Speech Communication Association.

Perelman, C., & Olbrechts-Tyteca, L. (1969). *The new rhetoric: A treatise on argumentation* (J. Wilkinson & P. Weaver, Trans.). Notre Dame, IN: University of Notre Dame Press.

Railsback, C. C. (1984, November). The contemporary American abortion controversy: Stages in the argument. *The Quarterly Journal of Speech, 70,* 410-424.

Saunders, D. J. (1993, July 19). Cultural war is hell. *San Francisco Chronicle,* p. A20.

Sawyer, K. (1994, August 7). Turning from "weapon of the spirit" to the shotgun. *Washington Post,* pp. A1, A8-A9.

Scheidler, J. M. (1985). *Closed: 99 ways to stop abortion.* Lake Bluff, IL: Regnery Books.

Shatz, S. F. (1993, March 29). Limiting the law. [San Francisco] *Recorder,* p. 10.

Sherman, M. (1988, July 30). Pro-lifers target city. *Atlanta Journal and Constitution,* p. A1.

Terry, R. (1992, November 4). *Letter to supporters.*

Tisdall, S. (1993, April 3). Storm troopers of the burning red line. *Guardian,* p. 23.

Totenberg, N. (Reporter). (1993, December 8). Anti-choice protestors could be made liable for damages. *Morning edition* (Transcript #1233-10). Washington, DC: National Public Radio.

Vanderford, M. L. (1989, May). Vilification and social movements: A case study of pro-life and pro-choice rhetoric. *The Quarterly Journal of Speech, 75,* 166-182.

Zarefsky, D. (1986). *President Johnson's war on poverty.* University: University of Alabama Press.

Holy Wars and Vile Bodies

The Politics of an American Iconography

David Slayden
Southern Methodist University

Editor's Introduction

In the past decade, the NEA has received critical attention from conservative spokespeople who have found in it a means to focus concerns over values and mount resistance in a rapidly changing society. The liberal response to such scrutiny further engaged the Right in a stringent exchange, which became increasing vitriolic and perhaps culminated with the media attention given to two NEA-supported artists: Robert Mapplethorpe and Andres Serrano.

In this chapter, David Slayden examines the issues and problems that have arisen surrounding the Right's attack on and the liberal defense of federally funded art. By looking at an episode of CNN's *Crossfire*—in which Pat Robertson, Christopher Reeve, Pat Buchanan, and Mike Kinsley discuss the NEA controversy— Slayden analyzes the politics implicit in the attempt to legislate values and mandate taste. Linking the problems of maintaining identity in a time of change to issues of community, Slayden calls into question not simply the concept of accurate representation, but also whether representation is finally possible.

===================

Call it *fin de siècle* angst or a typically postmodern event, but on July 16, 1990, Christopher Reeve, the Reverend Pat Robertson, Patrick Buchanan, and Mike Kinsley were gathered together on CNN's *Crossfire* to talk about art. Beyond the question of what, in the name of art, could assemble on a Monday night in midsummer this unlikely collection—an actor, a televangelist and sometime political candidate, a nationally syndicated columnist/television commentator/future presidential candidate, and yet another television commentator—arises the additional question of why this particular grouping of discussants? For if the question asked in the teasing title to the program, "The NEA: Art or Outrage?," had any hope of being credibly addressed (much less answered), might a viewer not expect to see at least one fine artist, one official from the NEA, and perhaps one art critic? Instead this mixing of speakers, speaking for others not present. The rationale for the program's timing was the impending vote of the House of Representatives on whether to restrict or possibly to abolish the National Endowment for the Arts. (This vote was delayed, in fact, until October in order to consider 26 amendments to the bill proposed by Congress [Bolton, 1992, p. 358]). But the selection of speakers on *Crossfire* typifies recent mass media discussions of art, representation, and the NEA: Since the early 1980s contemporary art has been increasingly appropriated by spokespeople from outside of the arts community as a problematic subject. Questions of representation have had less to do with establishing aesthetic standards than community standards, focusing instead on how art should be constituted in the public realm.

And discussions reaching the broad audiences of television and newspaper have repeatedly turned to the relationship between politics and art, with such considerations ostensibly motivated by a defense of the public interest. Underlying the question of the role of art in the political processes of a free society, however, has been the additional and even thornier question of who decides what is and isn't art.

Any account of the relation of avant-garde art to the public would be curious enough—perhaps a series of shocks and adjustments, condemnations and reassessments—but a chronicle of the exchange on NEA funding for controversial artwork reads like a lexicon of scatology, bestiality, and profligacy compiled to incite fear, make blame, and administer punishment. And this vocabulary, with its richly evocative imagery of the vile bodies of contemporary art, is employed primarily by conservative spokespeople and leaders from the Religious Right—those we might more typically associate with the purification of the spirit. Of course, a basic step on the road to salvation is to cleanse the gross body; so, the language of expulsion permeates conservative attacks on the NEA, attacks that only tangentially consider aesthetic issues to call repeated and concentrated attention to the political role of art. In doing so, the Right indulges prolifically in hate speech—defined for our purposes here as a speech act that is deliberately monologic, using tactics of negation and reduction to deny the validity of the opposition's voice; indeed, hate speech is devoted, finally, to removing oppositional voices through an eradication of reasoned discourse by invective. But to what end is hate speech directed in the Right's crusade against the NEA? And why this political battle in the symbolic realm of art?

The Right's use of hate speech to organize opposition to the NEA moves beyond any possible critical ire over a reinterpretation of art or the means of artistic production to condemn the artists and the groups or subcultures of which, in the conservative argument against contemporary art, they become representative. These groups or subcultures are configured by the Right as threatening "others," typically as vile bodies dangerous to the health of American culture. In this schema, art that gives voice to and carries the values of such subcultures does not simply call into question comfortable assumptions about the identity of the American public and its culture but threatens to destroy it. In its opposition to contemporary art's unacceptable

subjects or its violation of religious icons, expressions of hate dominate the Right's declamatory utterances, which often possess the tenor
of a holy war. And as in war, holy or otherwise, the enemy is both
personalized and objectified—objectified, because "they" are the
"other," the broad category of being not like "us." This tactic dehu-
manizes the opposition, removing them from any common ground
where exchange might take place and erode objectification. But the
enemy is also personalized as a local threat: Their very existence
endangers the basic values that inform and order the lives of the
American people. Questions of art and taste move from an exclusive
space to the realm of the everyday. In this manner, artistic production
not only expresses difference but also implicitly challenges the broad
category of American values that are synonymous with the values of
the traditional American family—a construct repeatedly naturalized
in the rhetoric of the Right.

This chapter examines the NEA controversy and argues that understanding the funding debate in terms of hate speech provides an
instructive example of the uses of populist rhetoric's appropriation of
elite discourse. The Right's scrutiny of art (and artists) and subsequent
reinterpretation of it (and them) as an attack on fundamental American values in fact works to deny free expression and the articulation
of difference—two values that would seem to be quintessentially
American. But in mounting a counterattack, the arts community is no
less opportunistic in its invocation of American values and similarly
reconstitutes the public realm and the iconography of America. Regardless of one's disposition and sympathies—aesthetic or political—
an analysis of the tactics of both sides suggests that their arguments
and actions are motivated less by a desire to protect public interest
than an attempt to redefine the public realm in order to gain and
expand power.

Private Art and Public Taste

Of the numerous titles I have considered in the writing of this piece,
the most recent to be discarded in favor of the one you see above was
"What We Talk About When We Talk About Art." Readers of
Raymond Carver will recognize this as a reference to a volume of his

collected stories, *What We Talk About When We Talk About Love* (1981). I first considered the title because art, like love, has some general definition on which most people can agree and yet in practice it can and often does differ greatly. And there lies the rub, for this gap between idea and actuality allows Carver functional ironic distance in the title story of his collection and in a number of other stories in the volume, a sort of cataloguing of the varieties of romantic experience. So with art as with love—ambiguous, at once private and public— considerable room for interpretation exists; and in the psychic area between individual expression and communal acceptance can arise an unsettling variety of responses: misunderstanding, confusion, affirmation, confrontation, and so on, all of which demand some sort of mediation between public and private realms. The comparison is further useful in pointing up the difficulties in such mediation, for once art becomes a political matter, legislating its practices almost immediately snags on questions of definition. But beyond a tacit agreement that the defining of art (as with love) is difficult, arises the question of why define it at all? What and whose purposes are served? Once defined, what sort of art can we expect to follow? As with arranged marriages, defining art and its place becomes manageable only after the object of definition and its two essential, involved parties—the artist and the artist's public—have been thoroughly re-ified. Although this arrangement may be satisfying for politicians with constituencies to placate, it is arguable that such maneuvering has anything much to do with artists or their publics.

Of course, when the federally funded NEA underwrites the production of art the government is involved; the public once removed is also involved because taxpayers' dollars support the NEA. In such a context, the relation of art to politics—linked like disharmonious Siamese twins—becomes a matter for public debate. The question framed as the title of the July 16th *Crossfire* offers us only two choices: art or outrage. If *binary opposition* has been an overworked phrase in recent critical language, perhaps this is because it has been so applicable to the subjects of public debate. Certainly in the numerous commentaries provoked by the tribulations of the NEA, two sides have typically been identified to depict what has been happening. These two sides are represented, regardless of whose version is received, as incompatible. The terms of the disagreement are absolute. The assumption of those defending the arts community is that the Right wants to abolish freedom of expression. The Right counters this charge—clearly unconstitutional even in the mind of the most ill-informed citizen—by asking why American tax dollars should be used to fund art that is obscene? Or as Pat Robertson puts it in a newspaper ad sponsored by his Christian Coalition and directed to Congress,

> You may find that the working folks in your district want you to use their money to teach their sons how to sodomize one another. You may find that the Roman Catholics in your district want their money spent on pictures of the Pope soaked in urine. But maybe not. (Bolton, 1992, p. 316)

The extrapolations used by both sides to gather support and polarize opposition are totalizing and tend toward the apocalyptic: "last stand" tactics to mobilize forces by touching on some cherished idea about being an American that amalgamates personal freedom and protecting one's beliefs, home, children—one's whole way of life—against the enemy. But what if we pull back both sides' operative stories from the apocalyptic/absolute conclusions and look at them as tactical maneuvers in an overall strategy? The Right wants to restrict where and how marginal topics are expressed. (The labeling of topics as marginal or mainstream is an essential yet naturalized tactic in this operation.) The Left wants to bring marginal subjects to equal ground with those now occupying the center. What is actually at stake is not a matter of abolishing but of codifying, of deciding where what is said to whom and how. It then becomes a matter of privileging certain types of representations over others. If this authorization of one subject as the proper subject of art and the exclusion of others is the case, we can then see how and why the NEA comes into play. (For that matter, we can then understand the Right's interest in cultural institutions and their activities—universities, museums, dramatic workshops, and other sites of federally subsidized productions—that qualify as ideological state apparatuses.) Once addressed in this manner, beyond the responses organized by questions of individual freedom or civic responsibility, is it not obviously the institutional nature of the operation that has both the Right and the Left concerned? Viewed as a battle for institutions and authorization, the Right's objective might be seen as a reinscribing or reconfiguring of artistic production in a conservatively acceptable outlet if not form, a recognition that though artistic content cannot necessarily be determined or restricted, audiences can. (Read *audiences* also as *publics* or *markets* to understand the impact of this tactic.) The arts community's actions are then seen as counter-insurgent attempts to hold ground gradually, arduously taken. And, if this is accurate, expression is not repressed per se, but the public—the sites where the public might see or hear the work—is repressed, thus the Right's attack on the institutions of delivery by attacking what they deliver.

That the Right's attack is made in the name of the public as an operation to protect the public's rights may be one of the instrumental ironies of the whole affair. In taking the tack of protecting the public, the Right is in fact excluding the public—and it is uncertain who, actually, that public may be—admitting its range of available choices. Repression is enacted in the name of protection, ideology in the guise of natural law.

How else to explain *Crossfire?* The July 16th program is remarkable if for no other reason than to contemplate its crossover possibilities. Consider for a moment, beyond the incongruous cast of characters, that the topic of discussion is subsidies for the production of fine art and the degree to which congressional watchdogs should intervene. Kinsley offers a provocative recitation of the controversy's outlines: the NEA has awarded grants to artists whose work is regarded by some as obscene. Not one to miss a broad stroke in a medium that thrives on broad strokes, Kinsley concludes his summary of Robertson's attack on the NEA by asking: "A voice of sanity or cultural Kryptonite?" Cut to Buchanan who directs his first question—the "How often do you beat your wife" variety—to Christopher Reeve. "Christopher Reeve, let me ask—let's take the picture of that—the Pope that is dipped in urine. Why should Roman Catholics be required to subsidize this kind of assault on their fundamental beliefs?" (Bolton, 1992, p. 245).[1] And on with the show.

Credit Reeve with recognizing when he is on the defensive. He responds that he hasn't seen that particular picture and frames his answer with a recitation of a this-is-the-price-one-has-to-pay-for-living-in-a-free-society argument. The NEA, he says patiently, has, after all, "given out 85,000 grants over twenty-five years and had maybe twenty controversies. This whole thing," he adds, "is very blown out of proportion" (Bolton, 1992, p. 245).

Buchanan returns to descriptions of Andres Serrano's works—the crucifix in urine and the picture of the Pope in urine—and asks, given the offensive nature of these works, why the NEA can't simply admit that they made a mistake, apologize, and promise to be more vigilant in the future? It's the suggestion about the future and vigilance that Reeve objects to; in his objection he offers a justification of the artistic process and artistic freedom. But Buchanan responds with the nut of the argument, by this time conventionalized by conservatives in their attack on the NEA: "All right. Christopher Reeve, let's—we would all support an artist's First Amendment right to be free to produce or replicate the thought we hate. The question comes, why is he using my tax dollars? We can't use his tax dollars for my thoughts he doesn't like, and for my expression he doesn't like." Reeve agrees. Buchanan continues: "Why should the tax dollars of the American people be used to fund this character?" (Bolton, 1992, p. 246).

So the NEA is reduced, at this point in the program, to one artist —Andres Serrano—who, through its support, created work offensive to all Americans—a reduction to which Reeve remarkably agrees. The appeal to fundamental American values continues when Robertson joins the discussion and buttresses his viewpoint with that of Thomas Jefferson's that "to compel a man to provide contributions of money to propagate concepts of which he disagreed is sinful and tyrannical" (Bolton, 1992, p. 246). Certainly it's difficult to disagree with Jefferson, but was he really talking about art and politics? And we're back to the economic argument, to the misuse of taxpayers' money. Robertson now refers to the work of artist number two—Robert Mapplethorpe—and the homoerotic photographs included in "Robert Mapplethorpe: The Perfect Moment," a retrospective assembled by the University of Pennsylvania's Institute for Contemporary Art: "People out there don't want to pay more taxes to show two men engaged in anal intercourse. For instance, they just don't want to do that. And it's my money and I don't want it going for that" (Bolton, 1992, p. 247). Robertson's monologue then takes an odd turn, one of those fundamental shifts in logic when religious and economic belief collide. Kinsley is jolted but Robertson seems unaware of the larger implications of what he is saying.

Robertson: Now, if we've got surpluses in the federal till, we've got plenty of money, no raised taxes, well, of course—

Kinsley: Wait a minute. If there were surpluses in the federal till, then it's okay to fund two men going at it—

Robertson: That's right. As soon as you get—Michael, as soon as you get surpluses where you don't have to raise my taxes, then by all means, let's have a little surplus for art. My companies are spending—

Kinsley: So, in other words, as long as there's a federal deficit, you're against any—even a single penny for art, offensive or otherwise? Is that your position? I mean, you're purposely ambiguous about that.

Robertson: No, my position is not that way. I'm just telling you. If you read Naisbitt's book, *Megatrends,* he tells that more people go to art galleries, museums and plays and spend more money than they do on all the professional sports in America. We funded the private sector six and a half billion dollars. My companies are producing in co-production over $100 million worth of motion pictures this year. And—

Kinsley: Pat, are you or are you not for government funding of the arts?

Reeve: May I interject something, please?

Kinsley: It's a very simple question. Leaving aside—

Reeve: May I interject something?

Kinsley: —the things that offend you, yes or no?

Reeve: May I—

Robertson: I do not think the federal government can afford it right now. I think we're wasting money. And I think with six and a half billion dollars being spent on art in America, the $175 million of the NEA grants amounts to 2.6 percent. We can do without it. But if the guys—I will not oppose it, Michael. I will not oppose it if Congress will put adequate safeguards so they won't be used to attack my religion. I don't think that's—

Reeve: May I please—

Robertson: —too unfair. (Bolton, 1992, p. 247)

Reeve does eventually interject and, when he does so it is to defend the $175 million NEA budget against the amount of money the government spends annually on military bands—it is roughly the same—and to suggest that if Robertson thinks that the arts aren't as important as military bands then he and Robertson are, perhaps, "light worlds apart." Perhaps. But from here Reeve quickly turns to the matter of obscenity, community standards, and who decides what is and what isn't art. It is an attempt to defend the NEA's peer panel review system and keep art funding decisions out of the hands of politicians. Robertson immediately devolves the discussion, asking Reeve, "Is it art to have one man urinating into the mouth of another? Is that creative art? It was one of the things we paid for, do you agree with that?" (Bolton, 1992, p. 248).

Reeve concedes that he probably doesn't agree with calling this particular work art—a photograph from Mapplethorpe's X Portfolio —but counters Robertson's charge of sex with one of violence, arguing that, as a taxpayer, he also paid for the Stealth bomber, which he thinks obscene. And then he concedes further by assenting that it is a problem to subsidize work from which children need to be protected but—and this is the ending of a story told repeatedly by the arts community—"the problem is you . . . are going to end up with a country which is second-rate culturally if you go ahead with this chilling deadening of the whole artistic life of the country" (Bolton, 1992, p. 248). He continues with a justification of art that defines its role socially, as a means of keeping a society healthy. "Art has got to be on the edge of society. It's at the cutting edge. Artists have got to be the leaders and, if I may finish, they bring up points which often are uncomfortable to us" (Bolton, 1992, p. 248). He cites the case of Karen Finley, whose grant was pulled in the wake of conservative scrutiny of the NEA. But Buchanan interrupts him to announce that the show will break for a commercial and then return to take up the question of Karen Finley, "the young lady, semi-nude, who smeared herself in chocolate as a form of moral statement against what she called sexism" (Bolton, 1992, p. 248).

Reeve's argument is sincere yet hardly convincing; he repeatedly pursues a return-on-investment sort of justification of art: A few objectionable works are a small price to pay for 25 years of symphony orchestras, ballets, and plays such as *Driving Miss Daisy*. By conceding this much, by agreeing at all, Reeve does what so many spokespeople for the arts against conservative attacks on the NEA have repeatedly done: He allows the Right to define the terms of the argument, terms that are specious at best—a speciousness that is evident when Buchanan asks him what "Clark Kent" would have said about Karen Finley who—and Buchanan repeats himself just in case those people "out there," have joined the program following the commercial break—"smears chocolate on herself, she's half nude and it's a form of artistic protest, as she calls it, a social statement against sexism and all the rest" (Bolton, 1992, p. 249). Buchanan dredges up Clark Kent like an indictment in light of Reeve's current role as defender of NEA outrages. How could you? Wasn't this controversy, after all, really about what the Clark Kents of this country—beyond being a mild-mannered reporter Clark is also a public citizen—would have said about funding semi-nude women making social statements? Before Reeve—AKA Clark Kent AKA Superman—can answer, Buchanan answers in his place: "Now, these are political views. . . . Why in heaven's name, should we be required to subsidize Karen Finley's political statement?" (Bolton, 1992, p. 249).

Is anyone liminally aware, in Buchanan's framing of the question, of the odd juxtapositions taking place here? Of the substitutions? The role playing? The impersonations? Beyond the delivery of Buchanan's derisive reductions and summary judgments is it possible to recognize the symbolic weight of the role he assumes as an *exposeur* of artists who speak "against sexism and all the rest?" Studying the program transcripts, Buchanan's appropriation of Reeve's most popular role seems obvious now: This real-life reporter who, in Superman-like fashion, transcends the limitations of the law to protect the public like a good vigilante, fighting for truth, justice, and the American way. Why not, in a television show where the other representatives are speaking for art's interests and God's interests, why not citizen Buchanan speaking for the public's interest?

That there may be more than one public and that Buchanan is in the same relation to his public as Finley, Serrano, or Mapplethorpe are to theirs is a comparison that may escape him, but it is a comparison in the context of *Crossfire* that begs to be made. In the NEA controversy there resides the possibility that neither side, after all, has the interest or attention of a numerically significant demographic: the mainstream American public. And if neither side does, the mainstream American public is no other than a rhetorical device, a tool in a system of discourse for defining social and political relationships. This acknowledged, we come possibly to the point of view taken by Michel Foucault and elaborated by Gilles Deleuze and other theorists, that speaking for others is itself a form of repression (Ferguson, Olander, Tucker, & Fiss, 1992, p. 10). We can agree, at least, with Madan Sarup's suggestion that "discourses are perhaps best understood as practices that systematically form the objects of which they speak" (Sarap, 1989, p. 70).

Buchanan characterizes the NEA as the "spotted owl" of American politics and suggests that the NEA is in its position through an act of denial, a refusal to apologize for the outrageous work it has supported. If the arts community would simply apologize, he tells Reeve, "you would not be in the kind of problem you are now which is defending this [objectionable art] and even demanding funding for it from a public which is really fed up with it" (Bolton, 1992, p. 249). But the question of the apology raises another question, possibly *the* question of the controversy. Among those who claim to be speaking for others who exactly are the others for whom they are speaking? Who has the numbers? Reeve responds to Buchanan, by raising the question, more or less, of why should artists apologize to a tyrannical minority point of view? When Buchanan objects and replies that Robertson is speaking for a majority point of view—"about 99 or 96 or 97 percent majority"—Reeve responds with statistics from a recent poll, taken by Forecast, Incorporated, that "93 percent of the people say that even when they find a particular piece of art offensive, quote, 'others have the right to view it' " (Bolton, 1992, p. 249). When Buchanan interrupts, asking if we—citizens, taxpayers, the public—have an obligation to subsidize such works, Reeve continues, adding that the poll,

also found that the public sides with the National Endowment for the Arts in the current controversy. According to the survey, when asked to choose between the sides favoring and opposing NEA funding cuts and content restrictions, 61 percent chose the pro-NEA side opposing cuts in restrictions. Only 13 percent favored cuts in restrictions. (Bolton, 1992, p. 250)

The representative sampling techniques of national polls not with-
standing, it is difficult to know who to believe or on what a belief can
be based. It becomes less a matter of whom to believe than perhaps,
finally, an admission that the public as both Reeve and Buchanan
conceive it is unknowable, devolving into an unknowable mass, a black
hole in a Baudrillardean universe into which information and opinion
may fall but from which nothing issues. "The mass is without attribute,
predicate, quality, reference. This is its definition, or its radical lack
of definition. It has no sociological reality" (Baudrillard, 1983, p. 5).
If Baudrillard is right, *the* public becomes simply a rhetorical projec-
tion, a noun signifying a concept to give credibility to an agenda. If
he is right, the public is credible, finally, only as an adjective.

Return for a moment to Foucault, Deleuze, and the question of
representation and repression. If the battle to save the public is a
symbolic one—questioning what is and what isn't art, what representations can and can't be federally funded—perhaps the public
ostensibly being saved is also symbolic, an object formed systematically through speaking of it. Once recognized as a discursive element
within a totalizing conservative strategy, the NEA controversy becomes not about censorship so much as about containment, not about
abolition so much as quarantine, repressing rather than eradicating.
It is not an attack on art per se but an attack on official recognition of
a certain type of art and the need and desire to unauthorize it. Such
representations as Serrano's or Mapplethorpe's, like categories of
behavior, can be acknowledged to exist but must be removed from the
realm of the accepted, the normal. Labeling such work as unacceptable, aberrant, abnormal leads to the withdrawal of NEA funding and
the official imprimatur of the government. Like pornography, prosti-
tution, and other vendors of illicit pleasures, it must have a largely
invisible or contained existence in the marketplace.

In a tone of compromise, speakers from the Right repeatedly uttered
the seemingly reasonable concession that this type of thing could be
allowed if it were privately funded and privately shown—in other words,
excluded from all forms of public life. In this action is an acknowledgment that although such representations cannot be prevented—
this would dangerously attack the fundamental American rights of the
individual—they should be cast as misrepresentations. The Right's

repeated use of military and disease metaphors to describe Serrano and Mapplethorpe and their work configures their art as an enemy to be met at the borders, indeed that borders must be erected to keep out the invaders—and this term works for both physical force and diseases, the language of medicine and war having in our daily usage become so intermingled (Sontag, 1989). By negating such work as not art and then labeling it perverse, the Right invokes a whole realm of ideas, operations and procedures—military and medical—that mobilize to exclude, perceptually and physically such productions from legitimate consideration. The Right's name-calling and reductive descriptions are tactical maneuvers in an overall strategy to invalidate the work, to reduce it from the privileged realm of consideration as art to the outlaw domain of pornography. Serrano's work is merely pissing on a crucifix. Mapplethorpe's work is abusive and obscene. Karen Finley is some half-naked woman who smears herself with chocolate. These summary descriptions function primarily to encourage audiences to rule out that the works under fire might have value as well as a public judgment—a judgment that would be reinforced by the withdrawal of NEA funding. The stance is humble yet effective in the broad strokes of the mass media. Perhaps such works cannot be kept from being made, but they can be kept on the periphery, contained like enemies from a hostile land or a virus carried on an ill wind. Hence, the border patrol language mentality of Helms, Buchanan, Wildmon. . . .

Negation and Definition

In a reading that he has delivered often to, as he says, "many receptive university audiences," William S. Burroughs (1987) preaches the gospel of M.O.B—"My Own Business"—in which he draws a line between the Johnsons and the Shits. "This planet," he tells us, "could be a reasonably pleasant place to live, if everybody could just mind his own business and let others do the same. But a wise old black faggot said to me years ago: 'Some people are shits, darling.' " According to Burroughs, the "mark of a hard-core shit is that he has to be RIGHT. He is incapable of minding his own business, because he has no business of his own to mind. He is a professional minder of other people's business." A Johnson, however,

> minds his own business. He doesn't rush to the law if he smells pot or opium in the hall. Doesn't care about the call girl on the second floor, or the fags in the back room. But he will give help when help is needed. He won't stand by when someone is drowning or under physical attack, or when animals are being abused. He figures things like that are everybody's business.

Burroughs' simple delineation of the world into two sides is as flawed in logic as the Religious Right's, but what is worth remarking on here is the affective difference: Burroughs is preaching tolerance; the Right is preaching intolerance. If both sides imagine a simpler America of shared values, Burroughs' side conceives of it as a place of free expression and nonintervention into private life of, as he says, minding one's business. The distinction between the Johnsons and the Shits reinforces what he sees as a fundamental practice of the other side—conservative politics in the 1980s—and their agenda characterized by "Ronnie and Nancy, hand in hand, to tell us nobody has the right to mind his own business."

Himself a celebrated junkie, Burroughs is referencing primarily the war on drugs and the directive of its theme line to the average citizen to "just say no," a line that, coupled with the metaphorical "war" on drugs, evokes a "home front" mentality and draws heavily on a nostalgia for an America past, a unified America where we could all agree on some one thing, such as values. This sort of populism sounds simple and wholesome enough but just saying no is organized around a negation and it functions through exclusion and assigning blame—a process reminiscent of the politics of race in the Third Reich.

The repeated invocation and appropriation of populism remains one of the more remarkable symbolic victories of Reagan-Bush era politics; that the symbolic victory translated into votes was the result of a mapping of an imagined America of which conservatives proclaimed themselves the protectors. It is an America whose mythic space, as the historian Richard Slotkin (1993) has called it, is informed by nostalgia for the frontier, its virtues, and possibilities. But it is inevitably also utopian. When Reagan's advertising team captured the spirit of his candidacy with the tag line "It's morning in America again," they evoked that imagined place; we had returned to the mythic garden and it myriad possibilities. The problem with this place, as Slotkin (1993) tells us in his identification and discussion of the crisis of public myth, is that "myth is the language in which a society remembers its history, and the reification of nostalgia in the mass culture and politics of the 1980s is a falsification of memory" (p. 660). Of course, much of the politics of the campaigns of 1980 and again of 1984 focused on economics, so why the attack on the NEA? Why the Right's interest in defining the country's culture? Buchanan, for example, offers his own version of recent history: "While the right has been busy winning primaries and elections, cutting taxes and funding anti-communist guerrillas abroad, the left has been quietly seizing all the commanding heights of American art and culture" (Bolton, 1992, p. 32). To corroborate his narrative, Buchanan then cites a review of a recent exhibit at the New York Museum of Modern Art, which identifies a new site for the battle against communism: "Political leaders in Washington believe that the battle against communism is being fought in the jungles of Asia and Central America, while failing to realize the war is raging on the battlefield of the arts within our own borders." So Buchanan asks, expectantly, predictably, "What is to be done?" And he quotes further,

> Conservatives and the religious community that comprise the vast middle-American population should actively support those artists that advocate the same values and ideas as they do. They should also choose to withdraw support and funding from the modernist culture they profess to despise. In short, they should do what the liberals did long ago— "capture the culture." (Bolton, 1992, p. 33)

But why the mixing of culture and politics? Why the consumer-activist approach to art? Buchanan concludes,

> A nation absorbs its values through its art. A corrupt culture will produce a corrupt people, and vice versa; between rotten art, films, plays, and books—and rotten behavior—the correlation is absolute. The hour is late; America needs a cultural revolution in the '90s as sweeping as its political revolution in the '80s. (Bolton, 1992, p. 33)

The Politics of Values

If the NEA controversy is simply a question of values, there is an aesthetics of a sort that is put into operation, although not exactly a contemplation of the beautiful or a consideration of perceptual categories. But in the Right's practice of distinguishing an acceptable center from an unacceptable periphery, certain aesthetic judgments are evoked to constitute a definition of art that combines economic verities with a moral populism. In this operation there is repeatedly a negation, an anti-aesthetic never dreamed of by the Dadaists, guided by a knowing what art isn't rather than what it is. And this anti-aesthetic and the values it expresses through an act of refusal—such expression being offered on behalf of the populous largely by politicians and those in the political arena—are positioned somehow as being both above politics and free from the relativism of a corrupting modernism. In short, real art is universal because it is moral. By a tautology that masquerades as an argument, real art is moral because it is universal. Good versus evil, center versus periphery, permissible versus forbidden, and the Shits, finally, versus the Johnsons. We speak for the people who speak the truth, all others lie. Even though we may not be authorities on art (sorrily, the NEA was supposed to do that) we are authorities on matters such as decency, and the values the public wants and needs.

This attempt to authenticate certain values and the ideas that support them is disturbing but certainly not without precedent. In his examination of sex as a subject of scientific discourse, Foucault questions the authority invoked by science to authenticate its views, to objectify its judgments of what was and was not normal. His aim is to expose the operational assumptions of scientific discourse, its naturalizing of its own method to validate what it had to say. He writes: "In the name of a biological and historical urgency, it [science and its objectivity] justified the racisms of the state, which at the time were on the horizon. It grounded them in the truth" (Foucault, 1990, p. 54). Substitute *homophobia* for *racism* here and the passage applies to recent activities of the Right, certainly the Religious Right. And the state, depending on one's point of view, corresponds to the state as conceived by the Religious Right or now, simply, the actual state.

Declaring that there is a war for America's culture justifies extreme actions. In the conservative myth of what constitutes America—and there is only one America—culture is spatialized, like so much territory to be held or lost in battle. This battle is not yet lost, but it is in danger of being lost. If it is lost, all will be lost: to the communists "within our borders." We don't even realize such a battle is being fought because we have failed to recognize the locale—the battlefield of the arts. And what's more, that it is occurring right here within our borders is even further cause for alarm because the enemy has infiltrated. The scenario for erosion or attack from within is a familiar one and anyone with even a nodding sense of history will find it quite easy to cite examples, from political polemic to popular culture. Pick a decade, or a century: *The Invasion of the Body Snatchers* (1956) and cold war anxiety, Burke's *Reflections on the Revolution in France* (1790) and warnings of the perniciousness of revolutionary ideas. Buchanan's paranoid rhetoric employs the well-worn reactionary trope of a creeping or unseen enemy working covertly from within through a perversion of traditional ideas and, thus, ideals. How has this happened? Here? To us? Buchanan explains: "While the right has been winning primaries and elections, cutting taxes and funding anticommunist guerrillas abroad, the left has been quietly seizing all the commanding heights of American art and culture" (Bolton, 1992, p. 32).

In the progression from metaphor to exhortation to an actual cultural revolution (although a cultural revolution perhaps is by definition both literal and figurative), Buchanan draws from a long-standing American reservoir of myth and associations. His invocation and adaptation of a capture narrative and necessary rescue of the culture from the liberals draws from a by-now-mythically saturated construct, the captivity narrative, which Slotkin identifies as one of two genres of personal narrative—the other being the wilderness fighter, typically characterized as the man who knows Indians—used repeatedly since colonial America to justify regeneration through violence (Slotkin, 1993, pp. 14-15). As Slotkin notes, the

> narrative formulas and ideological themes of the captivity tale (redemption through suffering) are integrated with the triumphalist scenario of

the Indian-war story to make a single unified Myth of the Frontier in which the triumph of civilization over savagery is symbolized by the hunter/warrior's rescue of the white woman held captive by savages. (Slotkin, 1993, p. 15)

We understand the Right's agenda as the triumph of civilization over savagery, but who is the hunter/warrior? The white woman?

This mythic scenario of the justly provoked retaliation has repeatedly been used to rationalize extreme action, such as the Bush administration's "War on Drugs," which Slotkin says,

has invoked the traditional myths of savage war to rationalize a policy in which various applications of force and violence have a central role. Here the Myth of the Frontier plays a classic role: we define and confront this crisis, and the profound questions it raises about our society and about the international order, by deploying the metaphor of "war" and locating the root of our problem in the power of a "savage," captive-taking enemy. (Slotkin, 1993, p. 650)

Such a myth has an almost incantatory power by virtue of association and presence and, once invoked, can be highly effective both symbolically and instrumentally, because, as Slotkin notes, "what begins as a demand for symbolic violence ends in actual bloodshed and in the doctrine of 'extraordinary violence': the sanctioning of 'cowboy' or (more properly) vigilante-style actions by public officials and covert operatives who defy public law and constitutional principles in order to 'do what a man's got do' " (Slotkin, 1993, p. 651).

The Right has applied a vigilante approach to a number of areas of contention—abortion activists, Wildmon and the American Family Association's consumer boycotts, Quayle's attacks on *Murphy Brown.* That the attacks on the NEA bear these marks of vigilante justice is evident in the repeated efforts of a small number of highly active groups to punish the NEA and simultaneously force legislation that would place it effectively under their control. The appeal of the Religious Right's crusade to restore American values can be understood any number of ways. But its simplest attraction is an insistence on the positive versus the negative, on a wan sort of utopia that denies the tendencies of negation and nihilism in modern art. Critique? What Critique? Everything's just peachy here if those people would only behave. That this desire is itself a denial the Religious Right would find absurd, but what can one call the refusal to acknowledge expressions of entire segments of society? The America that the Religious Right wants to inhabit becomes conceivable as a sort of religious theme park devoted to a monolithic faith. Still, the question remains, why the NEA? Why this most readily available exemplar and widely understood example of culture with a capital "C?" Why, in the name of the populous, attack what functions, finally, as an elite institution? Samuel Lipman writes,

> In a free society, it is neither possible nor desirable to go very far in prohibiting the private activities that inspire this outre art. People have always had their private pleasures, and as long as these pleasures remain private, confined to consenting adults, and not immediately injurious, the public weal remains undisturbed. But now we are told that what has been private must be made public. We are told that it is a true function of art to accommodate us to feelings and actions that we—and societies and nations before us—have found objectionable and even appalling. (Lipman, as quoted in Bolton, 1992, p. 358)

After talking about cultural decline as evident in new art and citing also a media culture that profits "hugely from the pleasing, and the lowering, of every taste," Lipman concludes that the best way to fight this decline and decadence is by refusing to support or consume it. The best actions are private and individual and, of course, must continue:

> There is still more to be done. Acting on our behalf as citizens, our Government agencies—in particular the National Endowment for the Arts—can redirect their energies away from being the validators of the latest fancies to hit the art market. Instead, public art support might more fully concentrate on what it does so well: the championing of the great art of the past, its regeneration in the present and its transmission to the future. This would mean saying yes to civilization. (Lipman, as quoted in Bolton, 1992, p. 42)

Yes. But whose civilization?

In its characterizations of art and society the Right invokes the market repeatedly and contradictorily. Art has sunk to its current low quality because it has promiscuously served the marketplace; it will do and does anything for a buck. But in proposing the withdrawal of NEA funding the Right argues that NEA-funded artists should test the "magic of the marketplace." In a press release the American Family Association under the direction of Rev. Donald Wildmon argues that they [Serrano and Mapplethorpe] should "meet the same test as other artists in our society—the demand of the marketplace. The NEA will receive their millions from private grants, and if the 'works of art' have merit they will succeed in the marketplace" (Wildmon, as quoted in Bolton, 1992, p. 72). He continues, taking a populist approach, "Artists such as Serrano and Mapplethorpe will still be free to produce their art, but not with the tax dollars of truck drivers, brick masons, carpenters, and factory workers who must compete in the market-place" (Wildmon, as quoted in Bolton, 1992, p. 72).

The addendum to the populist appeal carries symbolic weight. "Artists such as Serrano and Mapplethorpe" contiguous with "truck drivers, brick masons, carpenters, and factory workers" creates an understood dividing line between the average, the everyday, the normal and the abnormal, the deviant, the homosexual. In speaking of and against "their art," the initiative is against admittance into the public realm of what should be kept private. This exposure, particularly in the case of Mapplethorpe, becomes itself criminal. No separation exists between representation and action, a distinction made more problematic in that both Mapplethorpe's and Serrano's medium is photography. Wildmon writes,

> One of Mapplethorpe's government-funded photos, entitled "Honey," is that of a little girl about four years old. She has a sad face and looks scared, but the focus of the camera is on the child's genitals below her uplifted dress. The government helped fund the violation of this innocent little girl and the exposing of her private area to the public. (Wildmon, as quoted in Bolton, 1992, p. 71)

Public exposure of that configured as private becomes violation. Agreement that such an action is a violation is not difficult, but deciding on what is public and what is private is difficult—perhaps impossible.

The disputed Mapplethorpe exhibit is titled "The Perfect Moment," which signifies a lack of absence, the presence of fullness and completion crystallized in a single moment of experience, captured in and by the photograph—and several pieces in the retrospective were homo-erotic and/or sadomasochistic. Confronted with the public display of moments conventionally unseen and unheard, critics from the Right—Helms, Kramer, Robertson, Buchanan—frequently chose silence to express their disapproval of the works; they condemn the works as unspeakable. That these men who have made their professions of speaking and describing experience a failure of their medium through confronting Mapplethorpe's must necessarily be construed as an offensive tactic, as a deliberate refusal to put or admit into public discourse a subject that they deem unacceptable. The homoerotic photographs in the Mapplethorpe retrospective, like the fable of *Les Bijou indiscrets,* give public utterance to a subject that, if spoken of at all, is addressed in private (Foucault, 1990, p. 77). The Right's staking out discursive territories is a type of quarantine, a means of identifying what is normal and what is aberrant, implicating Mapplethorpe's work as socially dangerous. The work is typified as threatening, as not being merely representational but an actual and actively malignant force. The proper domain for such discourse is assigned through tactics of silence and exclusion from the public realm.

Subject and Subtext

If homosexuality, religion, patriotism, and family values provide the main themes of the Right's activism in the NEA controversy, the backstory is AIDS, epitomized in the death of Mapplethorpe. This narrative is present in every NEA discussion for or against free expression as a reminder of the very real limits of certain freedoms that, as Susan Sontag (1989) argues, are now being actively restricted as a matter of hygienic prudence. Mapplethorpe's death suggests punishment for an immoral lifestyle represented in the photographs; for the defend- ers of free speech Mapplethorpe's death provides all the more reason not to silence legislationally those who are speaking for or about those who may be silenced physically. This subtext or backstory is pres- ent, at times more nuanced than at others, but always present, giving a dramatic urgency to the showing of the controversial

work. Maplethorpe's death reinforces the necessity of admitting the
subject into public discourse. So, there is the association of art and culture with the AIDS virus, with a contagion and the need to contain it,
to isolate it in order to protect the public from artists like Mapplethorpe.
Buchanan overtly makes the association of AIDS with lifestyle and
with art when he writes,

> The gays yearly die by the thousands of AIDS, crying out in rage for what
> they cannot have: respect for a lifestyle Americans simply do not respect:
> billions for medical research to save them from the consequences of their
> own suicidal self-indulgence. Truly, these are lost souls, fighting a war
> against the author of human nature, a war that no man can win. (As
> quoted in Bolton, 1992, p. 138)

Such art becomes only propaganda for deviant un-American (and
un-Godly) lifestyles, and for the Right's purposes the connection between image and action is one to one. As on *Crossfire* when Kinsley
asks Robertson about a fund-raising ad paid for by his organization:
"Now, your ad said that the NEA is teaching our sons how to sodo-
mize one another." Kinsley then extends the logic of the ad. "Now
you don't seriously think someone's going to go to this exhibit
[Mapplethorpe], turn to his buddy and say, 'Hey, so that's how it's
done. Let's go try it ourselves.' Is that what you mean?" Robertson
answers, "It's very possible" (Bolton, 1992, p. 251).

Characteristic of the Right's critique is the easy transit from the
realm of art to the realm of society, for the effect of the Right's action
was to call attention to particular acts of art and to interpret them, to
examine them as objects with real effects in society rather than isolated
acts of the arts community without a wider scope. They took high
culture and disseminated it, popularized it, made Mapplethorpe, at
least, a name known to many who may not have heard of him before.
(They accuse his and all other contemporary art of being corrupted
by the market. Yet their devices, the attention and readings that they
give such artists, are what provide the sensational attention that increases market value.) And all of this, all of their activities, their examining, complaining, campaigning, brings Mapplethorpe the attention
that they don't want him to have, brings to the public's attention that
which they want to be kept private. Their avowed purpose is to

quarantine and to repress the subject of Mapplethorpe's photographs. It is essentially a medicinal procedure: Expose or reveal the source of distress in order to isolate it and prevent it from spreading. For they state repeatedly, like a party line, that they aren't against freedom of expression; what they oppose is the use of public funds to support sacrilegious and obscene (homoerotic) art—which is described as dangerous to the public—like an infectious disease of potentially epidemic proportions.

In the NEA controversy isn't the Right's objective, after all, to codify how certain subjects can be put into discourse, to decide which subjects can enter into public discourse? Outrage over homoerotic art or antireligious art is a tactical maneuver in an overall effort to proscribe who may speak and the conditions of that speech. Certainly in matters of Mapplethorpe it is an attempt to proscribe pleasure—what is pleasurable, where it can take place and be presented and discussed. With Serrano, once again, discourse is restricted; how religion may be discussed is ossified, prescriptive, and unidirectional. The Right's objective in the NEA controversy is a reclaiming of territory, a reconfiguring of American culture and its iconography that suits the politically conservative agenda of the Right—Buchanan's capturing of the culture. The broad claim that they speak for America, that they represent American values, defines America as a moral amalgam comprised of antigay, pro-family, pro-religion, and pro-American elements. The amalgamation is created through opposition, motivated by fear of something lost or about to be lost, and informed by a politics of the last stand. And like the Last Stand, such action may well be futile, which lends a certain fatalist energy to the cause to capture the culture.

But why must culture be captured? And can it be caught and kept like something dangerous that must be contained? In such a conception of culture, art and representation become clinical matters; there is simply right and wrong, our side against theirs, and the Right has claimed the voice for our side against a modernist American art and culture defined in Buchanan's paraphrase of Reagan's farewell address as a culture that is "more and more, openly anti-Christian, anti-American, nihilistic" (Bolton, 1992, p. 32). Such addresses work as rallying cries but meaning becomes lost in the terms and name-calling;

"anti-Christian" and "nihilistic" are perhaps manageable, but "anti-American" is appropriated to imagine the reclamation of an America that never existed. The conflation of imagination and memory becomes fatal for, as Slotkin reminds us, "the reification of nostalgia in the mass culture and politics of the 1980s is a falsification of memory" (Slotkin, 1993, p. 655). The simple "us against them" logic generated by recourse to labeling some representations "anti-American" follows from a mythical America that we have outgrown and whose very basis is questionable: the Myth of the Frontier. It is a myth that, "even in its liberal form," Slotkin reminds us,

> was exclusionist in its premises. . . . A new myth will have to respond to the demographic transformation of the United States and speak to and for a polyglot nationality. Historical memory will have to be revised, not to invent an imaginary role for supposedly marginal minorities, but to register the fact that our history in the West and the East, was shaped from the beginning by the meeting, conversation, and mutual adaptation of different cultures. (Slotkin, 1993, p. 655)

But in the conversation about American culture that July evening on *Crossfire* which America was being addressed? In the business of television where audiences are packaged and sold, which American public was listening may have been more a question of consumption communities than communities of shared values. The public described in the rhetoric of Buchanan and Robertson seemed to be itself like the program—produced, presented, fabricated. And the arts community's public did not seem any less of a contrivance.

One point made repeatedly by those defending the NEA is that the Right is assigning blame to the NEA and totalizing what they want to have happen from a judgment formed on just a few artists. Why? Because these artists provide them with convenient symbols to attack: homosexuality and minority viewpoints. Such artists and their works are not representative of the NEA by and large, but they are representative of what the Right wants to attack. In the Right's scenario of a country in decline, this nationally sponsored art is symbolic and actual at the same time. When Buchanan says that such art is representative of what America is becoming, that we must recapture the culture, and, when his readers assent, they are participating imagina-

tively in a capture narrative, a collective fantasy about the restoration
of an imagined past. Furthermore, this fantasy of restoration will be
realized through a scenario of containment, whose metaphors are
characterized by restriction, discipline, enclosure, and isolation. That
what they want to capture perhaps never existed is one matter, but
that the culture that they want to reclaim or create is a singular,
monolithic, and exclusive utopia is evident in the hateful discourse
organized around the NEA. For the Right has construed an idea of
culture that, apart from never having existed—Slotkin's false myth—is
reified, and if it were called into existence would be imposed, manu-
factured, and trickle-down.

In the idea of culture as envisioned by the Right, the dialogue becomes a monologue; art's purpose is to preserve rather than challenge,
to credential rather than articulate, as in Napoleon's appropriation of
David's neo-classicism to authenticate historically a regime without
precedent. When Robertson asks why the NEA can't simply say "this
stuff is horrible, let's ban this little bit and go ahead with the funding,"
he redefines the role of art as conceived in the National Foundation
on the Arts and the Humanities Act of 1965, which created the
Endowments. Public Law 89-209 states that,

> The practice of art and the study of humanities requires constant dedica-
> tion and devotion and that, while no government can call a great artist or
> scholar into existence, it is necessary and appropriate for the federal
> government to help create and sustain not only a climate encouraging
> freedom of thought, imagination, and inquiry, but also the material con-
> ditions facilitating the release of this creative talent.

In its report on the bill, the Senate Labor and Public Welfare Committee stresses that "fullest" attention be given "to freedom of artistic and
humanistic expression. One of the artist's and humanist's great values
to society is the mirror of self-examination which they raise so that
society can become aware of its shortcomings as well as its strengths"
(Bolton, 1992, p. 332).

Such a definition of culture in society is inherently political. To deny
that culture and politics are not interrelated is to move cultural production from the everyday, to divorce it from the actual processes of
a society's development—an act that is no less political than sponsor-

ing artistic production. This point is played out in the closing moments of *Crossfire* in one last exchange between Buchanan and Reeve:

Buchanan: Christopher Reeve, it is not—we are not telling the artist what to create. When they come in with this piece of trash, why don't you artists have the awareness—

Reeve: Sir—

Buchanan: —and the guts to get up and say, this is garbage, it's not what we expected, we're sorry.

Reeve: If you—if you have this authorization to go through with restrictive language, you are telling artists what to create. You are having politicians tell artists what to create. That's unacceptable. Now, the NEA provides money for the cultural diversity and life of this country. If every now and again something obscene comes up, that's the price you have to pay. And the other point I wanted to make is without—

Kinsley: Very quickly, please.

Reeve: Without the NEA, this country is going to culturally go down the drain and I certainly don't want to see that happen.

The question regarding federally funded expression as framed by *Crossfire* is one of prescription or permission and the living with the consequences of one or the other. But the debate on *Crossfire*—and throughout the NEA controversy—begs the more fundamental question of the politics of representation, whether inclusive or exclusive. Sarah Schulman, a lesbian artist who has benefited from NEA funding, writes of the predicament of being designated representative.

> Up until about five years ago, lesbian artists were almost completely excluded from the rewards system. . . . Now, through the new tokenism, a few political and apolitical sensibilities are permitted to be contained within the dominant culture. Individuals are even easier than political movements to contain. As a result, a single style is declared to be representative of a hugely diverse community that it cannot represent. At the same time, racism, class bias and the emphasis on trendy, marketable genres (like detective novels and stand-up monologues) keep other voices from the public arena. . . . In the end, the permitted aesthetics encourage new artists to work in precisely the same styles so that they, too, can be

rewarded. In this manner, much of the development of lesbian arts are [sic] taken out of the hands of the audience and given instead to a small group of critics and administrators. (As quoted in Bolton, 1992, p. 258)

Thus the problem and the politics, from any side, of speaking for others. To become representative and stand in the spotlight for others is an ironic reversal. It renders the representative as a participant in the resignation to the shadows of those whom one represents. Exclusion and discrimination are not prejudicial tactics exclusive to the Right but the effects of representation.

Conclusion

I close with one last irony. In an interview in the early 1970s, Deleuze speaking to Foucault, summarizes what Foucault has said elsewhere. So, speaking for Foucault, Deleuze says,

In my opinion you were the first—in your books and in the practical sphere—to teach us something absolutely fundamental: the indignity of speaking for others. We ridiculed representation and said it was finished, but we failed to draw the consequences of this theoretical conversation— to appreciate the theoretical fact that only those directly involved can speak in a practical way on their own behalf. (As quoted in Ferguson et al., 1992, p. 11)

This is the lesson of the NEA controversy and its value: Whether the expression is art or politics, entertainment or sports, abortion rights or gay rights, those involved can, should, must be allowed to speak on their own behalf. Certainly what is said may be ugly, offen- sive, and disturbing but not to allow it is equally ugly, offensive, and disturbing. Beyond the question of what may be said, then, is the question of who allows it. Speaking of the penal system, Foucault re- marks that, "when the prisoners began to speak, they possessed an in- dividual theory of prisons, the penal system, and justice. It is this form of discourse which ultimately matters, a discourse against power, the counter-discourse of prisoners and those we call delinquents—and not a theory about delinquency" (quoted in Ferguson et al., 1992, p. 11).

It is the same with art, for what matters is the art and not a theory or theories about art. Unlike the imposed iconography of the Right's America, the America I want to imagine would learn to live with the varieties of icons emerging from individual and community practice—however hateful these voices might be—would learn to acknowledge a continually emerging discourse of difference and assimilation to take place. When, at the end of *Crossfire,* Reeve says that with art you don't know what you'll get, he offers possibly the one workable definition of art presented throughout the NEA controversy. And this definition —one we could learn to live with or must decide to live with—of art as a form that is becoming rather than fixed seems as good a definition as any. Such a pluralistic definition is admittedly postmodern in its acknowledgment of the new alongside the old and the destabilization of the center in order to allow rather than assimilate difference. Accepting this definition further means accepting an art that is every-day rather than utopic, an art of emergence rather than stasis, of uncertainty rather than prescription. Accepting not knowing what we will get—and risking art that some will see as vile, obscene, and offensive—is not just the price one pays for living in a free society but the dividend as well. Such acceptance allows art that speaks to the public and not for them. Perhaps this acceptance—at once diverse and unified—is what truly constitutes our common culture; certainly it is the basis for an art with the potential to yield a truly American iconography.

Note

1. All *Crossfire* quotations from Bolton (1992) used by permission of Cable News Network. © Cable News Network, Inc. All Rights Reserved.

References

Baudrillard, J. (1983). *In the shadow of the silent majorities.* New York: Semiotext(e).
Bolton, R. (Ed.). (1992). *Culture wars: Documents from the recent controversies in the arts.* New York: New Press.
Burroughs, W. S. (1987). *Just say no to drug hysteria.* Address delivered at University of Kansas, Lawrence.

Ferguson, R., Olander, W., Tucker, M., & Fiss, K. (Eds.). (1992). *Discourses: Conversations in postmodern art and culture.* Cambridge: MIT Press.

Foucault, M. (1990). *The history of sexuality: Vol. 1. An introduction.* New York: Vintage.

Sarap, M. (1989). *Post-structuralism and post-modernism.* Athens: University of Georgia Press.

Sontag, S. (1989). *Illness as metaphor* and *AIDS and its metaphors.* Garden City, NY: Anchor.

Slotkin, R. (1993). *Gunfighter nation: The myth of the frontier in twentieth-century America.* New York: HarperCollins.

There's Such a Thing as Free Speech

And It's a Good Thing, Too

Stephen A. Smith
University of Arkansas

Editor's Introduction

To be for hate speech is to take a position that itself can expect to provoke hostility and invite outrage. In this final chapter, Stephen Smith would seem to do just that by questioning what is perhaps our most commonly held assumptions: that hate speech is bad and that, once it arises, it must necessarily be repressed. But Smith defends hate speech as a form of free speech, and this position in fact calls for seeing hate speech as allowing possibilities for understanding and reconciliation in a polyglot culture.

As Smith points out, the United States is unique among nations in its lack of legislation prohibiting hate speech. Although those who favor hate speech regulation see it as a means of protecting equality, Smith disagrees. He argues that once we see hate speech as free speech we admit it into an important cultural realm, making it part of discussion rather than an instrument of blame.

Bringing hate speech into the open allows dialogue, actually promoting rather than restricting the free flow of ideas. Such a practice also fosters the critical reception of ideas rather than blind acceptance. Hate speech is not a pariah. Hate speech promotes an open society where both sides of a conflict are examined, a practice that encourages tolerance, engenders respect for ideas, and may even result in more robust dialogue.

Persecution for the expression of opinions seems to me perfectly logical. If you have no doubt of your premises or your power and want a certain result with all your heart, you naturally express your wishes in law and sweep away all opposition. . . . But when men have realized that time has upset many fighting faiths, they may come to believe even more than they believe the very foundations of their own conduct that the ultimate good desired is better reached by free trade in ideas—that the best test of truth is the power of the thought to get itself accepted in the competition of the market. . . . That, at any rate, is the theory of our Constitution. It is an experiment, as all life is an experiment.

Oliver Wendell Holmes, Jr.
Dissenting in *Abrams v. United States*, 250 U.S. 616 (1919)

The discourse and the consequences of hate are issues of considerable concern in our lives, both public and private. Though the chapters in this volume make clear that hate can transcend categories, racial and ethnic differences have historically bred suspicions, misunderstandings, fears, and resentments, and the frustrations in resolving those feelings have often resulted in hateful speech and actions among such groups. The often tragic reality of those tensions in the United

States in recent years has been framed between the memory of Nazi Germany and the hopes of the civil rights movement, but contemporary ethnic conflicts around the globe demonstrate that the American experience is not unique.

The most notorious international example is the continuing Iranian *fatwah* against Salman Rushdie for publication of *The Satanic Verses*, but it is by no means the only instance of official action taken to punish authors and silence words that offend ("Iran Says Rushdie," 1994). Canadian authorities canceled a planned speech, denied an entry visa, and threatened to arrest the openly racist Khalid Abdul Muhammad, former aide to Nation of Islam leader Louis Farrakhan (Swardson, 1994). British historian David Irving, whose revisionist views question the Holocaust, has been arrested for his speeches and expelled from Canada, fined and denied entry into Germany for a speech, and denied a visa to speak and promote his book in Australia (Berton, 1992; "Germany Bars," 1993; "Historian Irving," 1994). In a case arising from a 1991 National Democratic Party rally in Munich, the German Constitutional Court recently said that the extermination of 6 million Jews in Hitler's concentration camps is a fact and that Holocaust denial is a "proven untruth"; therefore, those who spread the "Auschwitz Lie" are not protected by the Basic Law's guarantees of freedom of opinion and may be banned from stating their inaccurate views in public (German Information Center, 1994; Miller, 1994).

The United States, alone among Western industrial nations, does not have national legislation prohibiting hate speech, and it has not fully ratified the International Covenant on Civil and Political Rights or the International Convention on the Elimination of All Forms of Racial Discrimination, which require signatory members to adopt such provisions (see Lee, 1990; Walker, 1994). Proponents of hate speech regulation such as Richard Delgado and Jean Stefanic (1993) interpret that fact as demonstrating that we "have simply not caught up to other societies in protecting equality" (p. A23). Counter First Amendment advocates, "they got it backwards. We protect freedom of conscience, religion and speech like no other country. The rest of the world, Western industrial or otherwise, needs to catch up with us" (Hodges, 1993, p. A25). Nonetheless, Congress recently passed resolutions condemning the message of hate spewed by Khalid Abdul Muhammad[1] and state statutes, municipal ordinances, and campus speech codes have been adopted by well-meaning officials seeking harmony, decorum, and an ordered society.

This chapter considers the political and constitutional implications inherent in the efforts to censor and punish public expression and communication of "racist hate speech." Among those most prominently advocating or defending the enactment and articulating the rationale for such measures are Stanley Fish (1994), Catherine MacKinnon (1993), Kent Greenwalt (1989), Cass Sunstein (1993), Laura Lederer (1993), Richard Delgado (1991), Mari Matsuda (1989), Charles Lawrence (1990), and Julianne Malveaux (1993). They argue not only that hateful speech should be suppressed to achieve a more civil society but that it can be done within our constitutional scheme. The First Amendment does not protect hate speech, they variously argue, because it falls within the exempt categories of defamation or "fighting words" or because the words become speech "acts" rather than mere ideas, statements, or arguments. On the other hand, Franklyn Haiman (1993), Nat Hentoff (1992), Samuel Walker (1994), Jonathan Rauch (1993), and Henry Louis Gates, Jr. (1993) have cogently countered those arguments and questioned the constitutional validity of the enterprise, and the efforts to sanitize campus conversation have been attacked more broadly on ideological grounds by Dinesh D'Souza and others (D'Souza, 1991).

The authors on both sides of the above question have stated their positions clearly and eloquently; therefore, I do not intend to engage in a summary or analysis of the arguments in the speculative literature. I will, instead, focus upon and consider the issues in First Amendment jurisprudence by examining the various fact situations in which, and the legal arguments by which, the federal courts have consistently upheld the rights of speakers against the challenges of individuals and groups claiming to be offended or damaged by the symbolic manifestations of hate in public discourse.

Although the constitutional theories are not especially innovative, the traditional assumptions behind such constitutional protection do not always appear obvious in the case of hate speech. The speech can hardly be said to lead easily to the discovery of new truth, and it is difficult to categorize most such verbal exchanges as rational discourse about wise public policy. Moreover, it would be quite naive to pretend that such expressions are not hurtful to the sensibilities of those to whom they are directed, individually or collectively. Yet, I will argue that the government is without power to censor hate speech, that such speech not only demands constitutional protection, but that its protection is both politically beneficial and worth the cost.

Words as Weapons

The issues raised in the current hate speech controversy are not new. Although First Amendment doctrine has developed far beyond where it was four decades ago, the case of *Beauharnais v. Illinois* (1952) already anticipated most of the contemporary arguments, including the concept of group libel. Though the holding is now of dubious authority, a review of the facts and arguments in that case are very much worth examination as background to our current controversies, if for no other reason than to distinguish the path of American constitutional law from the legal approach embraced by other nations. The case arose when Joseph Beauharnais, president of the White Circle League, organized a meeting and distributed admittedly racist literature in Chicago. He was arrested and convicted for violation of an Illinois statute making it a crime to publish or distribute any material that,

> portrays depravity, criminality, unchastity, or lack of virtue of a class of citizens, of any race, color, creed or religion which said publication or exhibition exposes the citizens of any race, color, creed or religion to contempt, derision, or obloquy or which is productive of breach of the peace or riots. (§224a, Illinois Criminal Code)

Writing for the majority in a 5-4 decision, and citing the dicta in *Chaplinsky v. New Hampshire* (1942), Justice Frankfurter said,

> There are certain well-defined and narrowly limited classes of speech, the prevention and punishment of which have never been thought to raise any Constitutional problem. These include the lewd and obscene, the profane, the libelous, and the insulting or "fighting" words—those which by their very utterance inflict injury or tend to incite an immediate breach of the peace. It has been well observed that such utterances are no essential

part of any exposition of ideas, and are of such slight social value as a step to truth that any benefit that may be derived from them is clearly outweighed by the social interest in order and morality. Resort to epithets or personal abuse is not in any proper sense communication of information or opinion safeguarded by the Constitution, and its punishment as a criminal act would raise no question under that instrument. (*Cantwell v. Connecticut*, 1940)

Such were the views of a unanimous Court in *Chaplinsky v. New Hampshire* (1942).

Then, treating the statute as group libel, extending the common law of individual defamation, and citing a state case that had upheld a libel on the American Legion (*People v. Spielman*, 1925), Frankfurter dismissed the constitutional challenge, saying that,

if an utterance directed at an individual may be the object of criminal sanctions, we cannot deny to a State power to punish the same utterance directed at a defined group, unless we can say that this is a willful and purposeless restriction unrelated to the peace and well-being of the State.

Then, recounting the history of racial conflict in Illinois and well aware of the recent experience of Nazi Germany, he continued,

In the face of this history and its frequent obligato of extreme racial and religious propaganda, we would deny experience to say that the Illinois legislature was without reason in seeking ways to curb false or malicious defamation of racial and religious groups, made in public places and by means calculated to have a powerful emotional impact on those to whom it was presented. . . . This being so, we are precluded from saying that speech concededly punishable when in groups with whose position and esteem in society the affiliated individual may be inextricably involved.

Admitting the difficulty of success but defending the purpose of the statute, Frankfurter then confronted a common objection to such legislation:

It may be argued, and weightily, that this legislation will not help matters; that tension and on occasion violence between racial and religious groups must be traced to causes more deeply embedded in our society than the rantings of modern Know-Nothings. Only those lacking responsible humility will have a confident solution for problems as intractable as the frictions attributable to differences of race, color or religion. . . . That the legislative remedy might not in practice mitigate the evil, or might itself raise new problems, would only manifest once more the paradox of reform.

Justice Black's dissent still resonates as well, asking,

In view of [our] prior holdings, how does the Court justify its holding today that states can punish people for exercising the vital freedoms intended to be safeguarded from suppression by the First Amendment? The prior holdings are not referred to; the Court simply acts on the blind assumption that the First Amendment is wholly irrelevant. It is not even accorded the respect of a passing mention. This follows logically, I suppose, from recent constitutional doctrine which appears to measure state laws solely by this Court's notions of civilized "canons of decency," reasonableness, etc.

Seeing the obnoxious pamphlets as pure speech, Black said,

My own belief is that no legislature is charged with the duty or vested with the power to decide what public issues Americans can discuss. In a free country that is the individual's choice, not the state's. State experimentation in curbing freedom of expression is a startling and frightening doctrine in a country dedicated to self-government by its people. I reject the holding that either state or nation can punish people for having their say in matters of public concern.

Anticipating arguments about "Political Correctness" and from the censors of the Religious Right, Black said, "This statute imposes state censorship over the theater, moving pictures, radio, television, leaflets, magazines, books and newspapers. No doubt the statute is broad enough to make criminal the 'publication, sale, presentation or exhibition' of many of the world's great classics, both secular and religious."

"The Court condones this expansive state censorship," he continued,

by painstakingly analogizing it to the law of criminal libel. As a result of this refined analysis, the Illinois statute emerges labeled a "group libel law." This label may make the Court's holding more palatable for those who sustain it, but the sugar-coating does not make the censorship less deadly.

Unimpressed with the good intentions of the legislature, Black still found the statute to be unconstitutional:

> This Act sets up a system of state censorship which is at war with the kind of free government envisioned by those who forced adoption of our Bill of Rights. The motives behind the state law may have been to do good. But the same can be said about most laws making opinions punishable as crimes. History indicates that urges to do good have led to the burning of books and even to the burning of "witches."

"Today Beauharnais is punished for publicly expressing strong views in favor of segregation. Ironically enough, Beauharnais, convicted of crime in Chicago, would probably be given a hero's reception in many other localities, if not in some parts of Chicago itself," he said, recalling the lessons of his own past just as Frankfurter had been cognizant of his heritage.

> Moreover, the same kind of state law that makes Beauharnais a criminal for advocating segregation in Illinois can be utilized to send people to jail in other states for advocating equality and nonsegregation. What Beauharnais said in his leaflet is mild compared with usual arguments on both sides of racial controversies.

Concluding, Justice Black warned, "If there be minority groups who hail this holding as their victory, they might consider the possible relevancy of this ancient remark: 'Another such victory and I am undone.' "

Justice Douglas, joining in dissent, stressed the distinction between speech and conduct:

> Hitler and his Nazis showed how evil a conspiracy could be which was aimed at destroying a race by exposing it to contempt, derision, and obloquy. I would be willing to concede that such conduct directed at a race or group in this country could be made an indictable offense. For such a project would be more than the exercise of free speech.

For Douglas, the First Amendment, applied to the states through the Fourteenth, trumped other concerns. "The First Amendment is couched in absolute terms—freedom of speech shall not be abridged. Speech has, therefore, a preferred position as contrasted to some other civil rights." Then, echoing Holmes and previewing the future, he said,

> The free trade in ideas which the Framers of the Constitution visualized disappears. In its place there is substituted a new orthodoxy—an orthodoxy that changes with the whims of the age or the day, an orthodoxy which the majority by solemn judgment proclaims to be essential to the safety, welfare, security, morality, or health of society. Free speech in the constitutional sense disappears. Limits are drawn—limits dictated by expediency, political opinion, prejudices or some other desideratum of legislative action.

Douglas was not unaware of the racial tensions, nor did he think they would be solved by repressing speech:

> Today a white man stands convicted for protesting in unseemly language against our decisions invalidating restrictive covenants. Tomorrow a Negro will be hauled before a court for denouncing lynch laws in heated terms. Farm laborers in the West who compete with field hands drifting up from Mexico; whites who feel the pressure of Orientals; a minority which finds employment going to members of the dominant religious group—all of these are caught in the mesh of today's decision.

Political debate, he knew, was not always, or even usually, conducted in temperate language:

> Debate and argument even in the courtroom are not always calm and dispassionate. Emotions sway speakers and audiences alike. Intemperate speech is a distinctive characteristic of man. Hotheads blow off and release destructive energy in the process. They shout and rave, exaggerating weaknesses, magnifying error, viewing with alarm. So it has been from the beginning; and so it will be throughout time.

Like Black, he relied on the intent of the founders and embraced their choice over the balancing and deference to the state legislature that Frankfurter favored:

The Framers of the Constitution knew human nature as well as we do. They too had lived in dangerous days; they too knew the suffocating influence of orthodoxy and standardized thought. They weighed the compulsions for restrained speech and thought against the abuses of liberty. They chose liberty. That should be our choice today no matter how distasteful to us the pamphlet of Beauharnais may be.

The breathing room for vigorous debate and strong language that Black and Douglas defended in Beauharnais as an adjunct of republican governments had been sanctioned in another Illinois case only a few years before, and subsequent decisions would go even further. The Court's evolving interpretation that the First Amendment protected sharp words in public debate and limiting the scope of *Chaplinsky* began with *Terminiello v. Chicago* (1949), and it is one especially relevant to the current hate speech controversy.

The case grew out of a racist speech that Father Arthur Terminiello, a former priest from Alabama, delivered in a packed auditorium in Chicago under the auspices of the Christian Veterans of America while an angry crowd of one thousand protesters were outside. In his speech, Terminiello "condemned the conduct of the crowd outside and vigorously, if not viciously, criticized various political and racial groups whose activities he denounced as inimical to the nation's welfare" (*Terminiello v. Chicago*, 1949). He was arrested and convicted for breach of the peace, which the trial judge defined as including any "misbehavior which violates the public peace and decorum"; and instructed the jury that the "misbehavior may constitute a breach of the peace if it stirs the public to anger, invites dispute, brings about a condition of unrest, or creates a disturbance, or if it molests the inhabitants in the enjoyment of peace and quiet by arousing alarm."

Douglas, writing for the Court, did not bother to determine whether the speech fell into one of the categories excluded by *Chaplinsky;* the standards stated by the judge were target enough:

The vitality of civil and political institutions in our society depends on free discussion. As Chief Justice Hughes wrote in *De Jonge v. Oregon,* it is only through free debate and free exchange of ideas that government remains responsive to the will of the people and peaceful change is effected. The right to speak freely and to promote diversity of ideas and

programs is therefore one of the chief distinctions that sets us apart from
totalitarian regimes

he said, advancing his own definition of diversity.

Then, Justice Douglas made clear that the right of free speech did
not forfeit First Amendment protection just because some in the
audience might find it offensive:

> Accordingly a function of free speech under our system of government is
> to invite dispute. It may indeed best serve its high purpose when it induces
> a condition of unrest, creates dissatisfaction with conditions as they are,
> or even stirs people to anger. Speech is often provocative and challenging.
> It may strike at prejudices and preconceptions and have profound unset-
> tling effects as it presses for acceptance of an idea. That is why freedom
> of speech, though not absolute, is nevertheless protected against censor-
> ship or punishment, unless shown likely to produce a clear and present
> danger of a serious substantive evil that rises far above public inconven-
> ience, annoyance, or unrest. There is no room under our Constitution for
> a more restrictive view. For the alternative would lead to standardization
> of ideas either by legislatures, courts, or dominant political or community
> groups.

Perhaps the most insightful Supreme Court decision on the function
of provocative language and the potential dangers in allowing government officials to censor particular offensive words was Justice Harlan's
opinion in *Cohen v. California* (1971). Paul Robert Cohen was convicted for wearing a jacket emblazoned with "Fuck the Draft" in a
courthouse. His conviction, said Harlan, making the distinction between words and acts, clearly rested "upon the asserted offensiveness
of the words Cohen used to convey his message to the public. The
only 'conduct' which the State sought to punish is the fact of communication."

Justice Harlan also noted that,

> much has been made of the claim that Cohen's distasteful mode of
> expression was thrust upon unwilling or unsuspecting viewers, and that
> the State might therefore legitimately act as it did in order to protect the
> sensitive from otherwise unavoidable exposure to appellant's crude form
> of protest. Of course, the mere presumed presence of unwitting listeners
> or viewers does not serve automatically to justify curtailing all speech
> capable of giving offense.

He did not find the argument convincing, because the

> ability of government, consonant with the Constitution, to shut off dis-
> course solely to protect others from hearing it is, in other words, depen-
> dent upon a showing that substantial privacy interests are being invaded
> in an essentially intolerable manner. Any broader view of this authority
> would effectively empower a majority to silence dissidents simply as a
> matter of personal predilections.

The issue, said Harlan, was

> whether California can excise, as "offensive conduct," one particular
> scurrilous epithet from the public discourse, either upon the theory of the
> court below that its use is inherently likely to cause violent reaction or
> upon a more general assertion that the States, acting as guardians of public
> morality, may properly remove this offensive word from the public
> vocabulary.

He thought not.

Diversity and autonomy were not inconsistent in Harlan's view:

> The constitutional right of free expression is powerful medicine in a
> society as diverse and populous as ours. It is designed and intended to
> remove governmental restraints from the arena of public discussion,
> putting the decision as to what views shall be voiced largely into the hands
> of each of us, in the hope that use of such freedom will ultimately produce
> a more capable citizenry and more perfect polity and in the belief that no
> other approach would comport with the premise of individual dignity and
> choice upon which our political system rests.

Admittedly, he said, liberty is often secured at the price of order,
but that is not necessarily bad:

> To many, the immediate consequence of this freedom may often appear
> to be only verbal tumult, discord, and even offensive utterance. These are,
> however, within established limits, in truth necessary side effects of the
> broader enduring values which the process of open debate permits us to
> achieve. That the air may at times seem filled with verbal cacophony is,
> in this sense not a sign of weakness but of strength. We cannot lose sight
> of the fact that, in what otherwise might seem a trifling and annoying
> instance of individual distasteful abuse of a privilege, these fundamental
> societal values are truly implicated.

Audience response to particular words was not reason enough to allow state censorship; individuals can make their own choices about the language they think most effective in expressing themselves on public issues. "How is one to distinguish this from any other offensive word?" he asked.

> Surely the State has no right to cleanse public debate to the point where it is grammatically palatable to the most squeamish among us. Yet no readily ascertainable general principle exists for stopping short of that result were we to affirm the judgment below. For, while the particular four-letter word being litigated here is perhaps more distasteful than most others of its genre, it is nevertheless often true that one man's vulgarity is another's lyric. Indeed, we think it is largely because governmental officials cannot make principled distinctions in this area that the Constitution leaves matters of taste and style so largely to the individual.

There were, in Harlan's opinion, two additional reasons for his take on the First Amendment. It was important to understand that,

> much linguistic expression serves a dual communicative function: it conveys not only ideas capable of relatively precise, detached explication, but otherwise inexpressible emotions as well. In fact, words are often chosen as much for their emotive as their cognitive force. We cannot sanction the view that the Constitution, while solicitous of the cognitive content of individual speech, has little or no regard for that emotive function which, practically speaking, may often be the more important.

Furthermore, he noted, language is closely tied to the ideas it symbolizes. We cannot, he said, "indulge the facile assumption that one can forbid particularly suppressing ideas in the process. Indeed, governments might soon seize upon the censorship of particular words as a convenient guise for banning the expression of unpopular views."

In another case, concerned with economic rather than political issues, *Old Dominion Branch No. 496, Natl. Assn. Of Letter Carriers v. Austin* (1974), the Court also afforded protection to offensive language under the First Amendment against a tort action filed under Virginia's "insulting words" statute (Va. Code Ann., 1957). When the union newsletter listed Austin as a scab, he said that he did not know what a scab was, but that he was going to sue the Union if he was called a scab again. A few weeks later the newsletter again listed him as a scab and provided a definition attributed to Jack London that would cer- tainly fall within the reach of many campus speech codes of today:

> A scab is a two-legged animal with a corkscrew soul, a water brain, a combination backbone of jelly and glue. Where others have hearts, he carries a tumor of rotten principles . . . Esau was a traitor to himself; Judas was a traitor to his God; Benedict Arnold was a traitor to his country; a SCAB is a traitor to his God, his country, his family and his class.

Austin and the others listed as scabs said the article could "be read to charge them with having 'rotten principles,' with lacking 'charac- ter,' and with being '[traitors]'; that these charges are untrue; and that appellants knew they were untrue." They also claimed that,

> their coworkers and others became hostile to them, referring to them as the "scabs" the union was talking about, and that this made them tense and nervous and caused headaches. There is no evidence that anyone took literally the use of the word "traitor" or that appellees were in any way concerned about or affected by this charge.

Justice Marshall and the Court found little merit in the action for damages. Citing Mr. Justice Clark in *Linn v. Plant Guard Workers* (1966), he argued that such labor

> disputes are ordinarily heated affairs; the language that is commonplace there might well be deemed actionable per se in some state jurisdictions. Indeed, representation campaigns are frequently characterized by bitter and extreme charges, countercharges, unfounded rumors, vituperations, personal accusations, misrepresentations and distortions. Both labor and management often speak bluntly and recklessly, embellishing their respec- tive positions with imprecatory language. (383 U.S., at 58)

"Rather than being a reckless or knowing falsehood, naming the appellees as scabs was literally and factually true," Marshall said.

> To be sure, the word is most often used as an insult or epithet. But Linn recognized that federal law gives a union license to use intemperate, abusive, or insulting language without fear of restraint or penalty if it believes such rhetoric to be an effective means to make its point.

Such language could not, however, be the basis for recovery in this case. Marshall explained that words like *traitor* cannot be construed as representations of fact in this context. As the Court said long before, "to use loose language or undefined slogans that are part of the conventional give-and-take in our economic and political controversies— like 'unfair' or 'fascist'—is not to falsify facts" (*Cafeteria Employees Local 302 v. Angelos*, 1943). Such words were obviously used here in a loose, figurative sense to demonstrate the union's strong disagreement with the views of those workers who oppose unionization. Expression of such an opinion, even in the most pejorative terms, is protected under federal labor law. Here, too, "there is no such thing as a false idea. However pernicious an opinion may seem, we depend for its correction not on the conscience of judges and juries but on the competition of other ideas" (*Gertz v. Robert Welch, Inc.*, 1974).

It was impossible, he said, that anyone

> would have understood the newsletter to be charging the appellees with committing the criminal offense of treason . . . Jack London's "definition of a scab" is merely rhetorical hyperbole, a lusty and imaginative expression of the contempt felt by union members towards those who refuse to join. The Court in *Linn* recognized that such exaggerated rhetoric was commonplace in labor disputes and protected by federal law.

The First Amendment has been held to protect a wide choice in language to make one's point in a variety of contexts, well before the current concern with campus hate speech codes. That choice is, significantly, one to be made by individual speakers, not agents of the state. The effective antidote is also a responsibility of individuals, encompassing the options to ignore it or to respond to offensive speech with better speech, but not the option to censor or punish through the agency of state police power or to chill speech by means of civil tort actions.

Codes and the Constitution

The campus speech codes that were enacted on numerous university campuses during the 1980s were first forced to confront the First

Amendment in *Doe v. Michigan* (1989), striking down the Policy on Discrimination and Discriminatory Harassment of Students in the University Environment at the University of Michigan. The judge acknowledged the basic value of conflict and said, "It is an unfortunate fact of our constitutional system that the ideals of freedom and equality are often in conflict. The difficult and sometimes painful task of our political and legal institutions is to mediate the appropriate balance between these two competing values." The Policy had been adopted by the Regents with good intentions in an attempt to curb a rising tide of racial intolerance and harassment on campus, and it prohibited individuals, under the penalty of sanctions, from "stigmatizing or victimizing" individuals or groups on the basis of race, ethnicity, religion, sex, sexual orientation, creed, national origin, ancestry, age, marital status, handicap, or Vietnam-era veteran status. However laudable or appropriate an effort this may have been, the Court found that the Policy swept within its scope a significant amount of "verbal conduct" or "verbal behavior" that it said was unquestionably protected speech under the First Amendment.

Despite the best of intentions, said the court, the University could not establish an antidiscrimination policy that had the effect of prohibiting certain speech because it disagreed with ideas or messages sought to be conveyed. As the Supreme Court stated in *West Virginia State Board of Education v. Barnette* (1943): "If there is any star fixed in our constitutional constellation, it is that no official, high or petty, can prescribe what shall be orthodox in politics, nationalism, religion, or other matters of opinion or force citizens to confess by word or act their faith therein."

Consequently, the University could not proscribe speech simply because it was found to be offensive, even gravely so, by large numbers of people (*Texas v. Johnson*, 1989, supra 105). As the Supreme Court noted in *Street v. New York* (1969), "It is firmly settled that under our Constitution the public expression of ideas may not be prohibited merely because the ideas are themselves offensive to some of their hearers." The principle that the state was prohibited by the First Amendment from banishing unsettling ideas from public discourse was said to be especially incongruous in a university setting, "where the free and unfettered interplay of competing views is essential to the institution's educational mission" (*Keyishian v. Board of Regents,* 1967; *Sweezy v. New Hampshire,* 1957).

The difficulty in achieving the desired results at the University of Michigan also encountered a familiar problem of overbreadth, prohibiting protected speech along with that deemed excluded from the First Amendment's shield under *Chaplinsky,* and the Supreme Court has consistently held that statutes punishing speech or conduct solely on the grounds that they are unseemly or offensive are unconstitutionally overbroad. In *Gooding v. Wilson* (1972), the Supreme Court struck down a Georgia statute that made it a misdemeanor for "any person [to], without provocation, use to or of another, and in his presence . . . opprobrious words or abusive language, tending to cause a breach of the peace." The Supreme Court found that this statute was overbroad as well, because it punished speech that did not rise to the level of "fighting words" as defined in *Chaplinsky v. New Hampshire* (1942) (see also, *Lewis v. New Orleans,* 1974). In *Papish v. University of Missouri* (1973), the Supreme Court ordered the reinstatement of a university student expelled for distributing an underground newspaper sporting the headline "Motherfucker Acquitted" on the grounds that "the mere dissemination of ideas—no matter how offensive to good taste—on a state university campus may not be shut off in the name alone of conventions of decency."

In response, the University repeatedly argued that the Policy did not apply to any speech that is protected by the First Amendment, but the court found otherwise. For example, it noted that a complaint was filed against a graduate student in the School of Social Work alleging that he harassed students based on sexual orientation and sex in a research class, when the student openly stated his belief that homosexuality was a disease and that he intended to develop a counseling plan for changing gay clients to straight. In another instance a complaint was filed against a student for reading an allegedly homophobic limerick during a scheduled class public speaking exercise. In a third case, a student stated that "he had heard that minorities had a difficult time in the course and that he had heard that they were not treated fairly." A minority professor teaching the class filed a complaint on the grounds that the comment was unfair and hurt her chances for tenure. These examples that the University considered serious comments made in the context of classroom discussion to be sanctionable and that the innocent intent of the speaker was apparently immaterial led the judge to conclude that the policy was overbroad both on its face and as applied.

Another common infirmity of campus speech codes was also evident in the University of Michigan policy. The policy did not make clear exactly what type of speech was to be prohibited, making students guess at its meaning and not providing adequate warning as to precisely what speech might constitute a violation. "Looking at the plain language of the Policy," said the judge, "it was simply impossible to discern any limitation on its scope or any conceptual distinction between protected and unprotected conduct," and the questions during oral argument "illustrated the plain fact that the University never articulated any principled way to distinguish sanctionable from protected speech." As a result of this vagueness, he concluded, "Students of common understanding were necessarily forced to guess at whether a comment about a controversial issue would later be found to be sanctionable under the Policy."

The judge recognized the University was only trying to meet its "obligation to ensure equal educational opportunities for all of its students," but he said, "such efforts must not be at the expense of free speech. Unfortunately, this was precisely what the University did." He then permanently enjoined the University from enforcing its 1988 policy "as to verbal behavior or verbal conduct," but allowed it to continue to enforce the policies regarding physical behavior or conduct.

The Michigan case was the first to reach the federal courts and fall to the commands of the First Amendment, but other schools did not immediately learn those lessons. A second such case, *UMW Post v. Board of Regents of the University Of Wisconsin* (E.D.Wisc., 1991) ultimately met the same fate, but it is equally significant because its analysis dealt with policy violations outside the classroom situations central to the Michigan case (see, e.g., Siegel, 1993).

When the case came to the court, at least nine students on various campuses had been sanctioned under the challenged policy. The UW-Parkside found that a student used inappropriate language when he called another student "Shakazulu." At UW-Eau Claire, a student was found in violation for yelling epithets loudly at a woman for approximately 10 minutes, calling her a "fucking bitch" and "fucking cunt"; and another student was disciplined for sending a computer message to an Iranian faculty member proclaiming, "Death to all Arabs!! Die Islamic scumbags!" The UW-Oshkosh disciplined one student for angrily telling an Asian American student: "It's people like you—that's the reason this country is screwed up" and "you don't belong here." The student also stated that "Whites are always getting screwed by minorities, and some day the Whites will take over." At the same institution, a female student was disciplined for referring to a black female student as a "fat-ass nigger" during an argument. At UW-Stout a student was charged in a physical altercation with two residence hall staff members with calling one of them a "piece of shit nigger" and the other a "South American immigrant." At UW-River Falls, a male student was sanctioned for yelling at a female student in public, "you've got nice tits." At UW-Parkside, however, the Administration declined to apply the rule when a student called another a "redneck," finding that "it would be very difficult to show that the term 'redneck' is by itself the equivalent of a discriminatory epithet."

To be a violation under the policy adopted by the University of Wisconsin, a comment, epithet or other expressive behavior must: (a) be racist or discriminatory; (b) be directed at an individual; (c) demean the race, sex, religion, color, creed, disability, sexual orientation, national origin, ancestry or age of the individual; and, (d) create an intimidating, hostile, or demeaning environment for education, university-related work, or other university-authorized activity.

The District Court, having the benefit of precedent in the Michigan case, approached the case with both the First Amendment and the intent of the regulation in mind, and said,

> Above all else, the First Amendment means that government has no power to restrict expression because of its message, its ideas, its subject matter, or its content. To permit the continued building of our politics and culture, and to assure self-fulfillment for each individual, our people are guaranteed the right to express any thought, free from government censorship. The essence of this forbidden censorship is content control.

The analysis in the Wisconsin case, however, dealt more specifically with the "fighting words" doctrine as articulated in *Chaplinsky*, wherein the Court stated that such words "include the lewd and obscene, the profane, the libelous, and the insulting or 'fighting' words—those which by their very utterance inflict injury or tend to incite an immediate breach of the peace."[2]

The judge noted, however,

> Since *Chaplinsky*, the Supreme Court has narrowed and clarified the scope of the fighting words doctrine in at least three ways. First, the Court has limited the fighting words definition so that it now only includes its second half. Second, the Court has stated that in order for words to meet the second half of the definition they must "naturally tend to provoke violent resentment." Finally, the Court has held that fighting words must be "directed at the person of the hearer." Then, finding that the policy included "a substantial number of situations where no breach of the peace is likely to result," he held that "the rule fails to meet the requirements of the fighting words doctrine."

Having disposed of the "fighting words" argument, the court then addressed a number of points raised by the University of Wisconsin, and the discussion here is especially helpful in explicating the preferred position of the First Amendment against other social concerns.

The Board of Regents argued that they had and the judge should strike a balance between an absolutist free speech position and the need for an appropriate learning environment and uphold the policy "because it only regulates speech with minimum social value and which has harmful effects." The court, however, found that uncensored speech itself was a considerable social value to both the individual and the community and thought that any balancing would have a negative impact. "The First Amendment's protection of speech constitutes a pre-commitment by the government to refrain from restricting the expression of ideas. This pre-commitment ensures the 'continued building of our politics and culture' as well as 'self-fulfillment for each individual.' "

The danger inherent in balancing away speech rights is often subtle and overlooked.

> This commitment to free expression must be unwavering, because there exist many situations where, in the short run, it appears advantageous to limit speech to solve pressing social problems, such as discriminatory harassment. If a balancing approach is applied, these pressing and tangible

short run concerns are likely to outweigh the more amorphous and long run benefits of free speech,

said the judge. "However," he continued,

the suppression of speech, even where the speech's content appears to have little value and great costs, amounts to governmental thought control. An individual instance of thought control may not appear to impose great costs on society. However, if a balancing test is used there are likely to be many such instances. Taken as a whole, these instances will work to dissolve the great benefits which free speech affords.

The balancing test would be improper, and even if it were applied, the policy would be found unconstitutional.

The Board then asserted that hate speech did not constitute argument intended to inform or persuade an audience and was, therefore, not the type of verbal activity protected by the First Amendment. Not so, said the court:

Most students punished under the rule are likely to have employed comments, epithets or other expressive behavior to inform their listeners of their racist or discriminatory views. Moreover, even if the UW Rule did not regulate speech intended to inform or convince the listener, the speech the rule prohibits would be protected for its expression of the speaker's emotions.

Here the court was advancing the ultimate rights of the speaker per se, not placing the First Amendment on the usual ground of the benefits to the audience of citizens at large.

The Board then contended that the regulated speech lacked First Amendment value because it is unlikely to form any part of a dialogue or exchange of views and because it does not provide an opportunity for a reply. The court, drawing on *American Bookseller Association v. Hudnut* (1985), a case that had earlier disposed of Catherine MacKinnon's (1993) theory in a different context, also rejected the argument "that when speech is 'unanswerable,' and the metaphor that there is a 'marketplace of ideas' does not apply, the First Amendment does not apply either." Wrong again, said the judge:

The metaphor is time honored; Milton's *Aeropagitica* and John Stewart Mill's *On Liberty* defend freedom of speech on the ground that the truth will prevail, and many of the most important cases under the First Amendment recite this position. The Framers undoubtedly believed it. As a general matter it is true. But the Constitution does not make the dominance of truth a necessary condition of freedom of speech.

Realizing the validity of the University's desire to promote diversity, the judge agreed that increasing diversity is "clearly a constitutionally permissible goal for an institution of higher education" (*University of California Regents v. Bakke,* 1978). However, he reasoned, "the UW Rule does as much to hurt diversity on Wisconsin campuses as it does to help it. By establishing content-based restrictions on speech, the rule limits the diversity of ideas among students and thereby prevents the 'robust exchange of ideas' which intellectually diverse campuses provide."

Though the University's motives were clear and the effects of hate speech upon the targets was unpleasant, he said, the proposed solution failed to pass constitutional muster:

The problems of bigotry and discrimination sought to be addressed here are real and truly corrosive of the educational environment. But freedom of speech is almost absolute in our land and the only restriction the fighting words doctrine can abide is that based on the fear of violent reaction. Content-based prohibitions such as that in the UW Rule, however well intended, simply cannot survive the screening which our Constitution demands.

The University of Michigan case dealt with certain applications of the hate speech code to classroom activities, and the University of Wisconsin opinion addressed instances involving individual students arising on campus but outside of sanctioned university activities. A third case, *Iota Xi Chapter of Sigma Chi Fraternity v. George Mason University* (1991), resulted from different circumstances. As part of a fraternity social activity that involved a skit to raise funds for charity, the Sigma Chi fraternity at George Mason University staged an "ugly woman contest," in the cafeteria of the student union. According to the undisputed record, one of the members "dressed as an offensive caricature of a black woman. He was painted black and wore stringy,

black hair decorated with curlers, and his outfit was stuffed with
pillows to exaggerate a woman's breasts and buttocks. He spoke in
slang to parody African-Americans."

Shortly thereafter, 247 students, many of them foreign or minority
students, signed a petition, stating: "We are condemning the racist and
sexist implications of this event in which male members dressed as
women. One man in particular wore a black face, portraying a negative
stereotype of black women." University officials held a number of
meetings and determined that the fraternity's behavior had "created
a hostile learning environment for women and blacks, incompatible
with the University's mission." The Dean of Student Services imposed
social restrictions on the fraternity and required it to "implement an
educational program addressing cultural differences, diversity, and
the concerns of women."

The Fraternity later apologized to the University officials for the
presentation and conceded that the contest was "sophomoric and
offensive," but they filed suit seeking a declaratory judgment that
sanctions for the skit violated their First Amendment rights to freedom
of speech. The University responded that the conduct was not protected speech and that even if protected speech, it had compelling
educational interests at stake that justified the discipline imposed on
the fraternity.

The district court ruled in favor of Sigma Chi, explaining,

> One of the fundamental rights secured by the First Amendment is that of
> free, uncensored expression, even on matters some may think are trivial,
> vulgar or profane (*Berger v. Battaglia*). Because that fundamental right
> extends to students at a state university, a state university may not hinder
> the exercise of First Amendment rights simply because it feels that expo-
> sure to a given group's ideas may be somehow harmful to certain students
> (*Gay Alliance of Students v. Matthews*, 1976; *Healy v. James*, 1972).

Even if the activity were protected speech, the University contended
that any infringement on the First Amendment rights of the fraternity
was permissible because compelling educational interests were at
stake. Specifically, it said, "the behavior undermined the education of
minority and women students, the university's mission to promote
learning through a culturally diverse student body, the university's

mission to eliminate racist and sexist behavior on campus and the university's mission to accomplish maximal desegregation of its student body." Certainly, the judge said, the university does have these interests, but there has been no substantial or material disruption of that educational mission. Rather, he noted, "The student activity at issue in this action is consistent with GMU's educational mission in conveying ideas and promoting the free flow and expression of those ideas."

In trying to advance a part of the educational mission, George Mason had exceeded the limits of its constitutional authority and forgotten about its mission to allow the free exchange of ideas. The judge reminded the GMU administration,

> The First Amendment does not guarantee that other concepts virtually sacred to our Nation as a whole—such as the principle that discrimination based on race is odious and destructive—will go unquestioned in the marketplace of ideas (*Texas v. Johnson*). As noted by the Fourth Circuit in *Berger v. Battaglia,* a more appropriate response to the activities of the fraternity, and one consistent with the First Amendment "would have been instead to say to those offended by . . . [the] speech that their right to protest that speech by all peaceable means would be as stringently safeguarded . . . as would . . . [the] right to engage in it" (*Berger,* 779 F.2d at 1001, 1986).

In short, the court said,

> a state university may not suppress expression because it finds that expression offensive (see *Piarowski v. Illinois Community College,* [racially and sexually offensive art work not subject to outright suppression by state school],) . . . "If there is a bedrock principle underlying the First Amendment, it is that the Government may not prohibit the expression of an idea simply because society finds the idea itself offensive or disagreeable" (*Texas v. Johnson,* 109 S. Ct. at 2544.) The First Amendment does not recognize exceptions for bigotry, racism, and religious intolerance or ideas or matters some may deem trivial, vulgar or profane.

George Mason University could and did disagree with the message presented by the Sigma Chi skit, and it could certainly say so. It may not, however, discipline the students by infringing on their First Amendment rights based on the perceived offensive content of the activity. One of the most persistent and insidious threats to first amendment rights has been that posed by the "heckler's veto, imposed by the successful importuning of government to curtail 'offensive' speech at peril of suffering disruptions of public order." (*Berger*, 779 F.2d at 1001). In this instance, GMU sought to discipline the students based precisely on the "heckler's veto." That is not permissible.

The District Court granted summary judgment for the fraternity, and George Mason University appealed to the U. S. Court of Appeals for the Fourth Circuit. Judge Sprouse's opinion in *Iota Xi Chapter of Sigma Chi Fraternity v. George Mason University* (1993) is worthy of attention for two reasons. First, it is the highest federal court decision on a campus speech code. Second, it provides further illumination on the tension between the exercise of First Amendment and other legitimate goals of educational institutions.

The University first argued that the skit was conduct and not speech and was, therefore, not protected by the First Amendment. This is a frequent argument from those wanting to proscribe hateful ideas, even when expressed in "pure speech" ideas. The court, however, had a better understanding of communication theory and a different understanding of the scope of the First Amendment. The court said the skit was protected,

> because it is inherently expressive entertainment. Even if this were not true, however, the skit, in our view, qualifies as expressive conduct under the test articulated in *Texas v. Johnson*. It is true that the Johnson test for determining the expressiveness of conduct requires "an intent to convey a particularized message" and a great likelihood "that the message would be understood by those who viewed it." *Id.* (quoting *Spence v. Washington*). As Johnson and Spence point out, however, the intent to convey a message can be inferred from the conduct and the circumstances surrounding it.

"Thus viewed," said Sprouse, "the University's argument is self-defeating." The University's position was that "the message conveyed by the Fraternity's conduct—that racial and sexual themes should be treated lightly—was completely antithetical to the University's mission of promoting diversity and providing an educational environment free from racism and sexism." One official had stated that,

> the University does not and cannot condone this type of on-campus behavior which perpetuated derogatory racial and sexual stereotypes, tends to isolate minority students, and creates a hostile and distracting learning environment. Such behavior is incompatible with, and destructive to, the University's mission of promoting diversity within its student body [and] sends a message to the student body and the community that we . . . are not serious about hurtful and offensive behavior on campus.

The court said that affidavits from University administrators had taken action against the fraternity because

> its boorish message had interfered with the described University mission. It is manifest from these circumstances that the University officials thought the Fraternity intended to convey a message. The Fraternity members' apology and post-conduct contriteness suggest that they held the same view.

The University seemed to be contending that the skit sent a seriously wrong message and was no serious message, at the same time. On that point, the judge concluded,

> To be sure, no evidence suggests that the Fraternity advocated segregation or inferior social status for women. What is evident is that the Fraternity's purposefully nonsensical treatment of sexual and racial themes was intended to impart a message that the University's concerns, in the Fraternity's view, should be treated humorously.

In punishing the fraternity, the University did so because the message of the skit

> ran counter to the views the University sought to communicate to its students and the community. The mischief was the University's punishment of those who scoffed at its goals of racial integration and gender neutrality, while permitting, even encouraging, conduct that would further the viewpoint expressed in the University's goals and probably embraced by a majority of society as well.

The University urged the court to balance Sigma Chi's offensive conduct against the other substantial interests inherent in educational endeavors. The court was sympathetic with the University's goals but found the means to be unconstitutional.

> The University certainly has a substantial interest in maintaining an educational environment free of discrimination and racism, and in providing gender-neutral education. Yet it seems equally apparent that it has available numerous alternatives to imposing punishment on students based on the viewpoints they express. We agree wholeheartedly that it is the University officials' responsibility, even their obligation, to achieve the goals they have set. On the other hand, a public university has many constitutionally permissible means to protect female and minority students.

Selective punishment based upon message content, however, was unconstitutional under the First Amendment, and, the court concluded, the "University should have accomplished its goals in some fashion other than silencing speech on the basis of its viewpoint."

The final case dealing with campus speech codes, *Dambrot v. Central Michigan Univ.* (1993), is distinctive in that it concerns remarks made by a faculty member, and it resulted in the court's declaring it unconstitutional even though the speech in question did not merit First Amendment protection.

Dambrot, coach of the men's basketball team, used the word *nigger* in a locker room talk he gave to the players and coaching staff, addressing several players, both black and white, and one assistant coach, by the term. Dambrot testified that he intended to use the term in a "positive and reinforcing" manner during this closed-door locker room meeting, and the court found "absolutely no evidence to the contrary." Some time later, a former player reported the use of the word, the Athletic Director conducted interviews with the team, and all of the black players informed him that they were not offended by their coach's use of the term. The university's affirmative action officer, however, "confronted Dambrot, who admitted to using the term, though in a positive manner. The officer expressed to Dambrot her opinion that the term was incapable of being used positively and that, in any case, its use was a violation of the university's 'discriminatory harassment policy.' "

The officer recommended that Dambrot be disciplined, and he was suspended without pay for 5 days. A student demonstration was staged, accounts of a "racial incident" at the university were spread through the news media, and Dambrot was subsequently terminated. He brought suit alleging that his employment was terminated because he used the term *nigger,* and that the termination violated his First Amendment rights to free speech and academic freedom.

The District Court examined the issues and concluded, "There is no conclusion available from the evidence other than that a coach's disappointment with team play, and his attendant use of assertedly motivating language, was of private concern only to him and perhaps to his players. It was not speech on a matter of public concern." Nonetheless, Judge Cleland granted summary judgment in favor of Dambrot, declared the discriminatory harassment policy unconstitutional on its face, and permanently enjoined Central Michigan from further enforcement of the policy.

The CMU policy, in relevant part, prohibited

> any intentional, unintentional, physical, verbal, or nonverbal behavior that subjects an individual to an intimidating, hostile or offensive educational, employment or living environment by (c) demeaning or slurring individuals through . . . written literature because of their racial or ethnic affiliation; or (d) using symbols, epitaphs [sic] or slogans that infer [sic] negative connotations about an individual's racial or ethnic affiliation. [Plan for Affirmative Action at Central Michigan University, Section III(b)(1), Racial and Ethnic Harassment]

Although the University argued, "albeit half-heartedly," that the policy was not a "speech code" and was not equivalent to an ordinance or statute because it contains no real penalty mechanism, Judge Cleland found "such arguments disingenuous." He also found the speech code unconstitutional because it was overbroad, prohibiting much protected speech, and vague, almost impossible to interpret objectively. In addition, it was constitutionally infirm in that it constituted viewpoint discrimination in violation of the First Amendment.

On the point of overbreadth, the court said,

> The policy appears to have been drafted to include as much within its ambit as possible, and its language is sweeping indeed. It is not much of

a stretch to imagine a treatise (or a student's term paper or even a cafe-teria bull session), which explores the source of conflict among residents of some middle-eastern region and posits that one tribe involved in the conflict is the more blameworthy due to some ancient ethnic traditions which give rise to barbarian combativeness or a longstanding inability to compromise.

Especially troubling, said the judge, was that according to the policy,

it is of no import that the author or speaker was speaking in good faith about a plausible thesis, nor that he was not intending to refer to any particular individual, either on or off CMU's campus. Any behavior, even unintentional, that offends any individual is to be prohibited under the policy. The spirit in which the words are spoken is of no moment to this policy. The intent to inform rather than harm is irrelevant. If the speech gives offense it is prohibited. . . . On its face this policy is overbroad.

Relying on the rationale in *Doe v. Michigan* (1989), the court said,

The policy at issue here goes even beyond suppressing "offensive" speech and suppresses "negative connotations" that are "unintentional." The policy instituted by CMU is even more overbroad than the U of M policy struck down in Doe, and, for that reason, all the more improper.

The court also found that the policy contemplated unconstitutional discrimination among viewpoints. The judge noted that it prohibited use of

"symbols, epitaphs [sic] or slogans that infer negative connotations about an individual's racial or ethnic affiliation." Negative racial connotations are prohibited, but positive (or at least non-negative) connotations, based on those same racial or ethnic affiliations, are allowed. . . . That speaker's tally of ethnic attributes, though, would be the only viewpoint allowed to be heard on the CMU campus, because all speakers with a differing view on that issue are prohibited by the policy from responding: in their words the speech police can "infer negative connotations about an individual's . . . ethnic affiliation" or something "hostile" on those ethnic grounds.

The policy was also found constitutionally void for vagueness:

The terms "offensive" and "negative" require subjective reference in order to define them; the meanings of these terms are as vastly divergent as are individual tastes and personalities. The difficulties experienced in trying to subjectively define and prohibit speech which is "offensive" become quite evident in the facts of this very case.

"Consequently," Judge Cleland explained,

the media and public also reacted in several ways, from outrage to complacent understanding, with many variants in between, so some of them appeared to be offended, and some not. The facts of this case exemplify the vast diversity of reaction to speech which is potentially offensive. For a person, even one as perceptive and intelligent as the average college student or professor, to accurately guess what a listener's reaction will be to something potentially offensive is nigh on impossible.

In fact, he said,

when asked to specify what kind of conduct would constitute a "hostile environment," the university's own President . . . was utterly incapable of defining the terms of the policy. With the leader of the university unable to describe the boundaries of prohibited speech under his own policy, it becomes a daunting task for defendants to argue that the policy provides "fair notice of the standard of conduct to which a citizen is held accountable."

Perhaps more intriguing even than the above cases using the First Amendment as a shield is the settlement of a lawsuit filed against the University of California, Riverside. Phi Kappa Sigma challenged its 3-year suspension from campus by administrators, based on complaints from a Latino student organization that they were offended by the fraternity's T-shirt logo for a "South of the Border" party. Backed by counsel from the Individual Rights Foundation and supported by new provisions in the California Education Code to guarantee student speech rights, the fraternity used the First Amendment as a sword. University officials, realizing that they would most likely lose the suit and facing adverse publicity and high legal costs, agreed to a settlement —one that included a requirement that the responsible university administrators undergo First Amendment sensitivity training (see,

Billingsley, 1993; Frammolino, 1993; "The Offense of Going Too Far," 1993; Hentoff, 1994).

A recent survey published by the Freedom Forum First Amendment Center at Vanderbilt University documented that campus speech codes are still widespread and suggested that the codes were directed more often at speech than against behavior (Korwar, 1994). Yet, in every case in which a campus hate speech code at a public institution has been tested against the commands of the First Amendment, the courts have rejected virtually every possible defense and found them to be unconstitutional. In addition, one court held that administrators and student judiciary board members might be held liable for § 1983 violation of a faculty member's First Amendment rights (*Silva v. University of New Hampshire*, 1994). Furthermore, even in the more limited public forum of a public high school, the district court held that a dress code prohibiting clothing that "harasses, intimidates, or demeans an individual or group of individuals because of sex, color, race, religion, handicap, national origin or sexual orientation" was unconstitutional (*Pyle v. South Hadley School Committee*, 1994, citing *Steirer v. Bethlehem Area School District*, 1993); "Even 'teaching values' must conform to constitutional standards. The constitutional line is crossed when, instead of merely teaching, the educators demand that students express agreement with the educators' values." At this writing, a case is pending in Santa Clara County Superior Court challenging the speech code at Stanford University, a private institution, under California's 1992 Leonard Law and the First Amendment. Drafted by law professor Thomas Gray, the Stanford speech code is among the most narrowly drawn of such policies, and no student has ever been charged with a violation since it was adopted in 1990. Nonetheless, Robert Corry, a law student and one of the plaintiffs, said the code has a chilling effect on free discussion and asserted, "The only valid speech code is the First Amendment to the U.S. Constitution" (Wildavsky, 1994).[3]

The above line of decisions by federal courts, reinforced by the U.S. Supreme Court decision in *R.A.V. v. St. Paul* (1992), invalidating a municipal ordinance with the same purpose, has led numerous other universities to avoid or repeal similar campus speech codes that appear certain to violate freedom of speech. The University of Pennsylvania, for example, has repealed the code that brought it national notoriety in the much-publicized "water buffalo" incident, and former President Sheldon Hackney told Congress that he believed ever enacting the code was a mistake (Russakoff, 1993). Gordon Baldwin, a law professor who helped draft the University of Wisconsin policy that was declared unconstitutional, now says universities should not enact such codes (Farrish, 1994). California State University-Northridge President Blenda Wilson has said she was "opposed to speech codes" and "would never initiate a speech ban" (Chandler, 1994). The University of Connecticut also dropped its hate speech code after, it was said, they realized the disservice they were doing "by teaching future judges, writers and others that policing speech is permissible" ("Free Speech on Campus," 1994).

Republican Responsibilities

Hateful thoughts and words are not, of course, limited to college campuses, nor are the conflicts between individual freedom of speech and the sensibilities of the communitarians. The fate of attempts to mitigate the effects of hate speech in the larger society have, however, been the same as that of campus speech codes. The U.S. Supreme Court, in a case styled *R.A.V. v. St. Paul* (1992), declared unconstitutional a St. Paul, Minnesota, ordinance that provided,

> Whoever places on public or private property a symbol, object, appellation, characterization or graffiti, including, but not limited to, a burning cross or Nazi swastika, which one knows or has reasonable grounds to know arouses anger, alarm or resentment in others on the basis of race, color, creed, religion or gender commits disorderly conduct and shall be guilty of a misdemeanor.

Treating the "fighting words" stance of the city much like that of university administrators, the Court found the ordinance unconstitutional on its face because it prohibited "otherwise permitted speech solely on the basis of the subjects the speech addresses. . . . The First Amendment does not permit St. Paul to impose special prohibitions on those speakers who express views on disfavored subjects."

Moreover, said the Court in stretching the scope of the First Amendment, "the ordinance goes even beyond mere content discrimination, to actual viewpoint discrimination." Justice Scalia suggested that the ordinance would allow a wide range of "fighting words" by advocates of tolerance and equality, but would make criminal those used by the opposition speakers. Under the First Amendment, he said, "St. Paul has no such authority to license one side of a debate to fight freestyle, while requiring the other to follow Marquis of Queensbury Rules."

Many viewed Scalia's opinion as an extended constitutional diatribe against not only what he saw as the excesses of the "politically correct" censors but also against the legitimate concerns and competing interests of hate speech opponents. "One must wholeheartedly agree," said Scalia covering that potential charge, that diverse communities have "the responsibility, even the obligation," to counter noxious and divisive attitudes, "but the manner of that confrontation cannot consist of selective limitations upon speech." In response to the city's assertion that "only a content-specific measure can communicate to minority groups that the 'group hatred' aspect of such speech 'is not condoned by the majority,' " Scalia replied, "The point of the First Amendment is that majority preferences must be expressed in some fashion other than silencing speech on the basis of its content."

The Court was even less impressed by the city's argument that the censorship imposed by the ordinance was only a secondary effect of its intent to "protect against the victimization of a person or persons who are particularly vulnerable because of their membership in a group that historically has been discriminated against." To which, Scalia replied, "As we said in *Boos v. Barry*, 485 U.S. 312 (1988), 'listeners' reactions to speech are not the type of secondary effects' " contemplated and excepted in *Renton v. Playtime Theatres, Inc.* (1986). "The emotive impact of speech on its audience is not a secondary effect," he said.

Neither did the Court accept the city's contention that the ordinance was narrowly drawn to serve the compelling interest of ensuring "the basic human rights of members of groups that have historically been subjected to discrimination, including the right of such group members to live in peace where they wish." Scalia acknowledged that the interest was compelling and that the ordinance promoted the end. However, he suggested, "The dispositive question ... is whether content discrimination is reasonably necessary to achieve St. Paul's compelling interests; it plainly is not." The city could demonstrate its opposition to discrimination, but it could not do so by subverting the First Amendment and "imposing unique limitations upon speakers who (however benightedly) disagree."

In summarizing his opinion, Scalia said, "Let there be no mistake about our belief that burning a cross in someone's front yard is reprehensible. But St. Paul has sufficient means at its disposal to prevent such behavior without adding the First Amendment to the fire."

Although I seldom agree with Justice Scalia's approach to First Amendment jurisprudence, and I suspect he was engaging in a bit of spirited ax-grinding against "political correctness" in the above case, I do think he reached the correct result and generally for the right reasons. That said, let me make it clear that I yield to no one in my passionate commitment to social justice and the belief that it can be best achieved through reasoned discourse. My training in rhetorical and communication theory that helped me to understand why free speech is essential to republican government also convinced me that words matter, that they can structure realities, cashier governments, inspire noble deeds, and deeply wound the innocent.

My position and my argument is not only that hate speech codes are patently unconstitutional under the First Amendment, it is also that they are a bad idea as a matter of public policy. When first asked to contribute to this collection of essays, I suggested that the editors might wish to enlist someone else to write about hate speech, because I am, in a sense, for it. But, let me explain that statement.

The corrosive emotion of hate is, I think, a manifestation of the emotion of fear, created by economic insecurity, relative status deprivation, lack of education, feelings of powerlessness, sexual insecurity, or a more general fear of all differences as disconfirming the validity of one's own personal security. The expression of these feelings and targeting them toward some "other" is, I think, what concerns the advocates of hate speech codes. Even if these codes were constitutional, they cannot be effective. Proscribing the words does nothing to change the underlying thoughts and fears; hate speech does not express the unthinkable, only the unreasonable. In fact, suppression of speech often exacerbates and intensifies the sentiments of those silenced by law, while denying to everyone the opportunity to seek and discover wisdom through debate and the clash of ideas. On the other hand, a convincing case can be made that fostering freedom of speech can result in greater tolerance among citizens with differing views (see, generally, Bollinger, 1986).

Hate speech is much like a canker sore on the body politic. Legal restrictions on hate speech only suppress the symptoms; they do not treat the underlying causes of the social disease. Applying the Band-Aid of a speech code might keep it from the sight of those who would be repulsed, but the infection would remain and fester. A better prescription would be to expose it to the air of speech and the light of reason, the healing antibiotic of counterargument.

Furthermore, hate speech can serve an important social and political function. Irrational expressions of hate based on the status of the targets can alert us to the fact that something is wrong—in the body politic, in ourselves, or in the speakers. It might suggest that some change is necessary, or it might only warn us against the potential for demagogues. Speech codes, ordinances, and statutes would (if they could be enforced) blind us to the problems and deny us the opportunity to solve them before they broke out into actions.

Senator Frank Lautenberg, in a Senate speech condemning the remarks of Khalid Abdul Muhammad and recognizing that the message was protected by the First Amendment, made the point quite eloquently:

> We condemn Mr. Muhammad and his message. But we must also reach out to the students who were moved by his rhetoric of hate and attracted by his words of violence.
>
> Mr. President, we must figure out why those words fall on receptive ears. We have to come to grips with the fact that some of our students liked what they heard.
>
> Why? Why did they like what they heard? The answer is they are like other people—capable of prejudice. The answer is that the poverty, the racism, the hopelessness, they have witnessed in their communities has stoked anger—and it is a small step from anger to hatred. The answer is that many have been treated badly—and feel the system leaves them out. The answer is that they have seen racist statements made by whites—prominent whites in some cases—go unchallenged.

Mr. President, we need to condemn what was said in the strongest possible terms. But, in the end, we have to do more than condemn. We have to respond so that we prevent prejudice from taking seed and growing and bursting into a deadly bloom.

We have not found a way to reach the students who cheered Mr. Muhammad's speech. We have not been successful in dealing with their pain and their anger—which can easily spill over to violent episodes of rage and hatred.

That, Mr. President, is the hard part of what we have to do. (Lautenberg, 1994, p. S1951)

Hate speech codes might have other negative effects as well; they might actually inhibit, rather than enhance, the education of students and the development of responsible citizens. Republican theory has long recognized that active citizenship is hard work, that tumults are often the price of liberty in self-governing republics, that tumultuous liberty was preferable to ordered despotism, and that good laws were of no avail if the people were corrupt (Machiavelli, 1970, pp. 158-159). The same rationale might be applied to analyzing the relationship between free speech and speech codes as they relate to the goals of the university and the realities of racism.

Adopting hate speech codes is much easier than working to change the attitudes that lead to their consideration. As one study concluded, university

administrators must weigh the value of punishing hate speech against the fundamental educational mission. Educating those who verbally abuse others requires a greater commitment of time, energy, and resources than does punishing such offenders. But the ultimate effect more nearly meets the goal of higher education: to expand the mind and heart beyond the fear of the unknown, opening them to the whole range of human experiences. (Korwar, 1994, p. 31)

Blenda Wilson, President of Cal State-Northridge, seemed to express such an understanding and make that choice. In describing the approach on her campus, she said,

What happens here is not only that there's tension but that it's a tension that as a university community we are charged to understand, to articulate, to respond to. We have a responsibility as a university not only to educate people in terms of knowledge, but to help create future citizens.

It would be inappropriate and wrong for a university and community to purport to be a homogeneous community in which there is no tension over ideas. So we don't back away from it in the ways that genteel society avoids these kinds of tensions. And more than that, we have young people, so we have emotions involved. We have deep feelings of growing up and maturing and what that means.

These will be the leaders and the citizens and the employees in a multiethnic, multicultural society. If we can provide a place where the tensions that come out of our past are understood better, then our graduates indeed will be able to lead in a moral and tolerant way. (Chandler, 1994, p. B5)

In conclusion, I argue unapologetically here for First Amendment protection for hate speech and against constitutionally unwarranted codes that only hide the symptoms of such social maladies. The solution I suggest is something much more difficult. It demands listening carefully, thinking rationally, judging critically, and refuting vigorously those ideas and ideologies we find offensive or wrong. Such an approach requires both skill and courage, but the *res publica* will benefit most from allowing such expression and by a public refutation showing it to be wrong. Even those who accept the communitarian diagnosis of the ills of contemporary society, do not advocate unconstitutional speech codes but recognize individual rights and stress the responsibility to exercise moral suasion urging the rejection of unacceptable ideas (see "Rights, Responsibilities," 1993, p. 22).[4]

In a thoughtful analysis of the costs and benefits of freedom of speech, Simon Lee (1990) noted, and I agree, that free speech controversies are almost always high constitutional moments or important episodes in our personal lives. They should make us aware not only of the free speech issues but of deeper cultural issues demanding attention. We might, he contends, facilitate better solutions to both sides of the conflict if we can strengthen broad public support for the free flow and critical reception of ideas. To make speech more valuable we should work to foster a society in which more people have the ability to analyze information and opinion critically, where minority groups and the minority have the self-confidence that comes from being respected and accepted, where tolerance is a general virtue, where people can reflect and argue, speaking rather than shouting.

Notes

1. For two of the most thoughtful analyses of the relationship between hate speech and the First Amendment concerning the debate on the H. Res. 343, see Mike Synar (1994), "First Amendment Rights," and Jolene Unsoeld (1994), "Disgusting, Abhorrent Comments Are Still Protected by Our Constitution."

2. The *Chaplinsky* Court set forth a two-part definition for fighting words, but it applied only the second half. The Court did this because the statute in question had been construed to regulate only language that tends to incite an immediate breach of the peace. The statute involved in *Chaplinsky* provided:

> No person shall address any offensive, derisive or annoying word to any other person who is lawfully in any street or other public place, nor call him any offensive or derisive name, nor make any noise or exclamation in his presence and hearing with the intent to deride, offend or annoy him, or to prevent him from pursuing his lawful business or occupation.

3. The Stanford code was subsequently declared unconstitutional in *Corry et al. v. Leland Stanford University et al.*, No. 740309, Supreme Court, Santa Clara County, 27 February 1995. For a discussion of the Leonard Law, assuring freedom of speech to students in public and private secondary schools and institutions of higher education in California, see Nat Hentoff (1993), "Magna Carta for Students."

4. For a general exposition of the communitarian position, see Amitai Etzioni (1993), *The Spirit of Community*.

Cases Cited

American Bookseller Association v. Hudnut, 771 F.2d 1197 (1985).

Beauharnais v. Illinois, 343 U.S. 250 (1952).

Berger v. Battaglia, 779 F.2d 992, 1000 (4th Cir. 1985), cert. denied, 476 U.S. 1159 (1986).

Boos v. Barry, 485 U. S. 312 (1988).

Cafeteria Employees Local 302 v. Angelos, 320 U.S. 293, 295 (1943).

Cantwell v. Connecticut, 310 U.S. 296 (1940).

Chaplinsky v. New Hampshire, 310 U.S. 568 (1942).

Cohen v. California, 403 U.S. 15 (1971).

Corry v. Leland Stanford University, No. 740309, Supreme Court of Santa Clara County, California (1995).

Dambrot v. Central Michigan Univ., 839 F. Supp. 477; (E.D. Mich., 1993).

De Jonge v. Oregon, 299 U.S. 353, 365 (1930).

Doe v. Michigan, 721 F. Supp. 852 (E.D. Mich., 1989).

Gay Alliance of Students v. Matthews, 544 F.2d 162, 166 (4th Cir., 1976).

Gertz v. Robert Welch, Inc., 418 U.S. 323 (1974).

Gooding v. Wilson, 405 U.S. 518 (1972).

Healy v. James, 408 U.S. 169 (1972).

Iota Xi Chapter of Sigma Chi Fraternity v. George Mason University, 773 F. Supp. 792;
    (E.D. Va., 1991).
Iota Xi Chapter of Sigma Chi Fraternity v. George Mason University, 993 F.2d 386 (4th
    Cir., 1993).
Keyishian v. Board of Regents, 385 U.S. 585 (1967).
Lewis v. New Orleans, 415 U.S. 130 (1974).
Linn v. Plant Guard Workers, 383 U.S. 53 (1966).
Old Dominion Branch No. 496, Natl. Assn. Of Letter Carriers v. Austin, 418 U.S. 264
    (1974).
Papish v. University of Missouri, 410 U.S. 667 (1973).
People v. Spielman, 318 Ill., 482, 149 N. E. 466 (1925).
Piarowski v. Illinois Community College, 759 F.2d 625, 630 (7th Cir.), cert. denied, 474
    U.S. 1007 (1985).
Pyle v. South Hadley School of Committee, 861 F Supp. 157 (D. Mass 1994).
R.A.V. v. St. Paul, 112 S. Ct. 2538 (1992).
Renton v. Playtime Theatres, Inc., 475 U. S. 41 (1986).
Silva v. University of New Hampshire, 1994 U.S. Dist. Lexis 13281 (D. NH 1994).
Spence v. Washington, 418 U.S. 405 (1974).
Steirer v. Bethlehem Area School District, 987 F.2d 989 (3rd Cir., 1993).
Street v. New York, 394 U.S. 576 (1969).
Sweezy v. New Hampshire, 354 U.S. 234, 250 (1957).
Terminiello v. Chicago, 337 U.S. 1 (1949).
Texas v. Johnson, 491 U.S. 397 (1989).
University of California Regents v. Bakke, 438 U.S. 265, (1978).
UMW Post v. Board of Regents of the University Of Wisconsin, 774 F.Supp. 1163
    (E.D.Wisc., 1991).
West Virginia State Board of Education v. Barnette, 319 U.S. 624 (1943).

References

Berton, P. (1992, November 14). The case of David Irving: Why muzzle the wackos?
    Toronto Star, p. F3.
Billingsley, K. L. (1993, November 10). Free speech sensitivity training for UC officials.
    Sacramento Bee, p. B11.
Bollinger, L. C. (1986). *The tolerant society: Freedom of speech and extremist speech in
    America*. New York: Oxford University Press.
Chandler, J. (1994, November 22). CSUN leader believes in facing tension, not in
    censorship. *Los Angeles Times*, p. B5.
Delgado, R. (1991). Campus antiracism rules: Constitutional narratives in collision.
    Northwestern University Law Review, 85, 343.
Delgado, R., & Stefanic, J. (1993, November 13). Controls on hate speech are not
    censorship. *Washington Post*, p. A23.
D'Souza, D. (1991). *Illiberal education: The politics of race and sex on campus*. New
    York: Free Press.
Etzioni, A. (1993). *The spirit of community: Rights, responsibilities, and the communi-
    tarian agenda*. New York: Crown.

Farrish, K. (1994, February 7). Wesleyan considers dropping hate-speech ban. *Hartford Courant*, p. A1.

Fish, S. (1994). *There's no such thing as free speech, and it's a good thing, too*. New York: Oxford University Press.

Frammolino, R. (1993, November 11). Free speech suit ends ban on UC Riverside fraternity. *Los Angeles Times*, p. A1.

Free speech on campus. (1994, February 14). *Hartford Courant*, p. B8.

Gates, H. L., Jr. (1993, September 20). Let them talk: Why civil liberties pose no threat to civil rights. *The New Republic*, p. 37.

German Information Center. (1994, April). Constitutional court: Denial of Holocaust is not protected as free speech. *The Week in Germany*.

Germany bars controversial historian. (1993, November 10). *Reuter Library Report*, BC cycle.

Greenwalt, K. (1989). *Speech, crime, and the uses of language*. New York: Oxford University Press.

Haiman, F. S. (1993). *"Speech acts" and the First Amendment*. Carbondale: Southern Illinois University Press.

Hentoff, N. (1992). *Free speech for me—But not for thee*. New York: HarperCollins.

Hentoff, N. (1993, January 30). Magna Carta for students. *Washington Post*, p. A21.

Hentoff, N. (1994, January 1). Sombrero scrap. *Washington Post*, p. A21.

Historian Irving again refused Australian visa. (1994, May 3). Agence France Presse.

Hodges, R. (1993, November 27). Speech codes off campus! *Washington Post*, p. A25.

Iran says Rushdie death decree "irrevocable." (1994, April 11). Agence France Presse.

Korwar, A. R. (1994). *War of words: Speech codes at public colleges and universities*. Nashville, TN: Freedom Forum First Amendment Center.

Lautenberg, F. (1994, February 25). A response to racism. *Congressional Record, 140*, p. S1951.

Lawrence, C. R., III. (1990). If he hollers, let him go: Regulating racist speech on campus. *Duke Law Journal 1990*, p. 431.

Lederer, L. J. (1993, September 13). Constitutional contradictions in speech, equality. *Chicago Tribune*, p. 15.

Lee, S. (1990). *The cost of free speech*. London: Faber & Faber.

Machiavelli, N. (1970). *The discourses* (L. J. Walker, Trans.). London: Penguin.

MacKinnon, C. A. (1993). *Only words*. Cambridge, MA: Harvard University Press.

Malveaux, J. (1993, August 18). Keep campus speech civil. *USA Today*, p. 10A.

Matsuda, M. J. (1989). Public response to racism speech. *Michigan Law Review, 87*, 2320.

Miller, M. (1994, April 27). German ban on Holocaust denial upheld. *Los Angeles Times*, p. 4.

The offense of going too far. (1993, November 21). *Los Angeles Times*, p. 4.

Rauch, J. (1993). *Kindly inquisitors: The new attacks on free thought*. Chicago: University of Chicago Press.

Rights, responsibilities. (1993, December 22). *Christian Science Monitor*, p. 22.

Russakoff, D. (1993, November 17). Penn is abandoning speech code. *Washington Post*, p. A1.

Siegel, B. (1993, March 28). Fighting words: It seemed like a noble idea. *Los Angeles Times Magazine*, pp. 14ff.

Sunstein, C. R. (1993). *Democracy and the problem of free speech*. New York: Free Press.

Swardson, A. (1994, April). Canadians cancel speech. *Washington Post*, p. A18.

Synar, M. (1994, March 2). First Amendment rights. *Congressional Record, 140,* p. E300.

Unsoeld, J. (1994, February 24). Disgusting, abhorrent comments are still protected by our Constitution. *Congressional Record, 140,* p. E259.

Walker, S. (1994). *Hate speech: The history of an American controversy.* Lincoln: University of Nebraska Press.

Wildavsky, B. (1994, May 4). War of words over Stanford's speech rule. *San Francisco Chronicle,* p. A14.

Afterword

Hate, or Power?

David Theo Goldberg
Arizona State University

In the past decade or so, the prevailing social characterization of racist expressions has been reduced to the category of hate. Public institutions like universities have constructed hate speech codes, and state criminal codes have introduced the category of hate crimes. Nowadays, media coverage on "racist incidents" in the public sphere—on college campuses or in shopping malls, in the United States or in post-communist Europe—speak almost exclusively of the expression of hate.[1] The Florida hate crimes statute, not untypical of state laws that have become increasingly popular throughout the United States, makes possible (without requiring) the imposition of harsher penalties whenever a criminal offense "evidences prejudice based on the race, color, ancestry, ethnicity, religion or national origin of the victim." (In *Mitchell v. Wisconsin,* the Supreme Court unanimously affirmed the constitutionality of such enhanced sentences.) This conception in terms of hate was not always the case: Not only in the 1960s but throughout the 1970s reference to the phenomenon of "hate" was largely absent. The absence of such reference was due not to the relative absence of or silence about racist "incidents" during these decades: The former was, after all, the decade of civil rights struggles and "Black Power," the latter, the decade of the "Soweto uprising" and the instigation of apartheid boycotts as well as of affirmative action and the charge of "reverse discrimination." Yet we should be careful not to erase the conceptual history that produced expressions of "hate" by simply insisting that its genealogy is limited to the decade that produced the claim to "the end of history." The explicit public use of "hate" to characterize racist (and by mapping onto them sexist) expressions emerges in direct response to the recognition in the 1980s of the return of visceral racism in the public sphere.[2] This return has had much to do with the way in which the public rhetoric opened up a space, a "window of opportunity" as the jargon would have it, for the reemergence, the reinvention of exclusionary expression—not only the collusive racializing by social science and the media of the so-called urban underclass and its perceived habituation to drugs, welfare, teenage pregnancy, and crime but also the strong administrative attacks on affirmative action and the undertaking to license private discrimination.

Nevertheless, the genealogy of racism as expression of hate can be traced more deeply to the decade that produced the "end of ideology" thesis, specifically to the way the social sciences—social psychology, sociology, anthropology, and economics—initially constructed an understanding of racism once they fully recognized, and named, the problematic phenomenon. Racism was formatively understood in the 1950s in reductive terms as a prejudice, as an irrational premodern bias presupposing arbitrary and scientifically vacuous distinctions between biologically conceived racial groups.[3] This picture has recently been subjected to scathing attack by critical theory. It nevertheless remains the view that misleadingly underlies the popular (mis)understanding of racist expression as hate speech, and of racist injustice as hate crimes.

Understood in this way, we can begin to see what the characterization in terms of hate leaves out, what it refuses to acknowledge, how it silences effective antiracist strategies. The first point to notice is that the concepts of "hate speech" or "hate crimes" make racist expression turn on a psychological disposition, an emotive affect(ation), on a dis-order—and so as ab-normal and un-usual. Racist and sexist acts are silently transformed into emotive expressions, into crimes of passion. We tend, if not quite to empathize with the agent of a crime of passion, to discount the crime in the calculus of wrongs, to downplay its wrongfulness. Thus, at the extreme, one philosopher has questioned what he takes to be the imputation of specialness to racist crimes in virtue of their racist nature, insisting that the racism adds nothing to the particular nature of the crime, that a lynching, say, is wrong because a murder and no more wrong because the murder of a black person. What is dismissed in this characterization is the terror against the group, in light of which its members may feel especially terrified, in virtue of which the daily life of the group's members is normally threatened. More generally, expressions of hate encourage their dismissal as abnormal, as not the sort of undertaking ordinary people usually engage in, as the irrational product of warped minds. This reduces all racist expression, or the criminalization of a racist expression, to a single form: What is not reducible in this way, and so not covered by the categorical reduction, is not criminalizable; perhaps it is deemed not even racist (or sexist), for it fails to fall under the reductive characterization of racism (or sexism). It therefore need not be considered serious, or at least need not be taken seriously.

Racist expressions, however, are various—in characteristic kind, in underlying disposition, in emotive affect, in intention, and in outcome. Moreover, racisms are not unusual or abnormal. To the contrary, racist expressions are normal in and to our culture, manifest not only in extreme epithets but in insinuations and suggestions, in reasoning and representations; in short, in the microexpressions of daily life. Racism is not—or more exactly is not simply or only—about hate. The refusal by a landlord or employer to rent to or to hire black people (at least for certain public positions—restaurant waiters rather than kitchen hands, say) because of the calculated effects on business has little to do with emotion; nor is it irrational. Similarly, the remark by a college departmental chair to a black interviewee that she is clearly capable of teaching a course on Afro-American thought despite the fact that nothing in her record or interview is indicative of this may involve prejudgment; but it is the prejudgment of normal inductive reasoning and not necessarily the prejudice of affective—hateful—animosity.

What unites these cases as racist is the fact that they involve race-based exclusions (or inclusions), putatively licensed in virtue of claimed racial membership.[4] It follows that in many instances the perpetrators of what counts—or at least should count—as racist or sexist expressions, including crimes, are not moved by nor need they display dispositions of hate toward the objects of such expression. Rather, what these expressions are all about, whether or not in a particular instance they involve hate, is *power*.

Power involves the control that can be exercised—at least in principle —over a person(s) or over resources, often over the former to effect the latter, or vice versa, or the capacity to effect an end. Racist expres- sions turn on the assertion of power where the perpetrators tend otherwise to lack it, or by extension on the maintenance of relations of power, or minimally on reminding those the expression is directed at, its object—whether an individual or class of people—who it is that occupies the position of power. Such expressions therefore involve the assertion of selves over others constituted as Other in a space of di- minished or threatened or otherwise absent control or self-assertion. In this sense, racism is—or becomes—normal: It is endemic, if not quite pandemic, in social formations of disparate, discordant degrees of socioeconomic power and powerlessness. The relatively powerless, or those who perceive their power at least potentially threatened, resort to asserting themselves over those who are—who are *created* as—more powerless than themselves. More precisely, then, racist expressions may serve ideologically to rationalize relations of domination, or they may serve practically to effect such domination by defining who are its objects and what they may be subjected to. So these expressions may be taken most centrally and generally as the condition of this domination and subjection, the mode and fact of racialized oppression.

Racist (and oftentimes sexist) exclusions (and inclusions) are not done only for the sake of gaining or maintaining power in economic or political or personal terms. Power is exercised in the promotion and execution of the exclusions, whether intended or not. So racist (or sexist) exclusions need not be sought only instrumentally to control the socioeconomic resources. They may be sought also for the recognition of some imputed value in the exclusions themselves, or for the sake of power in the execution of the exclusion. This suggests that the proper yardstick against which to assess the degree of racist (or sexist) exclusion, the depth of the condition, is not simply the level of inclusion in and access to social resources. It is rather the fuller measures of incorporation into *and* influence upon the body politic, whether economically, politically, legally, or culturally.

It may be admitted that although racist expressions are predominantly expressed by those who wield power, it is both conceptually possible and empirically evident that members of generally dominated racial groups can promote racial exclusions of nonmembers. But given the fact that the dominant by definition control the resources and social strictures from which exclusions are advanced, racisms are largely if not altogether exclusively expressions from dominance. This also suggests two reasons why resistance to racisms is so often, if not predominantly, cultural. First, the production, expression, and appeal of culture cannot be so easily controlled as material resources. And second, to wrest control over one's culture is at once to pry loose the hold over naming and (self-)representation. This is a first step to self-determination, for it enables one to assert power over self-definition. And it is a necessary condition for taking command of the power to rationalize actions, conditions, and relations, for representation is always mediated by the prevailing discursive culture.

It might be countered that characterizing racist expressions in terms of hate has the pragmatic virtue of enabling a counter to be mounted where there might otherwise be none—in the law, by way of regulations and codes. It is much more difficult to criminalize or otherwise regulate racist expressions conceived as (imposed) power, not least because relations of power *are* so socially usual, faceless features of the fabric of our social formation. Restricting the regulation of racist expressions only to those covered by the extension of hate, however, comes with a heavy cost. Not only does it encourage us to think that the range of racist expressions—or at least the range that is intolerable—is thereby exhausted. (So, it makes little sense to substitute for the designations "hate speech" or "hate crimes" the only seemingly more specific "racist or sexist speech or crimes" while leaving unchanged the conceptualizations they signify.) The designation of hate limits the appropriate response to racist expressions to the reactive. If the primary object of concern in this regard is hate, then we are largely reduced to waiting for the occurrence of hateful deeds, for how else do we recognize the existence of the phenomena. This encourages removal of all those racist expressions not properly reducible to hate from the realm of political contestation. It effects this eviction by silencing the historical record of racialized injustices, by wrenching contemporary manifestations from the long duration of historical exclusions in terms of which they are best understood.

By contrast, understanding racisms as relations of power leads us to acknowledge their diffusion throughout our culture and the history of its production. It is to conceive such expressions not as the idiosyncratic excesses of pathological individuals, groups, or societies, but as the much more disturbingly normal manifestation of modern rationality. To challenge this necessitates far more vigorous proactive campaigns, in some fundamental ways a cultural sea change. It requires not just that those the relatively powerful construct as Other be like them (which by definition they necessarily cannot be); nor simply that those in positions of power cease explicitly to engage in "othering." It necessitates rather that those occupying any position of power be open to the deep and abiding influences of the Other, of the Other's values and commitments. It requires that the society not minimally respond or react to "incidents" or "events," but that it engage in dialogic exchanges, taking seriously—and so moved by—the positions and ideas of those who have been relatively marginalized, that those in positions of relative power be open, in theory and practice, policy and social structure, to the transformative implications of the suggestions of those over whom they might exercise power.

Conceived thus, recourse to the social technologies of "hate crimes" or "hate speech" appear not just inadequate but paradoxical. These technologies find their rationale in the hopeful deterrence effected by extraordinary punishment of racist crimes. But if hate crimes or speech are the irrational products of pathologically disturbed persons it seems fanciful to expect their potential perpetrators to engage in a rational calculus of the likely outcomes of their expressions. The likely effects, rather, will be to turn true believers into martyrs among fellow travelers and capricious actors into sacrificial lambs in the eyes of true believers. Only those deeply committed to retribution for its own sake, victims of such crimes and their supporters alike, will gather much satisfaction from the punishment; the rest of us will take solace only in the fact that the racist criminal will be less able to perpetrate acts of this kind in the future. We can take no solace in the fact that perpetrators will be free even as punished to discriminate again.

We—especially the racially dominant but also the racially marginal-ized—thus need to address far more vigorously and dialogically than we have tended to what it is in our culture and the history of its production that enables racializing categories to take hold, to promote and characterize social relations of power and exclusion, to license violence against the marginalized. Of course, there is a sense in which it is better to have hate speech codes and hate crime legislation: better pragmatically for those who are objects of such speech and deed when weighed against the silence effected in the absence of any other mode of response. Nevertheless, it would help to reconceive "hate" crimes and speech in terms of what they actually are: violent acts of imposed power over and against those *this* culture and its members continue to marginalize as racial Others.

I am not thus arguing that those who commit racially prompted injustices go unpunished; quite the contrary. I am suggesting rather that they be dealt with on the understanding not simply that they have harmed a particular individual and society abstractly, but also that they have harmed the entire group—the body of particular people—with whom the object of the injustice identifies. In this sense racist wrongs are wrongs—as the Ku Klux Klan Act of 1871 has it—against an entire class of people. And for such wrongs perpetrators are to be held to standards of "strict liability." If we can do it for products, why not for people? Perhaps then we—again, collectively—will come to see racist injustices as wrongs against humanity, and treat them with the degrees of severity they deserve.

The invocation of humanity here as the reference point in terms of which to respond to racist marginalization, objectification, and harm is not meant to reinstate the essentialized abstraction of a universal, thereby to license a racializing reversal: If a harm to humanity, then whites must thus be harmed and this is what renders racist expression wrong. Rather, it is to promote a pragmatically grounded solidarity, a recognition that the specificity of the harm to individual black persons as black is a harm in which, but for the resistance of and by individual white persons, they are implicated. In this sense it is not insignificant—indeed, it is deeply significant—that crimes against humanity are committed invariably by the relatively powerful against the powerless, defined usually in terms of gender, class, and race. It must also be stressed that in a deeply racist society, nonracial social institutions become implicated in the extension of racialized marginalizations. Transforming racism from hate speech or crime to speech or crime against humanity is designed, then, to shift philosophical ground from the narrow psychologism of offensiveness to the multiplicities of individual and institutional marginalizations, and from the abstracted limits of nonracialism to the situated revisability and resistances of antiracist pragmatics.[5] "Humanity" here, then, stands as a trope of antiracist solidarity and a normative standard of what postracist social relations might aim for and effect.

Notes

1. See, for example, Hockenos (1993). Programs on network and public television about contemporary racism are indicative also: thus, a number of programs on the resurrection of neo-Nazi movements in Central Europe and the United States by Ted Koppel on *Nightline* invoked the generalized rubric of hate, as did one by Phil Donahue and Vladimir Posner. *Hate* was the title used by Bill Moyers for his PBS special on racism and prejudice. See also Leonard Zeskind (1993).

2. The disanalogies between racist and sexist expression run as deep as the analogies. Indeed, although identifying commonalities between racist and sexist assumptions, expressions, and movements, identifying them without strict qualification is evasively reductive on both sides of the equation. For simplicity's sake I restrict myself here largely to comments about racism.

3. It may be that expressions of racism were understood as prejudice by those critical of them as early as the mid-19th century. Nevertheless, definitions of racism were offered for the first time only in the late 1930s, and the prevailing contemporary understanding of racism as prejudice is firmly anchored in the social science of the 1950s, especially social psychology.

4. Not uncommonly, the prejudgment that turns out false will be made, where circumstances permit in future cases, to be borne out. It is not unusual for a white professor who, grading blind to students' identities in the semester's first test gives the top grade to the student who turns out to be the only black person in the class, to downgrade that student in later tests. I owe the example to Jan Boxill, "Affirmative Action as Reverse Discrimination," unpublished note on file with author.

5. For a fuller argument concerning antiracist pragmatics, see chapter 9 of Goldberg (1993).

References

Goldberg, D. T. (1993). *Racist culture: Philosophy and the politics of meaning.* Oxford, UK: Basil Blackwell.

Hockenos, P. (1993). *Free to hate: The rise of the right in post-communist eastern Europe.* New York: Routledge & Kegan Paul.

Zeskind, L. (1993, November 16). And now, the hate show. *New York Times,* Op-Ed, p. A17.

Author Index

Aarons, L. F., 67, 78
Abbey, A., 144, 159, 161
Abercrombie, N., 5, 25
Allport, G. W., 35, 44, 53, 134, 140
Almay, T., 45, 53
Althusser, L., 138, 140
Alvesson, M., 87, 120
Aristotle, 40
Asch, S. E., 33, 53
Attkisson, S., 173, 193
Aufderheide, P., 11, 25
Averill, J. R., 38, 53

Ballard, H. B., 4, 25
Banks, J. A., 11, 25
Banks, S. P., 88, 121
Barker, M., 5, 14, 25
Barnouw, E., 140
Barthes, R., 124-127, 140
Bateson, G., 117, 120

Baudrillard, J., 208, 224
Beneke, T., 150, 153, 161
Bennetts, L., 56, 78
Berk, R. A., 42, 53
Bersani, L., 155, 161
Berton, P., 228, 264
Bhabha, H., 103-104, 120
Billingsley, K. L., 255, 264
Biskupic, J., 178, 193
Bobo, L., 34
Bockner, A. P., 146, 161
Bodenhausen, G. V., 33, 53
Bollinger, L. C., 259, 264
Bolton, R., 197, 201-206, 207, 211, 213, 215-216, 218, 219, 221, 223, 224
Boodman, S. G., 170, 171, 173, 186, 193
Booth, W., 172, 175, 193
Bordwell, S., 147, 149, 161, 162

277

Bottomore, T. B., 4, 25
Bowers, J. W., 168, 193
Boyd, E. A., 42, 53
Brandt, G. L., 11, 25
Brehm, J. W., 34, 53
Brehm, S. S., 34, 53
Brewer, M. B., 35, 53
Brinton, M., 91, 120
Bruce, P. A., 30, 53
Bumpus-Hooper, L., 179, 193
Burke, K., 37, 53, 86, 95-96, 120, 124,
    140, 181, 182, 185, 193
Burroughs, W. S., 209-210, 224

Cacioppo, J, T., 40, 54
Carlsson, C., 83, 95, 108, 120
Carter, R. T., 45, 53
Chandler, J., 256, 261, 264
Chandler, K., 169, 170, 193
Chase, A., 14, 25
Chubbick, J., 45, 53
Clark, J., 175, 176, 193
Clarke, J., 16, 26
Clegg, S. R., 87, 120
Cobb, K., 168, 170, 193
Condit, C. M., 165, 166, 180-181, 182,
    183, 191, 193
Conquergood, C., 100, 120
Conrad, C., 87, 120
Corcoran, F., 156, 161
Critcher, C., 16, 26

de Certeau, M., 92, 120, 144, 157, 158,
    161
De Cillia, R., 27
Deetz, S., 82, 87, 120
Delgado, R., 228, 229, 264
Dennis, R. M., 45, 53
Dermody, C., 175, 176, 193
Domhoff, G. W., 4, 25
Donaldson, R. E., 117, 120
Dovidio, J. F., 5, 21, 25
D'Souza, D., 229, 264
Duster, T., 34, 53

Egan, T., 57, 77, 78
Eisenberg, E. M., 2, 82, 88, 93, 106,
    109, 120, 156, 161

Ellul, J., 33, 34, 35, 39, 46, 47, 53, 128,
    133, 136, 138, 140, 187, 193
Engstrom, R. L., 45, 54
Epstein, E. J., 69, 77, 78
Essed, P. J. M., 5, 14, 22, 26
Etzioni, A., 264

Falcon, P. L., 144, 162
Farrish, K., 256, 264
Faux, M., 184, 186, 193
Feeney, S., 171, 193
Fejes, F., 62, 64, 66, 67, 68, 71, 77, 78
Ferguson, R., 207, 224
Fernandez, J. P., 22, 26
Finkelhor, E., 144, 161
Fish, S., 229, 264
Fisher, W. R., 144, 160, 161
Fiss, K., 207, 224
Flanders, L., 59-60, 73, 77, 78
Ford, G., 17, 26
Foucault, M., 155, 156, 161, 208, 212,
    217, 223, 225
Frammolino, R., 255, 264
Franken, B., 171, 194
Frankl, V., 190, 194
Freiberg, P., 65, 67, 75, 78
Fromm, E., 134, 140
Furnham, A., 144, 162

Gaertner, S. L., 5, 21, 25, 45, 53
Galtung, J., 7, 26
Gans, H., 7, 26, 69, 77, 78
Gardiner, S., 59, 77
Gates, H. L., Jr., 229, 264
Gergen, K., 81, 120
Giddens, A., 84, 89, 108, 109, 120
Ginsburg, S., 180, 194
Giorgi, A., 146, 154, 161
Glazer, N., 11, 26
Goldberg, D. T., 267-275
Goldberg, J. G., 191, 194
Goodall, H. L., xvi, 80-119, 120, 156,
    161
Gordon, P., 17, 26
Gove, P. B., 32, 53
Gramsci, A., 111, 120
Greenwalt, K., 229, 264
Griffin, S., 156, 161

Grimshaw, A. D., 34, 53
Groth, A. N., 150, 161
Gruber, H., 27
Gutierrez, F., 6, 7, 27

Haghighat, C., 14, 26
Hahn, H., 45, 53
Haiman, F. S., 229, 264
Hall, S., 16, 26
Hamm, M. S., 139, 141
Hammer, K. M., 42, 53
Hampton, J., 136, 141
Harbridge, J., 144, 162
Hartley, J., 26, 61, 77, 78
Hartmann, P., 6, 8, 26
Hawken, J., 117, 120
Hawley, J., 117, 120
Helms, J. E., 45, 53
Hentoff, N., 229, 255, 264
Hill, S., 5, 25
Hillard, J. W., 45, 53
Hockenos, P., 274, 275
Hodges, R., 228, 264
Hoffer, E., 189, 191, 194
Holmes, O. W., Jr., 227
Hummer, R. A., 144, 160, 162
Husband, C., 6, 8, 26

Ihde, D., 146, 162
Ivie, R. L., 156, 162

Jameson, F., 99, 120
Jaynes, G. D., 22, 26
Jefferson, T., 16, 26
Jenkins, R., 22, 26
Jensen, M., 162
Jensen, R. J., 168, 193
Johnson, K.A., 8, 26
Johnson, K. K., 144, 162
Johnson, M., 187, 188, 194

Kasindorf, J. R., 26, 56, 77, 78
Kaucauer, S., 128, 141
Kellett, P. M., 142-161
King, A., 32, 37, 38-39, 53
King, A. A., 156, 162
Kittell, R. E., 95
Klein, G., 11, 26

Klug, F., 17, 26
Knopper, S., 26, 68, 77, 79
Korwar, A. R., 255, 265
Kramer, R. M., 35, 53

Lake, R., 166, 194
Lakoff, G., 187, 188, 194
Lange, J. I., 189, 194
Langellier, K. M., 144, 162
Lanigan, R. L., 144, 146, 154, 159, 162
Laurence, C., 172, 195
Lautenberg, F., 260, 265
Lavie, S., 98-99, 121
Lawrence, C. R., 229, 265
Lawsky, D., 183, 194
Le Bon, G., 140, 141
Lederer, L. J., 229, 265
Lee, S., 228, 265
Leger, M., 83, 95, 108, 120
Leichtling, G., 59, 77
Lerner, M., 37, 40, 53
Levine, R., 26, 63, 77, 79
Lewis, L., 144, 162
Lichtenstein, M., 33, 53
Lichter, L., 10, 26
Lichter, S. R., 10, 26
Lieske, J., 45, 53
Lofles, I. L., 144, 159, 162
Lowenstein, L. F., 159, 162
Lynch, J., 11, 25

Machiavelli, N., 261, 265
MacKinnon, C. A., 229, 265
Malveaux, J., 229, 265
Manheim, J., 129, 137, 141
Mansfield, S., 56, 79
Martin, P. Y., 144, 160, 162
Martindale, C., 8, 26
Matsuda, M. J., 229, 265
McGuire, W. J., 40, 54
McLaughlin, J., 45, 53
Memmi, A., 45, 54, 101-102, 104, 106, 108, 121
Merleau-Ponty, M., 144, 156, 162
Merten, K., 8, 26
Miles, R., 5, 14, 26
Miller, M., 228, 265
Mills, C. W., 4, 26

Milner, D., 11, 26
Mitten, R., 27
Moritz, M. J., 55-77, 78, 79
Mozzochi, J., 59, 77
Muehlenhard, C. L., 144, 162
Muir, J. K., 163-191
Mumby, D., 87, 121
Murphy, J., 136, 141

Nakagawa, S., 57, 77
Nieburg, H. L., 35, 54, 121
Nowak, P., 27

Ochs, D. J., 168, 193
O'Connor, H., 77
O'Connor, J., 127, 141
Olander, W., 207, 224
Olbrechts-Tyteca, L., 182, 185, 194
Olsen, J., 145, 162
Olson, K., 172, 194
Orman, N., 177, 194
O'Shaughnessy, N. J., 124-126, 141

Panetta, E. M., 168, 184, 194
Papageorgis, D., 40, 54
Pelikan, J., 27
Perelman, C., 182, 185, 194
Peters, P. J., 58, 78, 79
Petrich, K., 62, 64, 66, 67, 68, 71, 77, 78
Pettigrew, T., 45, 54
Petty, R. E., 40, 54
Phizacklea, A., 5, 26
Porpora, D. V., 34, 54
Preiswerk, R., 11, 26

Railsback, C. C., 165, 194
Rauch, J., 229, 265
Reeves, F., 16, 26
Remak, J., 128, 130, 131, 141
Renwick, E., 45, 53
Riley, P., 88, 121
Roberts, B., 16, 26
Roth, B. M., 34, 54
Rothbart, M., 34, 54
Rothman, S., 10, 26
Ruge, M. H., 7, 26
Ruhrmann, G., 8, 26

Runkle, D. R., 30, 31, 32, 54
Russakoff, D., 256, 265
Russell, C., 34, 54
Russell, W. M. S., 34, 54
Russo, V., 60, 61, 62, 79

Sacks, H., 95, 121
Said, E., 104, 121
Salholz, E., 56, 79
Sarap, M., 161, 207, 225
Saunders, D. J., 186, 190, 194
Sawyer, K., 194
Scheidler, J. M., 167-168, 194
Schneider, L. J., 144, 162
Schult, D. G., 144, 162
Scott, J. C., 86, 87, 121, 144, 157, 162
Seeger, M., 82, 121
Seidel, G., 16, 26, 27
Shatz, S. F., 184, 185, 194
Sherman, M., 168, 194
Shimkin, D., 77
Shorris, E., 82-83, 111, 116, 121
Siegel, B., 265
Slayden, D., 196-224
Slotkin, R., 210-211, 213-214, 220, 225
Smith, C. L., 75-76, 77, 79
Smith, S. A., xiv, 226-262
Solomos, J., 22, 26
Sontag, S., 209, 217, 225
Spretnak, C., 117, 121
Sprouse, M., 108, 121
Staub, E., 33, 54
Stefanic, J., 228, 264
Sterba, R., 35, 54
Stolerman, H., 77
Strine, M. S., 158, 162
Sunstein, C. R., 229, 265
Sussman, L., 147, 149, 161, 162
Swardson, A., 228, 265
Synar, M., 265

TePaske, B. A., 162
Terry, R., 164, 195
Tisdall, S., 183, 195
Todorov, T., 14, 27
Totenberg, N., 184, 195
Troyna, B., 11, 27
Tuchman, G., 7, 27, 69, 79

Tucker, M., 207, 224
Turner, B. S., 5, 25
Turner, V., 88, 93, 109, 121

Ueda, R., 11, 26
Unsoeld, J., 265

Vanderford, M. L., 166, 195
Vanderleeuw, J., 45, 54
van Dijk, T. A., 1-24, 27

Walker, J., 45, 53
Walker, S., 228, 229, 265
Warren, C. A. B., 90, 102, 105, 108, 121
Weisbord, M. E., 118, 121

Wellman, D. T., 5, 27
Whillock, D. E., 122-140
Whillock, R. K., 28-48
Whyte, W., 111, 121
Wildavsky, B., 256, 265
Williams, J., 11, 27
Williams, R. M., 12, 26
Williams, S., 68, 79
Wilson, C. C., 6, 7, 27
Wodak, R., 16, 27
Wood, J. T., 158, 162

Yllö, K., 144, 161

Zarefsky, D., 186, 195
Zeskind, L., 274, 275

Subject Index

Abortion clinic access law, 174, 176-178
Abortion clinic bombings, 166, 167
Abortion clinic protests, 168-169
Abortion clinic violence, 170-176, 187
Abortion debate, 163-191
  Christian rhetoric, 187, 191
Academic discourse:
  elite racism, 14-15
  work-hate, 111-112
Advertising:
  anti-gay videotape, 59-61, 59-71,
    72, 74
  arts funding, 201
  racist political advertisements, 29-31
African Americans, stereotypes in
    politics, 41
AIDS:
  art and, 218
  news coverage, 66, 67, 72
Ailes, Roger, 32

Alabama gubernatorial campaign, 36,
    38, 40-41, 48, 49-52
Alexander, Dr. Clay, 171
Allegories, 98, 99
American Bookseller Association v.
    Hudnut, 246
Analogies, as expression of hate,
    182-183
Antiabortion rhetoric, as hate speech,
    163-191
Antidiscrimination laws, 18, 21
Anti-gay agenda, 55-77
Anti-Japanese sentiment, workworld, 99-
    101
Anti-Semitism:
  Alabama gubernatorial campaign, 42
  Nazi Germany, 34-35, 129-131
Art, politics in, 196-224
Assimilation, cultural assimilation to a
    new workworld, 101-103

Baldwin, Gordon, 256
Ballot initiatives, anti-gay (1992), 57, 59, 74, 75, 77
Beauharnais v. Illinois, 230, 233
Binary opposition, 200
Black, Justice Hugo, 232-233
Blacks. *See* African Americans
Boots, as symbol, 122, 123, 126, 139
Bray v. Alexandria Women's Health Clinic, 184-185
Britton, Dr. John, murder, 174
Buchanan, Pat, NEA controversy, 197, 202-208, 218, 220, 222
Bureaucracy, work-hate, 106-114
Bush-Dukakis presidential race, 29
Business world, hate speech, 80-119

California State University (Northridge), speech code, 256
Cambodia invasion, building support for, 137
Campaign rhetoric:
    anti-gay booklet, 57-58
    hate letters, 36, 38, 40, 42, 44, 49-52
    racism, 29-31, 47-48
Campus speech codes, 240-256
Central Michigan University, speech code, 252-255
Change:
    academic world, 111-112
    and power relations, 87-89
    work-hate, 88-119
Chaplinsky v. New Hampshire, 230-231, 235, 242, 245
Christian rhetoric:
    anti-gay pamphlet, 58
    pro-life movement, 174, 187, 191
Churchill, Winston, 137
Civil right, pro-lifers use of analogy to, 184-185
Civil Rights Bill (1991), 21
Closed: 99 Ways to Stop Abortion (book), 168
Cohen v. California, 236-238
Colonizer/colonized paradigm, 101-103
Colorado anti-gay initiative (1992), 57, 59, 74, 75, 77
Complicit resistance, 90-91

Conservatives, as protectors of American values, 210-211
Constrained self, business world, 106-115
Constraint, as rapists' issue, 154-156
Control:
    in the workworld, 83, 84
    power, 270
    rape, 144, 155
Corporate discourse, elite racism, 22-24
Countermythology, 104-107
Court decisions. *See* Supreme Court cases
Cramer, Michelle, 170, 183
Crossfire, arts funding debate, 197, 200, 202-208, 218, 220, 222
Crowds, images, 140
Cultural sensitivity, textbooks, 11-12
Culture, and politics, 221-222

Dambrot v. Central Michigan University, 252-255
Death Penalty for Homosexuals Is Prescribed in the Bible (pamphlet), 57-58
Discourse:
    academic, 14-15, 111, 112
    antiabortion hate rhetoric, 178-182
    corporate, 22-24, 25
    educational, 11-14, 24
    elite, 1-24
    media discourse, 6-10, 29-31
    parliamentary, 19-22
    political, 15-22, 24, 127-131, 137, 224
    public, 1-24, 42-44
    religious, 57-58, 174, 187
    scholarly, 14-15
    visual, 122-140
Divide and Conquer (film), 132-133
Doc Martens boots, as hate symbol, 122, 123, 126, 139
Doctors, hate targets of antiabortionists, 168-171, 178-179, 190
Doe v. Michigan, 240-243, 247, 254
Dominant group members, racism, 1-24
Douglas, Justice William O., 233-235, 236

Dress code, hate in visual discourse, 122-123, 139
Dukakis-Bush presidential race, 29

Earth First!, 189-190
Educational discourse, 11-14, 24
Elite discourse:
    corporate discourse, 22-24
    mass media, 4, 6-10
    political discourse, 15-22
    racist, 1-24
    scholarly discourse, 14-15
    textbooks, 11-14
Elite group, 4
Elite racism, 4-6
Employees, hate speech, 80-119
Empowerment programs, 93, 104, 106, 109
Ethnic affairs:
    in political discourse, 15-16
    mass media coverage, 8-9
Ethnic research, academia, 14-15, 24
Europe:
    corporate discourse, 23-24, 25
    pejorative names for minorities, 18
    political discourse, 18-19, 24
Evening the score, rape, 147-148
Extremism, 187, 189-190

Family values, 58, 63
Far Right:
    attack on gay and lesbian groups, 64, 76
    attack on NEA and artists, 196-224
    television programming, 64, 76
    vigilante justice, 214
Films:
    gay portrayals banned, 61
    Holocaust horrors depicted in, 124
    Second World War propaganda, 128-134
Finley, Karen, 205, 209
First Amendment doctrine, 229-262
Florida, hate crimes statute, 267
Frankfurter, Justice Felix, 230-232
Freedom, as rapists' issue, 153-156, 157
Freedom of Access to Clinics Entrances Act (1993), 176, 177, 183
Free speech, hate speech as, 226-262

Gay Agenda, The (videotape), 59-61, 69-71, 72, 74
Gay and Lesbian Alliance against Defamation (GLAAD), 68-69, 75, 76
Gay rights, news coverage, 65-66
Gays, portrayed in the mass media, 55-77
George Mason University, 247-252
Germany:
    economic hardship, 129-130, 135
    propaganda films, 128-131
GLAAD. See Gay and Lesbian Alliance against Defamation
Goebbels, Joseph, 128, 130
Gooding v. Wilson, 242
Government, hate symbols and war, 127-131
Graffiti, 100-101
Grenada invasion, building support for, 137
Griffin, Michael, 172, 179
Gunn, Dr. David, murder, 169, 172-173, 179, 190

Harassment techniques, anti-abortion movement, 170-171, 190-191
Harlan, Justice John, 236-238
Hate:
    as dialectical phenomenon, x-xi
    as operational tactic, xii-xiii, 28-48
    as symbolic defense, 136-139
    as symbolic experience, 134-135
    at work, 80-119
    crisis model, ix-x
    hate stratagem, 28-48
    love and, 191
    power and, xiii, 267-274
    strategic uses, 31-33
    to assert identity, xiii
    types, 136
    visual images, 122-140
    work-hate, 80-119
Hate acts:
    abortion clinic bombings, 166, 167
    abortion clinic murders, 169, 172-175, 179
    anti-abortion movement, 170-176
    coming to terms with, 47
    hate letters, 36, 38, 40, 42, 44, 49-52

hate speech and, 142-161
   rape, 144-161
   terrorizing abortion doctors, 170-171
Hate crimes statutes, xi, 267
Hateful resistance, rapist narratives,
   156-160
Hate letters, 36, 38, 40, 42, 44, 49-52
Hate, Lies, and Videotape (videotape),
   59-60
Hate narratives, 116
   business world, 86-119
   rapists, 142-161
Hate speech:
   analogies, 182-183
   anti-abortion rhetoric, 163-191
   as free speech, 226-262
   as statement of power, xiii, 267-274
   as taboo subject, 46
   court decisions, 226-262
   disease metaphors, xv, 209
   elite discourse, 1-24
   employees, 80-119
   gays and lesbians, 55-77
   hate acts and, 142-161
   legislation prohibiting, xv
   marketed in the mass media, 28-48,
      55-77
   metaphors, 185-188
   naming process, 178-182
   NEA funding debate, 196-224
   rapists narratives, 142-161
Hate symbols, 127-148
   German, 131, 135
Hidden transcripts, power relations, 86-
   87
Hill, Paul, 174-175
Hiring practices, 6-7, 21
Historical blame, 130, 132-133, 139
History, hate messages, 127-134
Hitler, Adolf, 34-35
   hate symbols, 135
   propaganda films, 128-131
Hollywood, gay portrayals banned, 61
Holocaust, xi, 34-35, 124, 186, 228
Holy war, 199
Homicide. *See* Murder
Homosexuality, anti-gay legislative
   initiatives, 57
Hyde, Rep. Henry, 183

Iconic message, 125, 126
   crowds, 140
   propaganda film, 130, 133
Iconography, politics of, 196-224
Identity, corporate change, 109
Ideological state apparatus, 138
Images:
   for crowds, 140
   of gays and lesbians, 68-71
   of Holocaust, 124
   representations of hate, 122-140
   used by antiabortionists, 182
   See also Symbols
Immigrants, corporate discourse, 18-20,
   24
Institutional control. *See* Power relations
Intolerance, 159
*Iota Xi Chapter of Sigma Chi Fraternity
   v. George Mason University*,
   247-252
Iraqi military action, building support
   for, 137
Irving, David, 228
Isolation, fostering stereotypes, 34-35,
   41

Jameson, Frederic, 99
Jews:
   stereotyped by Hitler, 34-35
   stereotype in politics, 42
Journalists, mass media, 6-8, 24

Keyishian v. Board of Regents, 241
King, Martin Luther, 184
Kinsley, Mike, NEA controversy, 197,
   202-208, 218, 222
Ku Klux Klan, xi
Ku Klux Klan Act (1983), 184, 273

Lambs of Christ, 169-170, 178, 186
Lautenberg, Sen. Frank, 260
Legislation:
   hate crimes, 267
   hate speech, 228
   See also Supreme Court cases
Lesbians:
   news coverage, 66-69
   portrayed in the mass media, 55-77
Liminality, 87-88, 93, 109, 113

Lindsay, Vachel, 127
Linguistic message, 125-126
   propaganda films, 130, 132-133

Machine, pro-lifer metaphor, 187-188
"Madwives," 89-90
Maguire, Lorraine, 173
Malicious hatred, 136
Mapplethorpe, Robert, 196, 203, 205,
   209, 216-217, 219
Marshall, Justice Thurgood, 239-240
Martell, Clark, 139
Massachusetts furlough program, 29
Mass media, 6-10
   ethnic affairs coverage, 8-9
   gay and lesbian community, 55-77
   hiring practices in, 6-7
   homosexual stereotypes, 62-65
   journalists, 6-8, 24
   marketing hate speech, 55-77
   news coverage, 7, 65-69, 72
   racist political advertisements, 29-31
   use of experts, 72-73
   white elite racism, 4, 6-10
Mein Kampf, 127, 130
Metaphors, 213
   disease, vx, 209
   symbols, 187-188, 209
Michelman, Kate, 179
Minorities, pejorative names, 17-18
Minority research, academia, 14-15, 24
Missionaries to the Pre-Born, 170, 178
Mitchell v. Wisconsin, 268
Monteith, Stanley, 72, 73
Moral hatred, 136
Movies. See Films
Muhammad, Khalid Abdul, 228, 260
Multiculturalism, textbooks, 11-12
Multinational corporations, resistance
   to, 99, 100-101
Murder:
   abortion clinic doctors, 169, 172-175,
      179, 190
   symbolic, rapist, 152-153, 155

Name calling, 190, 209
Names, as hate rhetoric, 17-19, 178-182
National Association of Letter Carriers v.
   Austin, 238-240

National Endowment for the Arts, fund-
   ing debate, 196-224
National Organization for Women v.
   Scheidler, 177
Nazis:
   propaganda films, 128-131
   symbol used by pro-life movement,
      182-183, 185, 186
Nazi symbols, 123
Neo-Nazis, 139-140
News coverage:
   AIDS, 66, 67, 72
   gay rights, 65-66
   Gay Rights March, 76-77
   lesbians, 66-69
   racist elite, 7
   use of experts, 72-73
Nicolosi, Joseph, 72, 73
Night and Fog (film), 124
Non-iconic message, 125, 127

Objectification, 190-191
Occupation, political and psychological,
   96-105
Operation Rescue, 168-169, 175,
   183-186, 190
Oppression:
   in the workworld, 90, 96
   rape, 157
Oregon anti-gay initiative (1992), 57,
   59, 74
Organizational behavior, hate speech,
   80-119
Organizational change, work-hate, 91-96
Out-class, denigrating, 39-42
Over-weighing, 180, 181

Papish v. University of Missouri, 242
Parliamentary discourse, 19-22
People v. Spielman, 231
Peters, Peter J., 58
Physicians, hate targets of antiabortion-
   ists, 168-171, 178-179, 190
PLAN. See Pro-Life Abortion Network
Political campaigns:
   anti-gay legislation, 59-61
   hate letters, 36, 38, 40, 42, 44, 49-52
   racist political advertisements, 29-31
   voting discussions, 45

Political discourse:
    elite racism, 15-22, 224
    hate symbols and war, 127-131
    propaganda, 137
Political goals, hate to motivate action,
    28-48
Political occupation, 98-105
Politics:
    art in, 196-224
    culture and, 221-222
    mixing art with, 211
Power:
    and hate, xiii, 267-274
    hate speech, 267-274
Power relations:
    denigrating the out-class, 39-42
    elite discourse, 1-24
    experts in the media, 72-73
    "madwives," 89-90
    rape, 142-161
    workworld, 85-92
Prelude to War (film), 132, 133
Print media:
    gay coverage, 65-69
    gay portrayals banned, 61-62
    minority journalists, 6-8, 24
    racist pamphlet, 57-58
Pro-Life Abortion Network (PLAN), 171
Pro-life rhetoric:
    as hate speech, 163-191
    Christian rhetoric, 174, 187, 191
Propaganda, defined, 136, 138
Propaganda films:
    German, 127-131
    United States, 132-134
Public discourse:
    elite racism, 1-24
    hate to deface or destroy, 42-44
Pyle v. South Hadley School Committee,
    256

Racism:
    campaign rhetoric, 29-31, 47-48
    elite discourse, 1-24
    power, 272
    voting discussions, 45
Racketeer Influenced and Corrupt Or-
    ganizations (RICO) Act, abortion
    clinics, 177, 178

Rape, 144
    as consumer advocacy, 148-150
    as debt collection, 147-148
    as justifiable homicide, 152-154
    as reclaiming voice, 151-152
    as revenge, 150-151
Rapists:
    in racist political advertisements,
        29-31
    narrative accounts, 142-161
R.A.V. v. St. Paul, 256, 257
Reeve, Christopher, NEA controversy,
    197, 202-208, 218, 222
Religious discourse:
    antiabortion, 174, 187, 191
    anti-gay pamphlet, 58
Repressive state apparatus, 138
Rescue America, 169, 171, 172-173
Rescue movement, anti-abortion
    rhetoric, 163-191
Resistance, hateful resistance of rapist,
    156-160
Retributive hatred, 136
Revenge:
    rape, 150-151
    work-hate, 114
RICO Act. *See* Racketeer Influenced and
    Corrupt Organizations Act
Rider, Cathy Ann, 173
Riefenstahl, Leni, 128-131
Rightwing debate:
    as hate speech, 196-224
    protectors of American values,
        210-211
    See also Far Right
Robertson, Pat, NEA controversy, 197,
    202-208, 218, 220, 221
Roosevelt, Franklin D., 137
Rushdie, Salman, 228

St. Paul (MN), speech code, 256, 257
Satanic Verses, The, 228
Scalia, Justice Antonin, 257-258
Scheidler, Joseph, 167-168, 170, 177,
    180, 189
Scholarly discourse, elite racism, 14-15
Schumer, Charles, 176
Self, corporate change, 109
Serrano, Andres, 196, 203, 209, 216, 219

Silva v. University of New Hampshire,
    256
Simple hate, 136
Skinheads, xii, 123, 126, 139
Snydle, Dr. Frank, harassment, 170-171
Social goals, hate to motivate action,
    28-48
Special rights, 70, 74, 76
Speech codes, universities, 240-256
Spiteful hatred, 136
Stalking, 173
Stanford University, speech code, 256
Star of David, as German hate symbol,
    131, 135
Steirer v. Bethlehem Area School District,
    256
Stereotypes, 33-39, 41
    mass media, 62-65
Stratagem:
    defined, 32
    hate speech as, 28-48
Street v. New York, 241
Supreme Court cases
    abortion clinic violence, 177, 185
    enhanced sentences, 268
    First Amendment issues, 226-262
Swastika, 126, 131, 134, 135, 139
Sweezy v. New Hampshire, 241
Symbols:
    metaphors, 187-188, 209, 213
    propaganda films, 128-134
    used by Hitler, 131, 135
    visual discourse, 122-140
    war on drugs, 210
    See also Images
Synecdoche, 38-39

Tartikoff, Brandon, 64
Teens Rescuing Unborn Tiny Humans
    (TRUTH), 170
Television:
    anti-gay videotapes in 1992, campaign,
        60
    depictions of homosexuals, 62
    family values, 63-64
    use of experts, 72-73
    visual cues, 123
Terminiello v. Chicago, 235-236

Terry, Randall, 164, 168-172, 176-177,
    178-180, 184, 186, 189
Texas v. Johnson, 241, 250
Textbooks, elite racism, 11-14, 24
Thompkins, Dr. Norman, harassment,
    171
Tiller, Dr. George, 173-174
Tolerance, 159
Treshman, David, 169, 172-173, 180
Triumph of the Will, 128-131
TRUTH. *See* Teens Rescuing Unborn
    Tiny Humans

*UMW Post v. Board of Regents of the
    University of Wisconsin*, 243-247
United States:
    building support for military actions,
        137
    propaganda films, 132-134
Universities, speech codes, 240-256
University of California (Riverside), free-
    dom of speech, 255
University of Connecticut, speech code,
    256
University of Michigan, speech code,
    240-243, 247, 254
University of Missouri, speech code, 242
University of Pennsylvania, speech code,
    256
University of Wisconsin, speech code,
    243-247, 256
U.S. Constitution:
    free speech cases, 229-240
    university speech codes, 240-256
U.S. Supreme Court. *See* Supreme Court
    cases

Values, and art, 211-217
Vanderbilt University, freedom of
    speech, 255-256
Videotapes, 73-74
    Hate, Lies, and Videotape, 59-60
    The Gay Agenda, 59-61, 69-71, 72,
        74
Vigilante justice, 214
Visual discourse, symbolism and the
    representation of hate, 122-140
Visual images. *See* Images

Visual message, crowds, 140
Voice:
    rape to reclaim, 151-152
    work-hate, 94-96
Voting discussions, racist, 45

War, pro-lifer's use of term, 185-187
Wars:
    building support for, 137
    creation of hate symbols, 127-128
    German propaganda films, 128-132
    United States propaganda films,
      132-134
*West Virginia State Board of Education
    v. Barnette*, 241

White Circle League, 230
Why We Fight (film series), 132-134
Wildman, Reverend Donald, 64, 216
Wilson, Blenda, 256, 261
Wishnatsky, Martin, 186
Work-hate, 80-119
World War II:
    hate symbols, 127-128, 131, 134,
      135
    origins, German history, 135
    propaganda, 137
    propaganda films, 127-134
Wright, Wendy, 183

Xenophobia, corporate work, 99-103

About the Contributors

David Theo Goldberg is Professor and Director of Justice Studies and serves on the Graduate Committee on Law and Social Science at Arizona State University. He is the author of *Racist Culture: Philosophy and the Politics of Meaning* and *Ethical Theory and Social Issues* (2nd ed.). He is the editor of *Multiculturalism: A Critical Reader* and *Anatomy of Racism;* co-editor of *Jewish Identity* (with Michael Krausz) and of *Social Identities: A Journal for the Study of Race, Nation and Culture* (with Abebe Zegeye). He is currently working on a book on The Racial State.

H. L. Goodall, Jr., is Professor and Head of the Department of Communication at the University of North Carolina at Greensboro. His primary research areas combine interests in organizational communication, resistance cultures and narratives, and interpretive ethnography. He is the author or coauthor of 11 books—most recently *Casing a Promised Land: The Autobiography of an Organizational Detective as Cultural Ethnographer* (1994), *Organization Communication: Balancing Creativity and Constraint* (1993; with Eric Eisenberg), *Living in the Rock n Roll Mystery: Reading Self, Others, and Contexts as Clues* (1991), and more than 70 articles, chapters, and conference presentations—most recently "Communication as the Material Manifestation of Spirituality" (1993, *World Communication Journal*) and "Empowerment, Culture, and Postmodern Organizing" (1992, *Journal of Organizational Change Management*).

Peter M. Kellett is Assistant Professor of Communication Studies at University of North Carolina-Greensboro. He received his doctorate from Southern Illinois University in 1990. He has published in journals such as *The Journal of Communication Studies* and *The Journal of Religious Communication*. He is particularly interested in the application of phenomenology to narrative analysis, and the promotion of tolerance in communication.

Marguerite J. Moritz came to the University of Colorado after 10 years with NBC-owned stations in Chicago, first as a producer of NBC's all-news radio network and then as a producer and field producer at the network's television station. She wrote and produced a documentary on the children of North Ireland that won three Emmy nominations and a national media award. Her series on minority businesses in Chicago was also nominated for an Emmy. Professional projects and scholarly pursuits have taken her to Ireland, West Germany, Japan, Mainland China, the Philippines, and Israel. She holds a Ph.D. from Northwestern, where she also holds her B.A. and M.A. in journalism.

Janette Kenner Muir is Assistant Professor and the Basic Course Director in the Department of Communication at George Mason University. Her primary research interest involves how citizens participate in the political process. She has published book chapters on citizen talk on the Persian Gulf War and on the Hill-Thomas Hearings, written reviews for the *Quarterly Journal of Speech* and *Presidential*

Studies Quarterly, and edited *C-SPAN in the Classroom: Theory and Application,* a volume coproduced by C-SPAN and the Speech Communication Association.

David Slayden has worked as an editor, writer, and producer in a variety of media—scholarly and popular, national and international—including journal publications, advertising, and television. He serves as a consultant on sponsored multimedia programs and public relations/marketing initiatives to several corporations and associations. He holds degrees in literature and art history from the University of Chicago and Indiana University. Currently an Assistant Professor at Southern Methodist University, he writes on issues of culture and society, focusing most often on questions of politics, representation, identity, and technology. He is also a contributor to KERA, the Dallas affiliate of National Public Radio.

Stephen A. Smith, Professor of Communication at the University of Arkansas, joined the faculty in 1983 after receiving his Ph.D. in Communication Studies at Northwestern University and completing special studies in First Amendment issues at Harvard Law School. He has been a visiting fellow at the University of Wisconsin's LaFollette Institute of Public Affairs; a Visiting Fellow in the Departments of Politics and Anthropology, Princeton University; a Visiting Scholar at Stanford Law School; an Andrew Mellon Fellow in the Department of History, University of Pennsylvania; a Visiting Fellow Commoner in Wolfson College, Faculty of Law, University of Cambridge; and a Visiting Professor of Rhetoric and Communication at the University of Virginia. He previously served as a member of the Arkansas House of Representatives, Vice President of the Arkansas Constitutional Convention, Chief of Staff to the Attorney General, and Executive Assistant to Governor Bill Clinton. Smith has published two books and contributed to 35 book chapters and scholarly articles. His research has been awarded the SCA Golden Anniversary Monograph Award, the SCA Wichelns Award for Communication and Law, the SCA Haiman Award for Scholarship in Freedom of Expression, the SSCA Madison Prize, and the Fulbright Research Prize in Communication Studies.

Teun A. van Dijk studied French language and literature at the Free University (Amsterdam) and Theory of Literature at the (City) University of Amsterdam, where he obtained degrees equivalent to a Master of Arts. He was granted his Ph.D. in linguistics from the Faculty of Letters of the University of Amsterdam. He is currently a professor of discourse studies at the University of Amsterdam. He is the author of more than 20 books including *Communicating Racism: Ethnic Prejudice in Thought and Talk* and more than 150 articles, and is founder-editor of *Text* and *Discourse & Society*. He is a frequent lecturer in Europe and the Americas on the role of power and ideologies in society and their reproduction and legitimation in discourse.

David E. Whillock is Associate Professor in Radio-Television-Film and the Graduate Director in Media Studies at Texas Christian University. He has written numerous articles on media images in journals such as *Literature and Film Quarterly* and *Journal of American Culture*. In addition, he has contributed chapters to several books on the American Vietnam War film. He has produced and directed a number of artistic films including *Chopper Blues,* a piece that featured the works of artist Charles Jones. The work was part of a traveling exhibition with the Mid-America Arts Alliance "Winds of War" collection that included the works of Jones and Goya.

Rita Kirk Whillock received her Ph.D. from the University of Missouri and currently serves as an Assistant Professor of communication at Southern Methodist University. She is the author of several articles in journals such as *Presidential Studies Quarterly, Political Communication, Southern Communication Journal,* and *World Communication Journal.* Her recent book, *Political Empiricism: Communication Strategies in State and Regional Elections* (1992) features analyses of election strategies based on a number of political campaigns in which she served as the primary communication strategist. The book received an award for the Outstanding Book in Applied Communication in 1992 from the Speech Communication Association. She frequently serves as a consultant specializing in the development of communication strategies for government and business leaders.